Maverick Mind

Maverick Mind

A Mother's Story
of Solving the
Mystery of Her
Unreachable,
Unteachable,
Silent Son

CHERI L. FLORANCE, PH.D.
WITH MARIN GAZZANIGA

G. P. PUTNAM'S SONS
NEW YORK

The names and identifying characteristics of clients have been changed to respect their confidentiality.

Additionally, although memory can be subjective and the subject of my son is one that I am passionate about, I have attempted to remain true to the essence of all exchanges quoted in this memoir.

⫿P

G. P. Putnam's Sons
Publishers Since 1838
a member of
Penguin Group (USA) Inc.
375 Hudson Street
New York, NY 10014

Library of Congress Cataloging-in-Publication Data

Florance, Cheri L.
Maverick mind : a mother's story of solving the mystery
of her unreachable, unteachable, silent son / Cheri L. Florance
with Marin Gazzaniga.
p.   cm.
ISBN 0-399-15100-1
1. Learning-disabled children—Education—United States.   2. Mothers
and sons—United States.   I. Gazzaniga, Marin.   II. Title.
LC4705.F62   2003   2003047298
371.9—dc22

Printed in the United States of America
1   3   5   7   9   10   8   6   4   2

This book is printed on acid-free paper. ∞

Book design by Stephanie Huntwork

Acknowledgments

I wish to thank John Whitney for being my son. Though at times the road has been a rocky one, Whitney has taught me more about how the brain works and how to repair the brain than any of my many prior educational experiences. Thanks also to my daughter, Vanessa. On the day of her birth, I promised her a joint venture that would be unforgettable, and together we have honored that promise. If I was the Chairman of the Board of the Maverick Minds, Vanessa was Chief Counsel. Her current desire to become an attorney seems like a continuation of the role she has been playing since preschool, when she learned how to use logical analysis to problem-solve the unpredictable Whitney dilemmas that would erupt like earthquakes without warning. Without her brother William, this story would not be written. William, nicknamed by his grandfather "the gentle giant," is the strong but high empathizer who feels situations so deeply that a passion to right injustices is always on his sleeve. A chemical engineering major en route to a career in medicine, William plans to use what he has learned from Whitney to help others as a practitioner and a researcher.

But the story begins with my mother and father, who brought me into this world and raised me to value the creative spirit in both the arts and the sciences. When I was faced with the challenges of raising three children and working full-time, with one of the kids seriously disabled, my mother, Dorothy, and my father, Jack, spun a web of support and unconditional love around us to protect us. Without this ecology of love for and dedication to our family, we would not have the successes we enjoy today.

You will see that my ex-husband, the father of Whitney, William, and Vanessa, is largely absent from this book. After a lot of soul-searching, wanting to focus primarily on Whitney's education and rehabilitation, the children and I decided to leave him out of *Maverick Mind*.

As a family, the children and I would also like to thank my agent, Mike Shatzkin, and his wife, Martha, for believing in this project. Mike once said to me that not many people in this world have a life story interesting enough that it can be made into a book. The kids and I must also thank Todd Williams and Melinda Inks for helping us all develop lifelong fitness habits and a love of the mind-body connection. My writer, Marin Gazzaniga, shared the laughs and tears as we relived many painful and often mentally stretching experiences. And my editor, Sheila Curry Oakes, painstakingly analyzed this manuscript sentence by sentence and thought by thought so that it will make a contribution to parents and professionals alike . . . not an easy job to do.

We also wish to thank a host of professionals with the mental flexibility that allowed me to think in nontraditional ways, including: Dennis Cantwell, M.D., UCLA; Elizabeth Weller, M.D., University of Pennsylvania; Ronald Goldman, Ph.D., University of Alabama; David Daly, University of Michigan; John Ratey, M.D., Harvard; and John Stang, M.D., and Judith Westman, M.D., Ohio State University College of Medicine. In addition, the educators who welcomed me into their classes as a parent-partner: Mrs. Jones, Mrs. Ludwizac, Mr. Niemie, Mrs. Moore, Mrs. Homon, Ms. Hutson, Mrs. Lindsay, Dr. Raffman, and Dr. Meske were major players in developing a community of support for our family as we followed our quest.

Whitney's story has changed my life, and I hope you will find elements of our saga that will change yours.

Contents

Preface

On an unseasonably warm day in December, my sons William, 17, and Whitney, 15, and I strolled through the gates of Columbia University in upper Manhattan. We came to New York to visit my oldest, Vanessa, a freshman at Manhattan College, and for William to interview at colleges in the area.

As we walked onto the impressive Columbia campus and gazed at the old Ivy League buildings, William got excited about this school. We were discussing his chances of being accepted when Whitney interrupted: "Why is Chi-kero there?"

We ignored him, caught up in our conversation.

Whitney persisted, as usual. "Why is Chi-kero there?"

I looked up, annoyed with the distraction. My gaze followed Whitney's outstretched arm, pointing at the names etched into the structure above Columbia's Butler Library: HOMER, HERODOTUS, SOPHOCLES, PLATO, ARISTOTLE, DEMOSTHENES, CICERO, VERGIL.

"You mean Cicero," I corrected his pronunciation. "They are all famous writers," I explained hurriedly.

It is always difficult to juggle a mother's attention among several children, but today was William's day to explore, and I wanted to get him excited about applying to schools.

"But he was a Roman senator, and the others were all writers and philosophers," Whitney said, staring at the list.

I was reminded of that *Sesame Street* game the kids used to sing along to: "One of these things is not like the others." Whitney had homed in on the one name that, in his mind, didn't exactly fit.

I looked at William in amused exasperation.

"He got you," William said.

"Where do you learn these things?" I asked in amazement. I didn't know enough to know if he was right or wrong.

Whitney doesn't gloat the way most teenagers do—the way my other two children certainly do when they are right and mom is wrong. Gloating, sarcasm, vengeance—these aren't Whitney's way.

"History class," he said matter-of-factly, adding: "And I think the Italian pronunciation is Chi-kero."

My awe at Whitney's pronouncement was more than typical parental pride, because Whitney was diagnosed as deaf, mute, and severely autistic when he was a baby. And while I've spent the past fifteen years stubbornly insisting that he would learn language, have a normal life, and go to college, I have also always fought a deep fear that none of these things would be possible.

We parents have big hopes and dreams for our children; we want to support them in every way so they can accomplish their goals. Through my work as a brain scientist and my own experiences as a mother, I've learned that for all of our best intentions, life surprises us and poses challenges we never imagined. For some, it's a child who takes drugs, or has a debilitating accident. For others, it's simply facing the daily frustrations of the mind-boggling commitment of raising another human being with a personality and will completely different from their own.

I must admit there have been times when, in the middle of an argument, something is said that hurt my feelings, or enraged me, or just baffled me, and I thought, *I can't do this. Where did this child come from? Why do I have to be the parent? Why did I take on this awesome responsibility?*

When a child has developmental problems, those concerns are magnified. Communication is a challenge. Reasoning is impossible. It's difficult to believe they aren't defying you on purpose. Not only is it hard to keep going, it's hard not to get so frustrated that you say something you will regret—yell, withdraw, or take up some self-destructive behavior in an attempt to cope. I know because I have done all of these things. I've gone through periods of eating too much, gaining weight, and abandoning my self-focus. I've lost friends and jobs, and alienated family members, and school and medical professionals.

The quest to "dream the impossible dream" can be quite powerful. My impossible dream was the desire to give Whitney a normal life. As a scientist specializing in the brain and communication who worked to fix the unfixable, I found that he became my impossible dream, my grand project. I'm driven, I'm single-minded, and I don't give up. These traits may not have always been appealing to all audiences, but the payoffs have always been worth it.

The day before our visit to Columbia, the kids and I saw the IMAX film about Ernest Shackleton and his attempted trip to the South Pole aboard the *Endurance*. He and his men lost their ship and had to try to find their way back home. For months they were lost, wet, trekking over mountains and bobbing along in lifeboats in the Antarctic. They endured the harshest physical circumstances you could ever imagine. I was deeply moved by the story of this arduous journey. While I've noticed recently that I cry easily at stories of people overcoming adversity, this was different. I wondered why I was so moved by the tale of this taxing physical journey—something I'd never undertake in a million years. Then I realized it was because I identified with what their trip was about: survival.

I could relate to their single focus, their determination, and their seemingly misplaced optimism. I had drawn on these traits and more in facing the challenge of getting through to my son, who seemed unreachable, unmovable, unteachable, and lost. But I found him and in the process found out something about myself—and something that I believe could change the face of science in the future.

When people hear the story of Whitney, they often find it hard to believe: *He must not have been autistic. He must have just grown out of it. It must have just been an emotional problem; how could you really have lived with him that way? How could you all have gotten through it? Didn't you all want to kill each other? Why didn't you give up? What was it like?*

For the first time in fifteen years, I have the mental space to look back and ponder these questions. While we were in it, we were like the men on that ship. When so many catastrophes happened in such short order, there was no time to assess, to weigh the costs and benefits. We simply did what we had to do to survive.

As I look back, I, too, wonder how we got here from there. I had a goal, yes, and I had ways to navigate the journey. But for most of the past fifteen years, I was clinging to a lifeboat in the middle of an ocean, unable to see the shore.

Standing in front of this library in Manhattan with Whitney correcting me, I realized I was safely on land. And so was Whitney.

Maverick Mind

The Hardest

Thing You'll

Ever Do

As I watched a beautiful young couple on television caught in a passionate embrace, I stifled a scream. It wasn't that a soap opera was the last thing I wanted to be watching—I was in labor. The nurse assigned to me apparently thought that the television would distract me from the contractions. She was wrong.

"Excuse me," I gasped.

"Just a minute." She was busy explaining the labor and delivery process to the student nurse she was training. I was in a teaching hospital and, as a Ph.D. and someone who had worked in hospitals all over the world, I had to respect her need to continue teaching. I had also worked as a consultant in this hospital for years, so everyone knew who I was. Unfortunately, this didn't seem to be working to my advantage. The nurse apparently assumed that because this was my third delivery, and I worked in the medical profession, I didn't need very much help or attention.

But because this was my third case of toxemia, and I'd miscarried once, I was concerned and nervous about this delivery.

From a very young age, I'd wanted to have lots of children. But child-bearing had proven difficult for me. My first pregnancy began smoothly. I was so excited to be having a baby that I took up knitting. My sister, who lived thousands of miles away in California, was pregnant at the same time I was, and because I was superstitious, I knit baby outfits for her future son rather than my unborn child, so as not to jinx anything. I even entered some of my unique creations in a local arts fair. I was the last person anyone expected to see getting excited about designing and knitting little sailor outfits with matching buttons, because most people thought of me as purely career-driven. In fact, I'd been working on my career since the age of twelve. In the past decade, I'd worked around the clock doing research and therapy and building my own consulting company to help people with communication disabilities. Having earned a double doctorate in speech and hearing science and psycholinguistic processing, I'd focused my practice on brain-based communication problems. My work ethic was strong.

Then, in my last month of pregnancy during a routine check-up, the doctor told me I had toxemia. I knew how dangerous this condition could be and that it was a leading cause of maternal and infant death during childbirth. The doctor ordered me to stay in bed for a week. When I developed visual disturbances and my urine tests still indicated toxemia, he told me they were going to induce my labor. Giving birth for the first time is scary enough; a medical complication can make it terrifying. I could barely pay attention to what was going on in the delivery room. I was scared and everything seemed to go by in a blur.

At the moment the doctor handed my baby girl to me, I heard the elevator door open in the hallway outside and I recognized the click-clack of my mother's high heels.

I was happy to see my mother and father in the doorway, beaming. "You look like an angel," said my father. I'll never forget that moment.

I was ecstatic—not only was I thrilled to meet my daughter, but I felt the incredible relief of knowing that we were both in fine health. I stayed up all night, holding Vanessa and talking to her nonstop. I told her about all the things she was going to get to experience in her lifetime, all the people who loved her, all the things she would get to see, hear, feel, and learn. I couldn't tell her enough. I poured out my feelings, hopes, and dreams to this new friend who was going to share my life. I swear she was listening to me as she snuggled at my breast, acting like it was the best news she'd ever heard.

My second pregnancy was an easy one. I had a new doctor, Dr. Russ, who was a nurturing ob-gyn with an excellent bedside manner. He monitored my pregnancy closely. However, as my due date neared, I tested positive for toxemia once again. I was admitted to the hospital, where I had to remain on complete bed rest until Dr. Russ felt it was safe for the baby to be delivered. I was allowed to get out of bed only to go to the bathroom. He waited until my due date to deliver. This labor was more difficult; I was in intensive care. But this time I was determined to watch my son be born. I will never forget the miraculous experience of seeing my body give birth. As soon as William was born, they whisked him away to the neonatal intensive care unit. The twelve hours before I was able to hold him in my arms seemed like an eternity. I worried that this time apart would interfere with our bonding, but as soon as I held him, I knew my concerns were unfounded. Again, my child and I fell in love as I stayed up talking to him all night.

When I got pregnant for the third time, I miscarried in the first trimester. I was in my late thirties, which was considered "old" at the time for childbearing. I was devastated but because I had always dreamed of a big family, I got pregnant again. As this fourth pregnancy neared full term, Dr. Russ was pleased with progress of both baby and mother. He again monitored me closely and had me on a strict prenatal health regimen. We had an amniocentesis study done this time because of my age, and the results were normal. The pregnancy progressed smoothly and I was able to maintain a full work schedule with no medical problems for me or the baby. Then, as my due date approached, toxemia was diagnosed yet again and I was confined to bed. Bed rest had been a challenge for me previously; now, with a thriving, demanding practice and two toddlers, it was even harder to stay still. I was, however, apprehensive enough to obey the doctors' orders.

I stayed home in bed, supervising my hospital-based practice by phone. My business had become so large that there was no one else to supervise it. We had research grants from the federal government, as well as a large hospital-based practice that included treating any patients who needed to have their communication skills evaluated (for instance, after a stroke, surgery, or head trauma). In addition to our own research, we were participating in two big research projects at the hospital, one on the impact of oto-toxic drugs used for hip and knee replacement patients (oto-toxic drugs could cause hearing problems) and one on the impact of endarterectomy (a procedure to clear out arteries to prevent stroke) on patients' thinking and communication skills. We tested hundreds of patients in these studies, and if they had a communication problem, we'd do follow-up therapy to improve their skills. I designed the tests and therapies, and taught quality control protocols for these studies to residents and post-master's professionals.

We were also providing speech and occupational therapy for Head Start programs in community centers and churches, providing inpatient care to a variety of nursing homes, and conducting speech and language therapy in a group of private schools as well as at the state penitentiary. My outpatient clinics were housed in a 9,000-square-foot old school building on the hospital campus that the hospital and I had jointly renovated. I also owned and supervised the Center for Independent Living, which was a brain studies laboratory in the hospital proper—an additional 1,500 square feet. We had people flying in from all over the world to get help with disorders ranging from stuttering to auditory processing. On top of this, I was consulting with corporations and government agencies, and giving speeches and media interviews about our work. It's not so surprising that I felt I couldn't be out of touch for a day. I was not only a parent to my children—my business was my brainchild.

After juggling all of that from bed, I was relieved to be at the point where I had the pitocin drip-feeding into my veins, starting my contractions. I'd done this twice now, and I had faith we'd be OK. I couldn't wait to meet my new baby.

I was about to ask that the nurse turn off the soap opera blaring overhead, when she announced, "Time for you to go."

The lack of attention from the nurse changed dramatically when I was wheeled into the delivery room. Suddenly the concern for my condition swung to the other extreme. The room was filled with medical students. This was not a time when I wanted to demonstrate my star quality. But no one asked if I minded the audience. If I'd had more energy, I might have objected. Instead, I focused on my breathing, my doctor's instructions, and the blipping of the fetal heart monitor.

Then the monitor stopped.

I looked up at Dr. Russ, whom I adored. He locked eyes with me and calmly called out, "Clear the room, please."

Dr. Russ spoke. "The umbilical cord is wrapped around the baby's neck four times. I have to unwind it while you push. If you push too hard, you'll strangle him. Listen carefully to my instructions." He paused. "Cheri, this is the hardest thing you will ever be asked to do."

I nodded and brought all of my attention to him. As a contraction came on, he told me to push gently as he worked to maneuver the cord around my baby's neck once. Then he ordered me to stop the pushing. Now I had to fight the pitocin drip and the contractions it had induced.

For what seemed like an eternity, Dr. Russ carefully guided me through pushing, and guided the cord around the baby's neck. Finally, I was told to give one final push.

I looked at Dr. Russ with concern because I heard no crying. He beamed at me as he showed me my son—Whitney. Then, as I waited anxiously, Whitney was whisked to an examining table to make sure everything was OK. In a few moments, Dr. Russ said, "He's a perfect ten," referring to the infant Apgar rating. My baby was totally normal.

He handed Whitney to me and I couldn't wait to take him in my arms. I was hungry for that wave of bonding. What I felt instead was a wave of concern bordering on nausea. Something was different. Something felt wrong. He wasn't cuddling. I cooed at him and smiled and started chattering. He didn't respond. Although Dr. Russ told me he was fine physically, I knew the labor had been difficult. Was there something he wasn't telling me? "He's a perfect ten," Dr. Russ repeated. I told myself I was tired, and as we both drifted off to sleep, I vowed that Whitney and I would have our chat later.

I couldn't allow myself to think about whether he'd suffered any brain damage in the moments when that heart monitor flat-lined. However, I found myself quietly trying some neurological tests while visitors and nurses came and went.

The famous Harvard pediatrician T. Berry Brazelton had devised an infant inventory to predict a baby's personality type and temperament at birth. Results of simple tests like noting how infants react to light, pinpricks, and other stimuli could classify how active your baby would be. I'd had fun experimenting with Dr. Brazelton's ideas with my two other children, but Whitney wasn't responding. I'd never seen a baby behave the way Whitney was behaving. He wasn't reacting to lights or sounds or voice or touch. I couldn't discern his temperament at all. Whitney was an enigma.

I tried to ignore the voices telling me something was wrong, that his nonreaction was bizarre. It was me who was having the problem, I told myself, not my perfect-10 baby. I reminded myself that this was my third child and the whole experience was wildly different. After all, everyone from my family to co-workers to the hospital staff had treated me differently this time around.

My family members, especially my parents, were worried about how I was going to raise three children basically on my own. (My husband was traveling or working out of town for most of our marriage, and we would officially divorce after twelve years.) My mother didn't see how it was going to work. She continued to remind me that children's first years of life were critical—for kids and for mom. "You've already had a good career," she'd argue. She had been a musician who had quit to raise my sister and me. Granted, she was from another generation, but colleagues of mine echoed her concern. Although it was now the mid-'80s, well into the era of working women, I knew very few women from my Columbus, Ohio, community who had full-time careers and several children. Those I knew who did have careers outside the home, worked part-time and had help.

It wasn't just the need to earn a living that kept me working; I was passionate about my work and I longed to share my passion with my kids. I considered myself very lucky because I'd felt as if my passion had "picked me" from a young age. From the time I was five years old, I would sit in my room and draw cartoon strips, like Brenda Starr, making up characters with different problems that I could solve. When I was in seventh grade, I got a job after school teaching in a dance studio. I worked with the kids who couldn't follow the instructor's directions. They were so frustrated—it wasn't that they couldn't dance, they just seemed to have trouble following the teacher. I'd take them downstairs and work with them after class until they were able to follow the steps. When a blind student came to the studio wanting to tap dance, I was the only person who the owner thought could help. In high school, my boyfriend's friends asked for help and advice about girlfriends. Ever since childhood I felt I'd had a calling to help people break through communication barriers.

I couldn't imagine giving up either my career or being a mom. So I became a mother of three children all under the age of four, as well as a full-time professional. I'd worked hard to find a way to include my children in what I did. I had some models to follow. My muse for my

graduate thesis (about how babies learn language) had been Lois
Bloom at Columbia University, who had taken a year off teaching to
study her daughter Alison and videotape her first year of life. I learned
a great deal from her book about that year, *One Word at a Time*. B. F.
Skinner, the famous psychologist, had also observed his children as
part of his research. To me, it sounded like an ideal way to combine a
career with having children. I was running Head Start programs when
the children were young, so I simply involved Vanessa and William in
that process. They came to work with me, and as my staff and I would
work on exercises for the Head Start programs, we'd try them out on
my children first. It gave the kids and me time together, I got work
done, they got educational play therapy, and the children in the programs
got highly effective activities that had been successfully de-bugged.
I wasn't trying to make my children into experimental subjects, but
rather merge our lives and share my passion with them.

Of course, I'd had to cut back on the extensive traveling I'd done
before Vanessa was born. Before I had children, I was traveling several
times a month to attend conferences, present papers, and consult on
research projects. I'd flown to Washington, D.C., to appear on a news
magazine show, *People Are Talking,* co-hosted by Oprah Winfrey, to
discuss my work with stutterers. Once I had children, this kind of traveling was difficult. I sometimes took short trips when I could, but
mostly I wrote about my research—submitting journal articles and
book chapters—in order to stay visible in my field. I missed the chances
to get out and learn about what others were doing, and to see the
world. My long-term plan was to start traveling again when the children were older; I thought it would be a great way to show them the
world.

In the meantime, I brought the kids to work and on nearby trips
with me—in my Firebird with two baby seats in the back. I thought
that the only thing that would change when I had Whitney was that I'd
have to either find a way to fit three baby seats in the Firebird, or trade it
in for a minivan.

All in all, I loved our life. I was devoted to my career and I adored my children; I thought I'd found a way to have it all.

Not everyone saw it my way. By the time you have three children, the atmosphere is different—even in the hospital room. When Vanessa was born, my room overflowed with gifts and flowers and well-wishers; that dwindled a bit with William; with Whitney, I got two pajama sets from my mother. Even the hospital workers were less interested in me. I knew how to breast-feed and get to the bathroom after my third baby, so there wasn't the parade of people checking up on me the way there had been with Vanessa. Also, hospital cost containment was in full swing, so they were anxious to get me on my feet and on my way.

Any of these issues could explain why I felt disconnected from Whitney, but they didn't appease my worry. I'd worked with enough handicapped children over the years to know that the "what ifs" and second-guessing could eat away at parents. Could something I'd done during my pregnancy have caused this problem? Was I too old to have this baby? Was it the toxemia? The difficult labor? Stress? Prenatal care? Genetics? Am I just overreacting? Is everything really OK? When there is no easy explanation, or no identifiable problem, these questions can spin out of control and become a haunting inner monologue that keeps mothers awake at night. As I lay there in the dark that first night, holding Whitney, cooing to him, trying to connect, I fought the feeling that there was a premonitory cloud hanging over the hospital room. I tried to block out the admonishing voice echoing in my head: *You wanted to have a big family, you made your bed. Now lie in it.*

By the time morning came, I was anxious to get home. Maybe the sterile hospital room was causing my discomfort, and Whitney was responding to that. Once we got home and could relax in our own surroundings, I reasoned, things would probably be better.

I called my mother to come pick us up. She arrived with William and Vanessa (now one and a half and two and a half, respectively) in tow, little bags of M&M's in their hands. "They wanted to give Whitney a baby gift," my mother explained, smiling. They were so cute dressed up in a suit and pinafore, offering their presents to their baby brother. I noticed that he didn't look at them either, nor did he startle. Nothing was making Whitney react. Still, my mother-voice was clinging to hope, saying, *You're tired, you've barely taken a day off throughout four pregnancies. It's just you. You're exhausted.*

My mother and I piled the children into the car and she drove us home. I imagined relaxing with Whitney in my own bed, visualizing the quiet time that would finally bond us.

When we walked into the house, I was surprised, to say the least, to see colleagues from the hospital sitting in my living room. For a moment I thought they were there to wish me well. Then I noticed the piles of charts and stacks of files. The hospital was up for recertification, and they needed me to check my charts to prepare for the upcoming audit.

I couldn't believe it. "Can't this wait a week?" I asked.

They insisted that the easiest way to get through the review was for them to ask me questions. "You rest, we'll do the work," they said.

Propped up in bed, I answered their questions in a daze. I could hear their words, but I couldn't understand what they'd said.

"That sounds good to me," was my fallback answer.

Once they left, I was completely drained. I think it took me hours to take a shower. Every step seemed like a major effort. Finally, I stumbled into bed and dozed on and off through the night, waking up to breast-feed Whitney every few hours. He didn't cry when he wanted to be fed. I simply tried to feed him every few hours and he would latch on. I felt more like a spigot than a mother. Breast-feeding Vanessa and William had felt different; it was a close and nurturing experience for mother and child. And even though neither of my other children had been fussy babies and hadn't cried much at all, there was something different about Whitney's quietness. I tried to tell myself it was the same, and that I should be grateful that my third baby was so silent. A nagging voice felt something was wrong.

There was a porch swing that I'd bought at an artists' street fair. I'd imagined rocking my new baby, relaxing in the early evening, using it as wind-down time. Instead, those first days home I found myself sitting there in a daze, holding Whitney while therapists who'd come over from the office sat across from me asking questions about how to handle various cases. Initially they claimed to be stopping by to see the baby or wish me well, but within minutes there were questions about work. I encouraged them to figure out the solutions on their own. It must have been too unsettling for them to have me go from the hyper-involved boss, to the dazed woman sitting in the swing. Although I seemed almost indifferent to their concerns, they appeared to become even more dependent on me, wanting to draw me out on every detail. My mind wasn't working quite right. I was so tired. I wondered if I'd stay like that forever or if I would ever get back to normal.

After about a week, I decided it would be less disruptive to my home life if I went to the office for a couple of hours a day. I had tried to tell my staff I needed some time off, but in the hospital world, which is twenty-four hours a day, seven days a week, patients want the doctor, not a substitute, and I was the only Ph.D. on our staff. The fact was, it was my business, and I was ultimately responsible for the patient care. I convinced myself, too, that having strangers coming and going might be upsetting to Whitney. I decided that having work come to me was more taxing on my energy. At least if I went to the office, my home would be my home, not just another place to answer questions many hours a week.

At the time, I had a wonderful woman named Tammi working for me. She was an elementary school teacher whom I hired to be my assistant with the kids, both at home and at work. She was a research assistant and child-care helper all rolled into one. Her job description was to be my second pair of hands—not a description that would have thrilled many. But Tammi was a savior. For the first few weeks, she stayed home with the children while I went to work for a couple of hours. Tammi was beautiful, tall, blond, and full of life. She was always bubbly and in a good mood, and there were times when her positive energy was the only thing that kept me from collapsing at the end of a hard day.

Within three weeks of Whitney's birth, I was back to a regular schedule at work. By the time Whitney was six weeks old, I started bringing him to the office with me for part of the day. I hired an additional child-care assistant to help Tammi so that the kids could be with me at work some of the time and also be supervised at home.

In those early months being back at work, I strove to incorporate Whitney into our activities. But Whitney was inconsistent in his response to the environment. If you clapped your hands loudly, he didn't always turn to look. He didn't seem to focus on people's faces, including mine. He didn't cry or laugh or coo the way my other children had. There is a widespread "wait and see" mentality with early development because there is such a range when it comes to normal development timelines. So when I took him to his well-baby checkups in his first year, his height, weight, physical appearance, and all of the standard measures were perfectly normal.

"Perfectly normal." That phrase rang in my ears. How did I explain to doctors that just because my baby was physically fine, and as adorable as could be, I could sense that something was not perfectly normal? I'd never had a problem connecting to any patient, no matter how severe the disorder. Alzheimer's, and stroke patients and schizophrenics will respond. You can connect to Down's syndrome patients. I even felt more connected to my dog Coco, whom I had adopted when she was six weeks old. Coco was more responsive to me at six weeks than Whitney was at six weeks or six months. With Whitney, it was as if his body was here, but he was hollow.

I never spoke these thoughts out loud to anyone. I think there were two reasons for this. First, there was the battle going on inside me between the mother and the scientist. The mother desperately wanted everything to be fine, but I also found it impossible to overlook that something wasn't quite right. Most mothers of handicapped children turn to experts to find out what's wrong. Many had turned to me. Here I was, the expert whom parents often came to when their child couldn't communicate or connect, and I had no idea what was going on with my own son. I was conflicted and confused. *If you can't figure out what is wrong, maybe there is nothing wrong,* said the mother to the scientist. *You have to accept that something's not right; I'm sorry I don't have the answer, but you have to keep trying to figure out what's going on,* argued the scientist with the mother.

The second reason I wasn't naming my fears about Whitney had to do with not wanting to label Whitney as having "a problem." This wasn't a conscious decision I made; it was an extension of a philosophy I'd followed in my practice.

Richard B. Stuart, a social psychologist, was the author of a book called *Trick or Treatment* that criticized the psychiatric mental health profession for focusing on what's wrong with patients. He critiqued "supportive counseling," in which those with a chronic malady get support or counseling for that malady, for focusing on the problem rather than on a solution. Stuart did a lot of marriage counseling, and one of his techniques was to hand each partner a clipboard during the first session and ask them to write down everything they liked about the other person. His theory was based on this logic: By devoting time to discuss what is wrong with each other, you may increase the number of things you don't like about your marriage, and that is probably not your goal. He argued that you couldn't improve mental health by talk-ing about what's wrong. If you track negative behavior, all you will get is more of it. If you locate those key elements that are the beloved com-ponents of the relationship, then you have a foundation upon which to build.

This approach had proven true with stuttering patients, with whom I had done much of my early therapeutic work and research. As a National Institutes of Health (NIH) fellow, I was trained that stutterers shouldn't be allowed to talk about stuttering. They weren't allowed to tell horror stories about how stuttering affected them. This was a difficult rule to enforce because patients come to you desperate to unload. We worked from the premise that if you're going to learn to be an ex-stutterer, talking about stuttering experiences was counterproductive. Instead, we focused on increasing positive behavior. In other words, we wanted to teach normal speech so it could replace stuttering. The book I cowrote on the subject was called *Stutter-Free Speech*.

We set the highest goal, and then got as close as we could. To do this, I worked with a hearing aid company in San Francisco to help design a device called the Delayed Auditory Feedback machine that altered how a stutterer hears himself during speech training sessions. This device delayed the sound of the patient's own voice so that it sounded like an echo. The patient heard himself talking in his headset, but slower than his mouth was moving. We would ask the person to slow down his speech until it was in sync with his hearing so that he could monitor his fluency. Once a patient mastered stutter-free speech at this speed, we adjusted the volume and speed. Although we didn't realize it at the time, while we were improving the way patients were talking, we also were improving how they were hearing.

These two approaches to treating a communication handicap would one day become the foundation for helping my son. First, we were doing basic scientific research to change the way patients heard so they could talk without stuttering. Second, we knew that tracking negative behavior wasn't going to get a positive result. Avoiding tracking the negative behavior was why I had a horror of labeling Whitney. I was afraid that if anyone started referring to him as "autistic," "handicapped," "brain-damaged," "learning disabled," "deaf," "mute," or *anything,* he'd be stuck with that definition. I wouldn't let my mind think that way. I vowed that I wouldn't dwell on the problem. I wouldn't label him; I wouldn't talk about what wasn't working.

Of course, every mother of a handicapped child wants to deny that a problem exists. But my training and work had me convinced that labeling Whitney could potentially be quite harmful. I had seen too many stroke patients in nursing homes where the treatment reinforces the permanency of the disability; I knew that simply offering supportive counseling to help stutterers cope with their problem didn't fix anything. I believed with all my being that focusing on the problem would become a self-fulfilling prophecy. Eventually, I would have to accept certain labels, such as "autistic" or "mentally handicapped," to get him into special education and classes where he could get special attention, but it was always a means to an end and never the way I viewed Whitney. I decided the only thoughts I'd entertain were how he was going to improve. Instead, I would do everything in my power to focus on what was working.

The problem was that with the stutterers, I knew the behaviors I wanted to increase to reduce the stuttering; with Whitney, I couldn't yet identify any behaviors to develop and work on. When it came to focusing on what was working, I had no idea where to begin.

When Whitney was a few months old, I decided we needed an outing. One of my favorite things to do with Vanessa and William had been to pile them into the car on Saturdays and drive down to The Gourmet Market in Columbus, a café owned by Chef Hubert, who'd served as chef for the king of Spain. One of our famous Ohioans, Dave Thomas, founder of Wendy's, had met Chef Hubert and hired him to cater a gala party he'd thrown for a Cincinnati Reds baseball game. Hubert enjoyed the experience so much, he decided to move to Columbus and start a restaurant and catering service. The Gourmet Market was very European, and unique for our Middle-American town. I'd lived in Paris when I was younger, and I adored taking the children to this Parisian-style café, sitting outside under an umbrella for Saturday brunch, listening to music. At night, the restaurant was too fancy for children, but as long as they behaved we were welcomed at brunch. In fact, we'd become regulars.

I got everyone dressed and we piled in the car and headed to the café for a taste of Europe. Vanessa had brought one of her stuffed animals to show the chef. They were happy to see us and the staff gathered round to fawn over Whitney, who sat unresponsive. Vanessa jumped in to show her stuffed animal and everyone's attention was drawn to her. William and Vanessa giggled and charmed the staff. My heart nearly broke looking at Whitney, propped in his baby seat. He didn't seem to be enjoying the outing. What was I doing wrong? Was I too tired? Was I not up to mothering three children? I didn't want to admit it, but looking at Whitney in that baby seat, it was as if we had brought along another stuffed animal—not a baby boy.

It was early evening by the time I packed the kids back into the car to drive home. I crept along the streets of the urban neighborhood, savoring the thinking time while my babies slept in their car seats. Between work and home, I no longer had a moment to myself when I could think. In the past, exercise had always served that purpose for me. Whether it was an aerobics class at the hospital, or riding my bike to the OSU (Ohio State University) pool, swimming for a half-hour, and riding home—I had used workouts as a time to meditate on and solve problems. After having Vanessa and William, I'd returned to working out soon after their births, but having three children was turning out to be exponentially more challenging than two, and I had been unable to find the time for my meditative exercise.

It was dusk and the warm lights coming from the windows of houses looked enticing. I had lots of colleagues and a large staff but spent no leisure time with other adults. Most of my colleagues in the hospital were men; there were not a lot of women in my professional circle. Of the professional women I knew, few had babies; I had no moms to spend time with. I imagined the families and couples inside their cozy homes having popcorn, watching a movie, chatting about their day—sharing problems and discussing how to solve them as well as sharing victories and stories.

I wasn't just lonely; I was profoundly sad. When you carry a child for nine months, and look forward to loving him, and he doesn't love you back—it breaks your heart. It was a sadness that was too hard for me to put into words with my parents, and no one else was available to share the heartbreak.

That morning in the hospital emergency room, when Whitney's fetal heart monitor flat-lined, Dr. Russ looked at me and said that it would be the hardest thing I'd ever do.

I was beginning to suspect that wasn't true.

2

A Stranger in

a Strange

Land

I was strumming the guitar and singing at the top of my voice. Vanessa and William were dancing around me, rocking and rolling their little bodies in time with the music. It was eight o'clock at night, long past the kids' bedtime, and it had been a long Saturday, but our days were so packed and there was so little time for relaxation that I couldn't bring myself to put an end to this much fun. Finally, the song came to a climax and we all collapsed on the floor, laughing in a heap. The kids jumped on me, shouting, "Again, again!"

I was beat. "All right, into your pajamas and I'll sing you a song in bed."

Vanessa and William headed upstairs to change and I took a deep breath. I turned to see Whitney, still sitting where we'd put him when we started working on our routine three hours ago. He was almost a year old and he still showed no signs of normal development. Of course, in my line of work, I knew that development could vary, and in my optimistic moments I clung to the hope that he was a late bloomer. In my less optimistic moments, I feared that his lack of engagement with any of us was a sign of something more serious. This first year especially, I watched him vigilantly for signs of what was working. After all, it is hard to assess a pre-toddler. Babies don't talk yet or even move all that much. If we went out in public, he appeared to be OK. Physically, he seemed to be developing normally. But his unresponsiveness to our voices or our behavior—to tonight's singing and dancing and laughing—was a big fact that was getting harder to explain or wish away.

I lifted his dead weight into my arms and carried him up to bed. Most children this age would cling to you, or cuddle—as my other children had. When I taught dance to children when I was a teenager, there were times when we would say, "OK, everyone, be like a limp dishrag, be like a sack of potatoes, pretend you have no bones." That's what Whitney was like a lot of the time: a sack of potatoes. There was no squirming, cooing baby boy grasping at my face or fingers.

We'd been up and out since early this Saturday morning to complete the household chores, and moved on to our second routine: shopping for materials to create activities for the Head Start programs I ran. The weekends were the only time I had to create preschool language kits, so I combined this task with playing with my kids. I'd spent the years 1970 to 1972 at Memphis State University in Tennessee working on the first Head Start programs. Now I was designing the early language-training program for six schools (each with a morning and afternoon session). Head Start was created for preschool children who lived below the poverty line. They were believed to be at high risk for communication disabilities because of a variety of factors including poor prenatal environment, poor nutrition, and little stimulation. Children in Head Start received language and speech assessments, and those who needed it received speech-language therapy as part of readiness for kindergarten.

I have always believed that the best way to engage someone in learning a new task was through fun, rather than rote repetition or boring drills. Because of my life-long exposure to the arts and music—my grandfather was a musician and ran a music store and my mother was a musician as well—I designed my therapeutic programs using dance, music, art, and theater to teach children basic skills, and then built on those skills so they could be transferred to everyday life. I even used music, dance, theater, and art teachers on my staff. I would create and then test a set of activities that were connected to a certain theme, such as dinosaurs or cowboys, and then take the activities to each group and train the teachers and parents to put the kids through the activities. It was a fun way to build communication and language skills in children, and an easy way to train adults to relate to the kids and draw them out. The results were striking.

Most of these children doubled their language age within a year. Three to five years old is a crucial time for language skills, and if these skills aren't worked on during this period, they usually get worse. You can also make a lot of progress if you stimulate children's language systems during this period—even in cases where children have language development problems. The brain is so plastic, especially at this age, that a little stimulation goes a long way. Results like this gave me hope for working with Whitney.

I had always found it rewarding to see the children drawn in by using activities that linked music, dance, story-telling and art. Head Start kids from the inner city, children of the poorest families, uneducated, little or no health care—the worst-case scenarios—were bused to our clinic in the summer. Even these extremely deprived children were responding. The children's mothers were very happy. It seemed like every day a mom took me aside to tell me I was a miracle worker.

Rather than feel inspired by this, I found it was getting harder and harder to hear compliments as my concerns about Whitney grew.

Whitney seemed to be developing OK physically. He could push himself around in his baby walker; he could sit up; he wasn't terribly mobile, but he could pull himself around crawling. But he was not vocalizing or making any sounds. There was none of the adorable cooing or babbling as he sat in his car seat, or coming from his crib in the mornings the way there had been with Vanessa and William. I'd always loved watching infants allowing sounds to roll around in their mouths, practicing and playing with the idea that they can use their larynx to create noise. That wasn't Whitney. Not only was there no "mama" or even "dada" uttered, there was no indication that he was aware if he did make a noise—an inadvertent gurgle or burp.

It seemed as if he had no reaction to himself or to the outside world, no curiosity about his siblings or me. If Vanessa took a rattle and shook it for him, he didn't respond—it was as if he looked right through her. If he reacted to mobiles or other hanging toys we had, it was more to stare at them than to poke or prod or reach out and try to touch them. He didn't react to the toys he had, or to the soft baby blanket I thought he'd curl up with.

Perhaps the most disturbing thing was that he didn't indicate any wants or needs. Babies are usually constantly trying to communicate needs and parents are running around trying to figure out what the need is. Is he crying because he's hungry? Needs a diaper changed? Wants to be held? When I was nursing Whitney, he would suck, and he would suck from a bottle. But he didn't make an effort to communicate any of this. Instead, I had to feed him on a schedule, check his diaper when we noticed something, hold him when I wanted to.

His lack of vocalization had me worried, although I knew there was a wide range of time when children begin to speak. I was left to question my instincts as mother and scientist. Was he simply slow to develop verbally and was I hypersensitive because of my profession? I found it hard to accept that it was too early to be concerned about language and communication skills. The lack of other normal language developmental cues had me worried. He didn't seem to have the prelinguistic skills that most babies have, such as attention, memory, pairing sights and sounds. Even before babies talk, you can get them to pay attention to you by making faces, or splashing the water in the tub— eventually they'll splash back, usually with glee. Most young children will turn their attention to a loud noise or startle at a jack-in-the-box. Research I'd done had led me to believe that from the moment of birth, a baby was able to pair sights and sounds. Every sound would have an associated visual image. Babies can select their mother's face because they recognize her voice. I'd watched with fascination as Vanessa and William developed these skills as precursors to language. But Whitney wasn't engaging in any of these behaviors.

If he was slow, I wanted to lay as much groundwork as I could for Whitney's future language development. I had decided to focus on auditory stimulation. In the 1960s, Hildred Schuell wrote about a therapy for stroke patients using a technique of "bombarding the auditory system." The auditory system fueled language, so she believed the best way to help someone get language back was to read or talk to the person repeatedly. In my practice, we'd had tremendous success with this method with stroke patients. Building auditory complexity also worked with Head Start kids.

I decided to bombard Whitney's auditory system, even though he didn't seem to be reacting. In a sense, what I was doing for Whitney was a baby version of what we were doing with the Head Start kids—trying to pair sounds and symbols, combine movement and listening, provide visual and verbal stimuli that he could then make associations with: singing to the baby, telling nursery rhymes, and showing finger plays like the "Eensy Weensy Spider," making noises and sounds while tickling the baby.

In addition, I'd bring Whitney to the office and put him in his baby seat so he could watch the art therapists, drama therapists, occupational and speech therapists engage the other children. On the weekends he'd "watch" us work on the activities for Head Start, and I would sing to the kids and play my guitar for an hour or two every night. I was doing this in the hope that the information was getting in there somehow, that his brain was processing the music and storing it in some way that would help him build language.

He was unresponsive. He would sit and stare at things that seemed uninteresting to us. He didn't look at the things other kids his age did; instead he would hyperfocus on a brick, or a crack in the floor. This bombardment technique was labor- and time-intensive, and continuing to provide stimulation to a nonresponsive child was extremely frustrating. Dancing and singing for a little boy who didn't make eye contact with us, who would look blankly ahead and didn't bounce or respond in any way to the music or to our expressions, was disheartening. There were plenty of times when I wanted to give up.

One day when I was at home working, I could hear Vanessa and William playing upstairs and I went in to check on them. Whitney was nowhere to be seen.

"Where's your brother?" I asked. They had no idea and said he must have crawled off. I searched the downstairs in a panic. Finally, I found him standing in the bathroom amidst a pile of toilet paper. He was madly unrolling the toilet paper off the roll. He looked fascinated with how the toilet paper was spilling onto the floor. It was the closest thing I'd seen to him engaging in anything that could be considered childhood mischief.

He had never responded to toys or mobiles, so engaging in "productive play" by unrolling the toilet paper roll gave me a moment's hope. But as I stood there watching, the repetitive nature of what he was doing started to concern me. When Vanessa or William got into mischief—unrolling toilet paper or banging pots and pans, there was laughter and a sense of fun. As I watched Whitney mechanically unrolling the paper, over and over in the exact same way, I began to fear it was not play but possibly perseveration—the persistent repetition of a verbal or motor response, a common behavior in those with brain disorders. I'd seen countless stroke patients or autistic children caught in these repetitive acts. It is as if their brains get stuck in a groove; like a broken record that keeps repeating, their brains go around in a circle instead of moving forward. Before I allowed my fears to take hold that this was a sign of autism, I chose instead to focus on the positive fact that he was standing, something that was developmentally normal.

That was when he started walking. There was no "cruising," no handholding. He simply started walking. It would be the same thing with toilet training soon after. He didn't seem to need language to learn physical things. Perhaps he learned them from visual modeling, by observing and copying. He was developing physically, but most important, he *was* learning. This gave me hope.

Just before Christmas, I'd gone shopping after work to get gifts for clients and colleagues. I'd splurged on some executive gifts at local upscale executive boutiques (mostly because I knew they'd wrap them nicely—which would be one less thing for me to do). While they wrapped the gifts, I sat and watched, mesmerized by the expert way the woman folded the corners with precision and scored the ribbons into extravagant bows. There was a time when I'd have enjoyed taking the time and care to wrap personal gifts that way myself, but time for such things was a luxury I no longer had.

When I got home that night, the lights were out and the children were asleep. I hid the presents in the basement to keep them out of reach of the children.

"Why did you do that? You shouldn't have done that! Your mother is going to be so upset!"

I was up early working on my computer in my home office while Tammi got the kids ready for breakfast—I was engrossed in getting my work done efficiently so I could have breakfast with the kids before we all left for the office at the hospital. I jolted at the sound of Tammi yelling and ran downstairs to the kitchen. I'd never heard her yell.

There was a huge pile of gift-wrapping, torn to pieces, and the fancy pens and desk sets I'd bought were strewn around on the floor. Vanessa and William were crying.

I looked around and saw Whitney in the corner. He was shaking his hands frantically, as if he was trying to shake off the bad feelings. *Oh no*. This was behavior I recognized, but I'd never seen Whitney do it. It was called "self-stim" for self-stimulation, and it was behavior you saw only in the most severely impaired. I wanted it to stop. I turned on Tammi, "Tammi, please stop *now*. We'll talk about this later."

I picked Whitney up and tried to comfort him by holding him close. He continued to shake his hands, not responding to me. After several minutes of this, he wore himself out and dozed off.

After Tammi had taken Vanessa and William to school, she returned to the house and we sat down.

She began, "Whitney needs discipline. He's developing bad habits and these habits will turn into big behavioral problems."

"I know he is not reacting like we would expect, Tammi," I said, "but we can't yell, he doesn't know what we're saying. He doesn't understand. There's no point in reprimanding him."

She looked at me in amazement. "He needs discipline."

As I tried to explain that I knew he didn't do it with malicious intent, he was just trying to find out what was in the colorful boxes, I realized that while I was shocked that she thought we could discipline him with words, she was equally shocked that I thought we couldn't. It was the first time it hit me that not everyone suspected, as I did, that Whitney had a problem. In spite of not wanting to, I saw a sort of hearing impairment I'd never observed before, developmental delays, and now symptoms of autism. I also realized that my attempt to focus on the positive was throwing Tammi off. She saw me as ignoring a discipline problem, rather than adopting a specific strategy for a difficulty I knew couldn't be overcome with firm parenting. I began to question myself—could I do this? Could I handle Whitney? Could I help him? Could I do it on my own?

I was starting to find the combined stress of my job and my family life quite difficult. What was perhaps hardest was that Whitney's problem

was perplexing me, whereas at work I could see solutions to complicated cases.

At about this time, I was working with a nine-year-old girl from
Florida whose parents had tried everything to get her to talk. She didn't
speak but would engage in two activities: jumping on the trampoline
for hours, or watching Disney movies. I diagnosed her with language-
processing disorder and created a program to help her develop the necessary verbal pathways. In addition to her speech problems, she was
also having problems decoding what she heard, and reading and writing. Her mother was attempting to homeschool her, as in the family's
opinion, school programs had not been successful.

As part of her therapy, we created index cards that had the names
and pictures of everyday objects and taped them to the objects in their
house: refrigerator, milk, chair, bed, TV. We used pictures from maga-
zines, and her mother, who was a good artist, drew pictures on the
cards as well. We also made a book of logos for familiar places, such as
McDonald's, Pizza Hut, Wal-Mart, and other places that the girl could
recognize. We started with groups of ten cards a day. The first ten were
things she saw every day, many times a day. Then we added another ten
cards of less familiar objects to work with each day. We had different
exercises we would do with the cards. For instance, we would show her
the card and repeat the word to help her make the association between
the image and the sound of the word. Or we would put out two cards:
one that had a hot dog and one that had the Cheerios logo and say,
"Give me the Cheerios," to train her to link the sound of a word with
the visual image and word. In this way, she began to associate the word
with the picture. This is called "sound symbol relationships." She
would remember that the picture went with the word, so she could
select the picture when asked to find it.

Next, we got her to begin to say the words aloud after we said them.
She wasn't just repeating sounds—these words now had meaning for
her. About two weeks later, the girl started saying the words on her

own. First just a few, but quickly she was saying about a hundred of these words regularly.

Her mother, rather than celebrating this gigantic breakthrough, became upset and complained that it wasn't normal for a nine-year-old to speak so few words. She was expressing her grief for the lost nine years. Once the key was found, and learning new words suddenly seemed easy, she was bemoaning the lost years and wishing they'd found a key to her daughter's speech when she was two. This is a common reaction among patients. Many become angry about the lost years, once it seems "easy" to unlock the door. It isn't easy. In fact it's like running a marathon. I can recall watching as two Nigerian runners crossed the finish line of a marathon in Columbus with ease. They looked as if they'd just taken a walk. It was probably an hour before the next people crossed the line, and those people looked like they were dying. When language works right, it seems to take no effort. But if it doesn't, it takes enormous work to get it going. What the mother didn't understand was that we had a found a way to open the door for language for her daughter. There was much work ahead, but I knew we'd found a way in.

I understood parents' frustrations over lost time, but more and more, I was fighting a feeling of resentment and anger. I was working to find a door to Whitney's language, but that Eureka! moment wasn't happening. I was finding it with other people, but not my son. He couldn't or wouldn't speak or even vocalize, he didn't seem to hear or respond; I was bombarding his auditory system with music and words, but didn't know if any of it was getting through. While working with parents of our patients, I was having to check the voice in my head that was shouting, *That's more than my son can do, you should be glad!* It was getting harder to go to work. I would sit in my car in the parking lot for half an hour getting my game face on, preparing myself, so I wouldn't think or say to the patients or parents, "Why don't you appreciate this? You should be grateful it's not harder."

I may have had an empathetic therapist face at work and an energetic mom face at home, but after the kids were asleep and I crawled
into bed, I often cried quietly, feeling frustration, fear, and despair over
how to help Whitney. It was the one time in my life when I felt words
were inadequate to communicate what I was observing because I just
didn't understand my own son.

Soon after Whitney could walk, he decided he could cook. He didn't
sleep very much, and would stay awake at night. After a while, he simply got up and tried to fix something to eat. I realized that he had no
way to communicate "I'm hungry." He couldn't cry or talk. So when he
was hungry, and it wasn't mealtime, I suppose he felt he had no choice
but to go make something himself.

One morning I came down to the kitchen to discover that he'd taken
everything out of the cupboards and the refrigerator. He'd poured
milk, syrup, cereal, and everything he could get his hands on in a giant
mess in the middle of the floor. It was ghastly. I couldn't believe it. I had
to hold back the frustration and tears as I cleaned up the mess. I'd told
Tammi there was no point in disciplining him because he couldn't
understand. Was I right? How was I going to get through this? How
was I going to teach him that he couldn't behave in this way? Could he
understand anything? Was it pointless? After I finally cleaned up the
mess, I started to make breakfast. I opened the oven door and inside
was a mixing bowl with chocolate cake mix, water, and oil—all
unstirred. Lying on top were three unbroken eggs, still in their shells.

Suddenly I flashed on the image of the mother of a young toddler in
a program I had set up for Down's babies at Ohio State a few years ago.
One day, a mother came to me brimming with news: She had been at
home in her kitchen, and her son handed a cookie tray to her. She took
the tray and set it aside. The boy got the tray and handed it to her
again, insistently. Again she took it and set it down. Again, he handed it
to her. Now she felt she had to pay attention. Then she realized that

this was the tray she always used to cook one of his favorite foods: hot dogs with cheese wrapped in bacon. As she got out the ingredients and started to make the snack, he became gleeful. She told me this story with tears in her eyes. "My baby thinks!" she said. The simple action of her child handing her the cookie sheet had conveyed to her that he was a thinking human being, trying to communicate.

That's how I felt when I saw that bowl with the three whole eggs sitting in the oven. *My baby thinks!* I realized Whitney, not yet two, was trying to bake a cake. It was as if he was reading the instructions on the back of the box, but because he didn't know how to read, he followed the pictures and didn't understand the need to crack open the eggs or stir the mixture. Suddenly it all made sense. When it hadn't worked, he'd gotten frustrated and made the mess. His thoughts were trapped inside, with no door—yet—to get out.

3

An Intelligent
Child Trapped
Inside

The only normal thing about Whitney's toddler years was that he went through the terrible twos. He was turning into a wild child, was into everything, and was extremely difficult to control. Many parents of two-year-olds will commiserate about saying "No" all of the time. Imagine if your child seems unable to hear "No," and you have no idea how to communicate that idea to him.

Whitney didn't seem to understand or hear us if we tried to speak to him, so there was no teaching him—and no way to discipline him. He would have tantrums, but they were silent. It was eerie to see him flail around, kicking and biting, but without crying or screaming or whining. It wrenched my heart to see that he was in such pain. I would get angry with strangers who would stop and stare at the strange sight of his silent scream. At times I wanted to yell and cry myself: *What? What is it? What's wrong? Tell me!*

I tried to let other professionals guide me. I knew the medical protocol: You cannot and should not treat your own child because you cannot be objective. When a pediatrician I had worked with, a friend of many years, suggested I have Whitney's hearing tested around age two, I readily agreed. They put him under anesthesia and determined that his hearing was normal, or at least the transmission from the eighth nerve to the brain was normal. I had an odd reaction to this news. While I was glad to hear the test didn't reveal nerve damage, I was perplexed about how his ears were malfunctioning.

In my work over the past twelve years, I had seen more than six hundred Head Start kids a year, and probably more than twelve thousand stroke patients, more than a thousand executives with stuttering problems, and a hundred schizophrenics. I had handled the worst-case scenarios of communication disorders. When faced with patients, it was my job to measure their thinking, speaking, reading, and writing abilities, determine what was going on in their brains, and find a way to correct it. Here I was with this little boy who was apparently physically healthy but was acting like the worst of the patients I'd seen.

For one thing, Whitney's perseverating seemed to be getting worse. Observing him flailing his hands, rocking back and forth, or twirling round and round in a circle for no apparent reason with no apparent trigger could make me feel hopeless: If I couldn't break through this behavior, there would be no way to teach him anything. Now I think his behavior was caused by his hearing alternating between hypo (low) and hyper (high) functioning. At the time, however, I had no idea what was causing it.

Even more frightening were times when Whitney would lash out at others. His older brother and sister were still almost babies themselves: William was three-and-a-half and Vanessa was nearing five. While William and Vanessa were wonderful with Whitney, I did have to worry about him hurting them. This was painful for me to admit as a mother, because Whitney's actions didn't seem to me to be intentionally malicious. The trouble Whitney caused didn't even have that impish side that most kids' mischief does—pulling out a chair, hiding something, taking away a toy—trying to annoy or get attention. His lashing out was random, with no apparent trigger. This meant keeping an eye on Whitney at every moment.

Our daily schedule was packed. The kids and I would get up at about six a.m. After getting the three of them fed and dressed with Tammi's help, we'd pile into the car and get to my office at around seven thirty. Tammi would take Vanessa and William to preschool and come back to help with Whitney. He would spend the morning with Tammi as well as various therapists and teachers, rotating in fifteen-minute intervals in an attempt to get him interested in various activities. Meanwhile, I would go straight to the hospital to make the rounds to check up on the in-patient consults. By nine a.m., I would finish and go to our prototype Head Start center, where I would work until about eleven. Then it was back to the hospital for another set of rounds to check on the in-patients, their treatment, and write up reports.

By this time, Tammi would have picked up Vanessa and William from preschool and brought them back to my office, where they would spend the afternoon doing various Head Start activities. Once they were engaged in practicing these activities with me or art, music, or dance therapists, she would take Whitney home and do an hour of the ten- to fifteen-minute "brain gym" circuit training routines I'd devised for him. I thought short routines were a good way to get him involved in productive play. We alternated trying to get Whitney interested in playing in the sandbox, with puzzles, listening to music, listening to stories, or water play, such as playing with bath toys, tub paints, shaving cream, or sponge toys. He might splash in the water while we were playing with the boats beside him, but then he'd run off. Or he would stare out into space and not appear to look at anything, swinging back and forth on the occupational therapy swing we had. He wasn't very responsive, but we kept trying, thinking the routine of doing the same thing every day might cue him to engage more. Maybe he would remember from day to day that we had done the same activities the day before. Maybe he would start to look forward to, for instance, playing in the sandbox. The plan was to bombard all of his sensory systems, to create routine, to engage him. I was desperately trying anything that had worked for others.

Meanwhile, from about one to three p.m., I taught in a residency program that trained doctors, social workers, psychologists, speech therapists, and occupational and physical therapists in the research protocols for the therapies we administered. Then I returned to the clinic where I'd see outpatients and check in on the after-school Head Start program. After one final set of rounds, it was time to go home. This was usually around seven p.m., and by now Tammi had all of the kids at home.

Not only had I had a full day, but the kids had too. Vanessa and William had put in about eight hours between preschool and playing at all of the activities and exercises at my office. I was continually redesigning my job so that my children could both play and learn in my office, and we could be together while I was earning our living. It was like a great after-school program that I was able to tailor to them. And because Tammi was there, they could always go for a treat or play out-side if they wanted. Still, when we got home there was another long stretch of work ahead of us. Because Whitney was seldom sleeping through the night, I tried to devise ways to wear him out so we could all get some rest.

I would grab my guitar and play music and we'd clomp through the house, running up and down the stairs. Or we'd put Disney videos on the TV and sing along, and William and Vanessa would jump up and down on the bed trying to get Whitney to follow. When I think back on the things we did to try to tire him out, I have to laugh. Of course, most of the time Whitney didn't join in. We were exhausting the wrong people.

If Whitney was particularly wound up—twirling, shaking, rocking, etc.—I'd pile the kids into the car and drive around. Sometimes the motion would calm him down and put him to sleep; other times it would make him so agitated that he'd try to get out of the car. There was no predicting his reactions, even to the same circumstances or situations.

I don't know what would have become of Whitney or me if William and Vanessa hadn't been there. They basically became Whitney's therapists; they were adept at helping me handle him. They would bring home some of their preschool activities and try to teach them to Whitney. Although our weekday hours were packed, there was a lot of time in the evenings and on weekends when it was just the four of us alone. We'd go to the park, and Whitney would run off headfirst into some dangerous situation. We were always darting off to find him and always trying to find ways to assimilate him into our lives. Better than anyone else, his brother and sister learned how to redirect his behavior, how to coddle him along. They were naturals. If I had to say what helped Whitney the most, it would be the love, care, and attention of his brother and sister. The four of us are bonded together in a different way from many families because we lived through this together; we had a unique shared experience in which William and Vanessa became problem-solvers and supporters from a very young age.

At the time, I wasn't sure we'd make it. It wasn't even his behavior that was hardest. It was the sleep deprivation. Often, Whitney would fall asleep in the afternoon and stay up all night. If I was able to get him to sleep in the evening—say, in bed at eight p.m., he would often wake up at one in the morning and get into trouble. There were countless times when he would get into dangerous situations—like getting the window open, the screen off, and climbing up on the roof.

One night, he got out of the house, got his little pedal car from the garage, and maneuvered it out on the road. His pediatrician, who lived across the street, happened to spot Whitney and grabbed him as he was peddling off down the street on a Whitney-created adventure. Just as I was wondering where Whitney had gotten to, there was our neighbor, dragging him back home. I am still amazed, when I think back on those early years, at how lucky we were. Many people kept him alive during his childhood performing similar rescue efforts.

I was determined to be more vigilant. I parked a rocking chair in his room and tried to read, or told myself I would only doze lightly so that I would be alert if he awoke, and able to prevent him from getting out of his bed and into trouble. I was so tired though, that I would often fall asleep and wake up with a start to the sound of clattering in the kitchen. I'd race in to see what he'd gotten into.

On nights like this, after getting him back to sleep, I would look around the room, exhausted, wishing I could find a way to get through to him. The therapist in me saw a child who was resistant to any endeavor of any kind—what we called "refractory to treatment." At the same time, he was doing odd things that I'd never seen handicapped children do. The scientist and researcher in me knew that Whitney's abilities to problem-solve when he had no language was unique. It's long been debated whether you can have thoughts without words, and Whitney seemed to be able to problem-solve, so I was starting to think he had a visual thinking system that existed without words.

In the moments when I could consider his skills, trying to quiet the mother's concerned voice and hear the scientist's objective observations, I saw that there was something miraculous inside him. Whitney seemed very attracted to the mechanical, cause-and-effect type of toys, like a Jack-in-the-box or others where you push a lever or button and a character pops up. He seemed to remember the Sesame Street and Disney characters from TV, and we bought him toys with those characters. He also was drawn to toys that you could wind up, and he would watch them for a long time, as if he wanted to figure out how they were made or what they did. If you tried to get him to play with you or with a particular toy, forget it—he would run off. But if left to select the toy for himself, once in a while he would, and this was the type of toy he would go for. Otherwise, Whitney was taking things apart. Taking toys apart. Taking pens apart. Taking cameras apart. We had to hide anything valuable that we didn't want taken apart and left in a pile.

———

One night I woke to hear William crying, ran into his room, and was terrified to see Whitney about to take a knife to his brother's arm. I tried to safety-proof the house, hiding anything that seemed as if it could be dangerous, or putting it out of reach. I had hidden the knives on the top of a cupboard. Somehow, he climbed up onto the top of the counter, reached above the cupboard by first standing on a doorknob and then pulling himself to the top of the refrigerator, getting the knife, and then crawling back down. How he knew they were up there I'll never know.

Thank goodness Whitney hadn't cut William. When I found him, he was pressing the knife to his brother's arm. I thought, *Is he trying to kill his brother? I can't take this anymore!* I gently pulled the knife from Whitney's hand to avoid a tantrum. As I sat there, hugging both boys to me tightly, William calmed down and dozed off. Whitney sat there, watching his older brother sleep. It didn't make sense to me that he was thinking, *I hate my brother, I'll kill him.* Whitney seemed detached, but not mean or jealous. It didn't seem that he was connected enough to us to feel any malice—or love—toward us. We weren't people with thoughts and feelings to him—or at least not in any way I could discern. I stared at him, trying to feel what he was thinking. He continued to stare at William. Could it be curiosity I saw on his face? Or was I imagining that? Could it be that Whitney was trying to figure out how his brother was made? After all, he was taking everything else apart; maybe he was trying to take William apart too and figure out how he worked.

Still, whatever the motivation, the results could have been disastrous. At that moment, I knew I needed help but I didn't know what to do. Because I was totally sleep-deprived, getting a good night's sleep was imperative.

I tried calling respite care—places that can take care of an ailing parent or dependent for a brief period of time, to give the caretakers a break. Nobody would take him because he didn't qualify. I tried to get home-care providers to take care of him at our house. Either they wouldn't come to watch a baby—or they'd come for a couple of hours but once they sized up the situation they would decide they didn't want the responsibility and would quit. The large repertoire of resources I had access to professionally was getting tapped out. Even Tammi was having to call me more and more to say, "I need your help with Whitney." It seemed I was having to drop everything and run home with increasing regularity.

Then I saw an ad in the paper for new "child-proof suites" at the Hyatt in downtown Cincinnati. The suites were specifically marketed as a place where parents could bring their children and not have a care in the world. They boasted childproof locks on the door so the kids couldn't get out or get into trouble. *Let your cares float away,* said the ad. That sounded good to me.

One Friday night I worked late, then packed the kids in the car and drove two hours from Columbus to the Cincinnati Hyatt. I was praying the drive would put Whitney to sleep, and it did. In fact, all three of them fell asleep en route. When we got to the hotel, I woke them up and they toddled inside. While I checked in, they all promptly fell asleep on the roller cart for the luggage. I rolled them up to the suite that had two large adjoining rooms. Gently, I moved the children to their beds in one room without waking them. I checked the childproof locks, ordered room service, and fell into a deep and sound sleep in my room.

The next thing I knew, an urgent knocking awakened me. I struggled to focus on the red numbers of the clock by my bed. It was three a.m. I fumbled for the light and found my way to the door. Standing there was the hotel security and local police. "Is this your child, ma'am?" they asked.

I looked down, and there was Whitney.

I grabbed him and ran toward the other room. As I flung open the door, the officers and I gasped. William and Vanessa were sound asleep, sprawled on top of the covers. But the room was a mess. Whitney had meticulously peeled off the veneer of the TV center, dismantled the "child-proof" lock, opened the door, and left. I couldn't believe it. I knew I had been in a deep sleep, but how could he have been that quiet? Not even his brother and sister had woken up.

Somehow he'd taken the elevator to the second floor, found the kitchen, and a Coke, taken off his clothes and fallen asleep on the floor.

A security guard discovered him, and the night manager called in the Cincinnati police who, along with the Hyatt security guards, had been searching the hotel room by room for this apparently deaf-mute child's parents. We, of course, were on the top floor, in the last room.

Cincinnati is an urban rough-and-tumble town. To have been awakened by the city police pounding on my door, with my missing child in tow, was terrifying. He'd found his way to the hotel kitchen. What if he'd wandered out into the streets? As the police left, one turned to me and said, "You should really take better care of your children."

Driving back from the hotel to home, all I could hear was that officer's warning. I was doing everything I could think of to take care of my children. What more could I do? Why wasn't it enough?

I was scared to death. *How am I going to live through this and keep my children safe?* the mother was saying. *I can't take this anymore. If I don't get some sleep, I'm going to have a nervous breakdown.* I was beginning to wonder how big a risk it was to have Whitney at home with us, but I couldn't bring myself to consider not having him there.

Then, somewhere on the highway, the scientist in me got curious. *Wait a minute,* I thought. How could a baby do all of that? How many two-year-olds could figure all that out? His curiosity was phenomenal. As a cognitive scientist, I'd never seen anything like this. When we arrived, he'd ridden up to our room asleep on that cart. How did he have the visual/spatial skills to find his way back downstairs? To take the lock apart, get the door open, and get to the elevator? What he had done required an enormously complex series of cognitive skills— executive planning, sequencing, logic, reasoning, and hypothesis testing. He'd finished dismantling the VCR station and he was thirsty. He found a way to solve his problem.

I realized I would never have been capable of doing what he did. The way Whitney was decoding and remembering his world was something I wasn't able to do. It occurred to me that people had different ways of thinking—not in the philosophical sense, but in the brain-mechanics sense. Some people, like me, think verbally (using language) and some people think visually (in pictures).

At that time, I was on a surgical research team at the hospital investigating how altered blood flow to the brain affected cognition (thinking), attention, processing, and memory. We were examining patients who were undergoing a new procedure, called an endarterectomy, that was intended to prevent stroke by clearing out an artery that brought blood to the brain. We tested patients before and after surgery with IQ, voice, and language tests, as well as questionnaires that the patients and their families filled out about how the patient functioned in day-to-day life before and after surgery. Dr. William Evans was the vascular surgeon heading the research. When we were working on articles about our findings for surgical journals, he wanted my findings boiled down to the patient's overall score before and after the operation.

Rather than distill the information, I would give long explanations, talking out loud to formulate my thoughts. I could see that although the surgeons liked and respected me, this kind of discussion drove them crazy. They were bottom-line people. Surgeons were visual—they saved lives by being able to see a problem and fix it. There was no need for language in this important task. On the other hand, I wasn't someone who jumped to the bottom line immediately. I found I needed to talk or write until I could find the answer via language. I was starting to think that our approaches to understanding a situation might be a function of differences in thinking.

Most of the cognitive tests we gave the patients were normal both before and after the procedure. The one test they consistently scored poorly on before the surgery, and improved on after the surgery, were

tests of attention and short-term memory. We were seeing fully functioning adults who had lost their attention span because of build-up of
plaque in their arteries. When their arteries were cleared, their attention span increased.

This made me begin to see attention as a "zoom lens" for communicating. I considered how this worked with other clients and patients. I
realized that using attention span to move thought into working memory was the first thing we addressed with Head Start kids. All of our
activities focused on getting the child to engage, think, and then understand. It wasn't that little preschoolers were noncompliant. If a preschool kid wanders off during story time to play a musical instrument,
you don't think he's bad, you think that you haven't held his attention
and engaged his thinking with your words. When a child is doing this at
seven or eight, however, it's often considered a behavioral problem
when often it is really a processing problem. In fact, a primary function of preschool is to lengthen attention—especially for listening
comprehension and following directions. Most of a kindergartener's
day depends on accurate listening. So to prepare kids for kindergarten, we had to train their attention, working memory, and listening
comprehension—skills that are the basis for early learning.

I realized the reason I couldn't teach Whitney anything was because
I couldn't get his auditory attention and I could not figure out how to
reach into his head to help him create verbal memories. Whitney didn't
attend to us as givers of information long enough for us to focus him or
teach him or model behavior. Any modeling he learned happened on
his own observation time not because we sat him down and showed
him. For instance, he learned toilet training by watching his brother,
not because we were able to specifically teach him. When language
development is abnormal, the development of behavioral control is dis-
rupted. Modeling is sequencing, and language trains the brain to
sequence. He was living off of some big picture, and trying to understand the parts mechanically rather than through verbal explanations.
Maybe if I could lengthen his attention-memory systems, I could begin

to teach him. I knew he had the ability to focus for a long period because I'd seen him get caught up in visual projects while he was taking things apart, or building things or watching a Disney flick. The trick was to train him to do it in response to others, not solely on his own timetable, so we could mold it into active and productive learning.

I'd spent my career "inside" unusual brains—schizophrenics, crack addicts, stroke patients. Never had I encountered a brain or mind quite like Whitney's. I decided I needed to get inside Whitney's brain to see how it worked so I could help him express himself in ways we could all understand.

4

The Wild

Child

Unfortunately, by the age of three, Whitney was getting harder and harder to control. We were constantly trying to keep on top of him, but it was too easy to get distracted for a minute, or assume someone else was watching him, and suddenly he'd zoom off and was into some sort of trouble. He was in constant jeopardy, and I worried he would suffer a fatal accident.

Because of Whitney's behavioral problems—we were never certain what would trigger a reaction—everyday chores became major strategic events. He was like a powder keg that could go off at any moment. Sometimes, interrupting what he was doing because it was time to go clearly caused his fit. Other times, there was no discernible reason for him suddenly running away, throwing himself to the ground, or kicking.

I was constantly trying to figure out how to get household chores done in the most efficient way. For instance, I'd tried going grocery shopping on Sunday nights or off hours, but discovered that many things were sold out by then. Because I could never set aside daytime hours for shopping during the week, we were forced to go on weekends, when I usually had all three kids with me. Trying to shop during peak hours while also keeping an eye on Whitney in case he ran off or had a fit, was such an ordeal that I tried to limit big shops to a once-a-month event, and then pick up other items when I could at a nearby 7-Eleven.

In order to make shopping as efficient and painless as possible, I bought walkie-talkies for Vanessa, then around five, William, just four, and myself. Armed with the shopping list, I'd send Vanessa and William off with their walkie-talkies and read out items for them to collect from our list. We would take turns keeping an eye on Whitney because it was easier to have someone follow after him, or hang out while he stared at a bunch of cereal boxes, than try to get him to follow along. We stayed in touch via our walkie-talkies and it made the process more fun.

Once when we were shopping, Whitney slipped our surveillance, and when I found him he was dragging a giant train—bigger than he was—from a toy display toward me. We ran over, and Vanessa and William tried to get Whitney's attention while I took the train from him and returned it to the display. It was too expensive to purchase, but we couldn't explain that to Whitney. He simply didn't understand why he couldn't get what he wanted. Everybody else was loading up the cart. Why not him? We couldn't separate him from the train. He started throwing a fit. Whitney's fits were very disturbing to see. He quickly became very red-faced, but there were no tears or sounds of crying. Often he would throw himself to the ground, thrash around, bite, kick, or bang his head. When this happened, we would have to abandon our cartload of supplies, get him to the car, and get him home. Everyone in the store watched us carry out this thrashing, but silent, wild child.

A woman approached me on the way out the door. "You know, there's a Positive Parenting workshop at the church on Thursday nights. I found it immensely helpful."

"Thanks," I said through clenched teeth as we struggled out the door with Whitney.

One of the most misleading things about Whitney was that he appeared normal. With his big brown eyes, he was a really adorable boy. He had plenty of clothes from Vanessa and William's hand-me-downs so he was always dressed in cute outfits. At times he was totally blank and aloof but at other times he had a sort of charisma about his face. It wasn't as though he was engaging you, but more like he was engaged inside himself—as if he was thinking his own thoughts actively. He didn't appear to have obvious handicaps, like someone with leg braces or someone who is blind. Whitney had a lot of sensory problems—he couldn't balance or determine his body in space—but these problems in addition to his communication problems were hard to see at first glance. You had to spend time with him to realize his inability to communicate; on the surface, he simply appeared to be a child who wouldn't obey. Thus, I got no sympathy from people when we were out in public and Whitney misbehaved. I only got lectured or reprimanded. No one considered that there was anything wrong with Whitney that a tough parenting approach wouldn't fix. I seemed to be a bad parent.

As we settled in the car, I looked in the rearview mirror at Vanessa and William. I could see this episode was extremely upsetting and embarrassing to them. What were we going to do? Then, William threw up all over the back seat of the car, Whitney stared out the window, and Vanessa chatted away about how to solve this problem in the future and how the train was too expensive anyway.

Visits to my parents were becoming difficult. They lived in a stately, gorgeous old home in Delaware, Ohio, thirty miles from us. Going to my parents' house involved sitting around the dining room table for a big family meal and conversation. Trying to get Whitney to sit at the table was impossible. If he wasn't hungry, he wouldn't sit still. Instead, he'd run around and get into mischief. This meant I'd chase after him, making sure he didn't damage or destroy anything.

My mother had gone to an elegant women's college in Nashville. Visits from her grandchildren were an opportunity for her to teach gracious table manners and how to act like ladies and gentlemen. The social skills my mother had taught me had been invaluable in my work. I could behave and feel comfortable in any situation. I knew how to make small talk and interact with a large variety of people, and what fork to use at formal events. However beneficial this kind of training was for Vanessa and William, it was not going to benefit Whitney. After a trip to my parents, we were exhausted—me from running after Whitney, my parents from trying to maintain a semblance of decorum amid the chaos.

One Saturday, Vanessa and William begged me to take them to the local public library. They loved to read and often spent time at their after-school library program. I was concerned about how I'd handle Whitney at the library, but they promised to be quick, so we went. When we walked in, Whitney immediately homed in on a puppet display and a special area where kids were able to play with puppets and toys while the parents checked out books. *Great*, I thought, *he's got something to entertain him*.

Vanessa and William each quickly rounded up a large stack of books and got on line to check out. After about ten minutes, I could see the line wasn't moving quickly. I glanced nervously at Whitney, but he was still engrossed in the puppets. The librarian was talking on the phone and seemed to be arguing with her husband, which was slowing down her ability to check out people's books.

As our turn approached, Whitney came over with an armload of puppets. I shook my head and had Vanessa hold our spot in line as I tried to guide him back to the puppet area to put them back. "They are just to play with in the library," I said. "We can't take them home." He didn't understand. He grabbed the puppets and again tried to go stand in line with his brother and sister. Vanessa tried next. She soothed him and guided him back, gently trying to remove the puppets from his arms. He started flailing around, kicking, banging his head, and trying to bite Vanessa. I ran over to get him. By this time we were creating a spectacle.

"Some people should learn how to handle their children," said the librarian, the phone receiver still clutched under her chin. Other parents on line murmured their agreement. "Parents shouldn't come to the library if they can't control their kids." "I agree, why would anyone come in if they can't control their child?" "This is ridiculous. What mother would do this?" The tsk-tsking rang in my ears as the three of us struggled to get Whitney out of the library and back to the car, kicking and biting the whole way. My face was flushed with anger and embarrassment. I wanted to go back inside and check out William and Vanessa's books, but they insisted we leave. It was too embarrassing and Whitney was too worked up to prolong the library time a moment more. William got so upset he threw up in the car again.

We drove off in defeat. I was certain that somewhere in Whitney's brain he had figured out that if his brother and sister could check out the books and take them home, he should be able to check out the puppets. He couldn't understand why you could take some things with you and not other things. I was concerned that I couldn't explain things to Whitney, but I was also concerned about Vanessa and William. They were the best brother and sister Whitney could have. They loved him and I couldn't handle him without their help. But what was happening to their childhood? Because of Whitney, they couldn't check out library books on a Saturday afternoon.

Was everyone—professionals, friends, family, strangers—right? Was I going to damage William and Vanessa by putting them through this? To this day, people ask me how William and Vanessa reacted to their little brother. They didn't see Whitney as odd, perhaps because they had virtually grown up in a speech and hearing clinic surrounded by people who were not the average middle-of-the-bell-curve types— spending their days with Head Start kids, stutterers, and other patients.

I never spoke to them about their brother as being sick or different. I'd say, "Let's try to get Whitney to play with us." And that's what they'd do. People find it hard to believe they never complained; but they never did. Maybe it was because when I started to realize the limiting impact, I worked hard to make sure that they had time apart from Whitney—at school and doing other outside activities.

One Saturday I took the kids out for a nature walk along the reservoir. It was one of the only times I could get some exercise and fresh air, and I hoped it would tire Whitney out and help him to sleep at night.

Whitney could spend an enormous amount of time sitting and staring at a leaf, a stone, or a blade of grass. It seemed his brain was busy working at understanding something—I just didn't know what. Although Whitney seemed to behave chaotically, maybe he was attending to an order I couldn't comprehend. After all, Albert Einstein, a visual thinker who saw order in chaos, was thought to be mentally retarded by his elementary school teacher. Was it just a mother's optimism to think that maybe Whitney's brain was seeing the world in the same visual way?

I was walking along, pointing out various wildflowers to the kids, thinking this was the closest thing to a relaxing day I'd had in ages, when I heard Vanessa shout. "Mom!"

I swung around to see that Whitney had scrambled over a tall fence and was headed toward the reservoir dam.

"Stay here!" I shouted to Vanessa and William. I ran toward the fence and struggled to climb up, swing my body over, and drop down to the other side. I took a deep breath and walked as quickly as I could to catch up to Whitney, not wanting to run and provoke him. I couldn't use my voice to lure him back, to calm him, or to yell at him to be careful. I knew he wasn't deaf—in fact, at times he would react strongly to noise and at other times he paid no attention to sound. But using sound to connect with Whitney never worked the way it works with most people. I couldn't demand that he come to me. As soon as I was close enough, I grabbed him, held him as tightly as I could, and carried him back toward the fence. Sure enough, he started thrashing in my arms, trying to get away.

Finally we both collapsed on the ground in exhaustion. I had never felt so powerless in my life. How do you save your child if they can't hear the fear and anger in your voice? Every parent has a moment when they cry *"No!!"* Those cries serve a purpose. They communicate fear that will alert a child and often stop him from doing something dangerous. Whitney didn't seem to hear that—or any other emotion.

He hated to be interrupted. I hated not being able to explain my actions. I sat there with him in my arms until he quieted down enough for me to be able to coax him back up and over the fence.

He also didn't seem to respond to facial expressions—a parent's face aghast or fearful would scare most babies. I wondered what he saw. I'd watched him stare at his face in the mirror for hours, moving his mouth, wrinkling his nose, touching his eyes. He could be fascinated with each individual feature. But he didn't seem to be able to respond to the whole of a human face.

A piece of the puzzle that was Whitney came to me one evening, when I had left Vanessa and William with the neighbors and went to pick up some carry-out food. Whitney fell asleep on the way over so I left him locked in the car and ran inside to retrieve the food. Minutes later, I came out and he was gone. Frantically, I looked around the parking lot, trying to figure out what would attract him. Then I remembered there was a drug store at the other end of the shopping mall that we'd visited a few weeks ago and he'd been taken with the toys in the back of the store. Somehow, I knew he'd gotten out, walked around the restaurant, gone to the shopping mall, and into the drug store.

When I came running in asking for a small boy, the shopkeeper said,

"Is he yours? He's been back looking at the toys. You shouldn't let him wander around alone like that."

I gathered Whitney up and drove him home. After my panic subsided, I felt a twinge of pride and excitement. We'd been to that drug store just once, several weeks ago. Yet somehow he had created some visual markers in his mind of where that store was so when he woke up, he recognized something in that parking lot that signaled "toys." He'd marked that territory in his mind. He knew that if he went from A to B to C, he'd find his way to the toys again. After the Hyatt, I'd thought that maybe he had immediate visual recall, because he'd been able to find the elevator and make his way back downstairs just hours after we'd arrived. This time it had been weeks since we'd been to these stores, and he seemed to know exactly where he was going. Was he building knowledge, storing long-term memories? It seemed as if he was using a whole parallel system of thinking that was non-linguistic.

There was no doubt in me now that he was thinking. To find that store required attention, problem-solving, memory, and analysis of some sort. The problem was, his thinking was so fast. We weren't only trying to keep up with him physically; we were trying to keep up with where his brain was taking him. Whitney's visual thinking was like a Ferrari, and we were all driving along in a minivan. It gave me a new way to frame his behavior. Maybe when he ran off from us he wasn't impulsive—after all, he wasn't easily distractible. Maybe his thinking was associative rather than sequential. He'd see water, and he'd be off and running to jump in and play. He didn't have language so there was no sequential logic—no way to teach that all water isn't for play, that some water is dangerous.

I began questioning what it meant to label a child hyperactive or impulsive. Had we just misread what some are doing, the speeds at which some are thinking? Often, stutterers think faster than they can talk. My job was to get their mind and mouth in sync. Whitney had a fast mind, but no language to communicate his thoughts. What good is visual thinking if you don't have any words?

If I can open that up, I thought, *if I can build a visual thinking system—maybe it could cross over and help the auditory/language system.*

I started to think about how to train the visual system in an orderly way. How could I build an architecture of visual thinking?

I was developing a program called *TV Teacher* for Head Start and my other clients, and I started adapting it for Whitney. I bought a portable TV with a built-in VCR that we could plug into the car. Watching videos sometimes calmed him down, so I wanted to have this tool on hand for when we were commuting, and also if he had a fit while we were out. For each video, I bought toys to represent the agents (characters), actions (things the characters did), and objects (the things they used to perform the actions). For a video *Donald Duck Teaches Math,* we had Donald in an airplane, Mickey in a truck, Minnie in a little car. We had *Snow White and the Seven Dwarfs, Winnie the Pooh, Sesame Street,* and others.

The purpose of *TV Teacher* was for the child to progress from watching the video, to understanding the interaction of agents, actions, and objects by playing with the toys and acting out the actions in the videos. I had spent a year studying how to do this as my doctoral dissertation topic, supervised in speech and hearing and psychology. It was eerie that I'd chosen to study how children acquire language years ago, and was now faced with trying to help my son with this very problem. I thought this same method might be a way to build sequential thinking visually, as opposed to verbally. If Whitney could start to discern that the Pooh toys went with the Pooh video, Disney with Disney, then he would be learning how to store information and recall it appropriately.

He seemed to be able to. His play was starting to parallel our play even though he wasn't talking. Parallel play is used to teach children to talk. A phrase is repeated and the parallel action demonstrated—"Mickey drives car"—until the child starts to say "Mickey" or "car" or "Mickey drive" and so on. While Whitney wasn't using words, he was starting to act out little actions and stories from our playtime when he played by himself.

Now I wanted to figure out how to get him to build these cause-and-effect ideas into paragraphs of thought. First, we started using dollhouses that went with the Disney and Sesame Street toys so that Whitney could replicate his own daily activities in order of occurrence. He could make Mickey or Big Bird go to sleep, wake up, eat in the kitchen, or play in the yard. Next, we advanced to the Playmobile sets that had characters and accessories to create scenes, such as a schoolhouse, fishing, or cowboys. We'd use the toys to act out different stories we invented. I thought this would help him start to classify objects and actions by helping him create the kind of "bin sort" we'd been teaching Head Start kids. With Head Start children, I used the words in rhyming songs to build this skill—getting the kids to remember groupings of words based on rhyming cues. With the Playmobile toys, I was trying to teach that mental filing skill visually rather than verbally.

It is hard to explain the importance of developing these basic skills, because most of us are born with them. Language is structured to make us think sequentially—first we do this, then we do that; first this happens, then that happens. Without language, Whitney's thoughts seemed to have no temporal or linear organizing principles. I was trying to find ways to make Whitney play that would make his visual mind work in a verbal way. We made Whitney's toys take turns going to sleep, eating in the kitchen, going to the bathroom, riding a bike, and playing on the playground—mimicking Whitney's every-day routine. Getting him to internalize these routines, and see these as sequential patterns for behavior, would perhaps build sequential thinking without language.

I knew the skills that were part of functional play were the foundation for learning to communicate. Most babies automatically associate sounds with symbols or objects, and this is how they acquire language. But Whitney was learning visually.

My job was to get his visual system to work well enough so that he could build long-term visual memory and knowledge for problem solving and thinking that was age appropriate. Once this was working, could I find a way to teach him language? I knew that there were visual aspects of thinking, but I didn't know if it was possible to have visual thinking without any verbal at all. Could I harness his visual thinking to teach his brain verbal skills?

5

The

Depths

of Despair

Now that Whitney's playing was becoming more functional, I thought he might be ready to make the leap from how the toys interact to each other, to how humans relate to each other. I knew that it was going to be very important for him in terms of social as well as academic development, and that the two spheres were quite inter-dependent.

He was only three, but I was becoming concerned about his inability to be around other children and adults and to separate from William, Vanessa, and me. One of the therapists at work told me about an older woman, a grandmother who ran an informal "Mom's Day Off" program at her home, five minutes from my office. "She has a swing in her back yard and even gives the kids lunch. It's very low-key," the therapist explained.

I decided to give it a try. The first day I brought Whitney for only an hour and stayed to observe. Whitney played by himself with toys, and didn't throw a fit or pose any behavioral problems. Pretty soon Whitney would stay for two to three hours at a time. He was not playing with the other children, but he wasn't harming anyone, and he was tolerating being around others. I was thrilled.

After about three months, the grandmother said she needed to talk to me. She didn't think Whitney should come anymore.

"Has he done anything wrong?" I asked.

She felt she didn't have the training to help him and that he wasn't normal—that he needed to be someplace where they knew how to make him better.

I was devastated. I tried to convince her it was a giant step for him to be around the other kids and not misbehave. But she stood firm; she didn't want us back again. It worried me that his abnormal behavior made everyone so uncomfortable, even though he wasn't acting out. If he couldn't be accepted here, in such an unstructured setting, what would happen in school?

I was determined that Whitney not lose any ground in his ability to be around others. Through my work at the hospital, I'd been going to preschools in the area for years, screening children for speech and hearing problems, and there was a preschool in the local Lutheran church that was one of my favorites. The school was very progressive, and I loved the director. I knew that they'd just been chosen to receive government funding to include handicapped children in 10 percent of their population. So far, they had no handicapped students. I thought it would be a perfect match: they'd want Whitney because of their new project, and he'd get to be in a great, mainstream school.

I spoke to the school's director, who was very empathetic. An artist herself (she was a gifted puppeteer), she'd always been very interested in the work I did because of our use of the arts. She was surprised to learn I had children, as she'd only known me professionally, and was supportive of my goals for Whitney.

"OK, bring Whitney here, we'll find a way to make it work," she assured me.

Whitney was three, but we put him in the two-year-old class. At the age of two, many children enjoy playing by themselves, so we hoped he wouldn't stick out as being especially different.

At first he didn't. I can still recall how nervous I was bringing him to school those first few days, lugging bags of toys from home so he'd have something familiar to play with. As I sat in the corner to make sure all went smoothly, I watched my big, brown-eyed toddler playing with his Disney characters. He didn't look any different from the other children. I believed that everything was going to work out perfectly. He fit right in—unless someone tried to get him to follow directions.

No one, not even me, had much success when it came to trying to get Whitney to do something he didn't want to. He wasn't obstinate or mean, but we had no way to teach or discipline him verbally. I'd been hoping that the structure and pattern of the school day would help Whitney model normal behavior. During this period, my morning routine was to get Vanessa, William, and Whitney in the car by 6:15 a.m. We would pick up Vanessa's friends in the neighborhood and take them to the bus stop on the busy main road (her friends' parents would pick Vanessa up after school). The bus came within a twenty-minute window, so we had to wait anywhere from one to twenty minutes to be sure we didn't miss it. Then I had to pick up William's friends and take the boys to kindergarten at Columbus Academy—a 45-minute drive in the other direction. During the time it took to collect all of these kids and get them to their destinations, we sang, told stories, and played games. We created entire plays in the car, made up songs—the kids enjoyed it so much they begged me to come as their "Show and Tell" act at school. I saw it as speech and language therapy for Whitney—he sat in his car seat, surrounded by young children laughing, talking, and telling stories. They especially loved Fridays, when we'd go to the drive-through at the Jolly Pirate donut shop. We'd drive up to the giant plastic pirate to place our order, and William and his friends would shout, "We want blood donuts, we want barf donuts!" and laugh hysterically. Whitney, meanwhile, was oblivious to all of the fun.

After two hours of driving, it was time to take Whitney to preschool. I was already exhausted from getting the other kids to school
before I even tried to get Whitney out of the car and into the church
building.

Whitney was going through a phase where his cowboy boots were
the only shoes he would wear. We'd been doing so much work with him
to mimic our stories that he wanted to be a cowboy. This posed a problem because the preschool had gym floors and required everyone to
wear tennis shoes. It was impossible to explain to Whitney that he had
to wear sneakers and couldn't wear his boots. It became a giant power
struggle between us. I could feel his frustration. I could see that if
someone came over and tried to change my shoes with no explanation,
I'd resist. He wanted to go play in the gym, where the big toys he could
ride were. I tried letting him wear the cowboy boots in the car and
bringing tennis shoes to change into. But he resisted. If his teacher tried
to change his shoes, he'd try to bite her. If he got really frustrated, he'd
pee on us. He would try to run out of the building. If we persisted, he'd
start banging his head and rocking.

I thought I was beginning to understand. He couldn't say, "Leave me
alone," so he peed on someone who was bothering him. It was his way
of communicating his opinion, his sense of right and wrong. He was
thinking and trying to "talk" back. It was hard to explain this to the
teachers. The person who got peed on didn't appreciate that this was a
sign that my son was thinking and trying to communicate.

But most of the time, his fits seemed to occur with no clear provoca-
tion. He was starting to have fits in which he would appear to have an
extreme reaction to his clothes. Sometimes he'd be fine and other times,
with no warning, it was as if his clothes were suddenly crawling on his
skin, as if he was suddenly highly sensitive to the feel of the material
and he would try to tear everything off. It could be snowing and cold
outside, but he'd want to rip off his shoes, pants, and shirt, and run.
I started to suspect he had a hypo-hyper brain—meaning he seemed
to fluctuate between extreme sensitivity and no response whatsoever.

Maybe this was why he had fits that sometimes seemed to come out of nowhere—maybe one of his senses, or part of his brain, would suddenly hyperfunction, causing him distress, and then because it had defueled itself, it would shut down and not function at all. David Caplan, M.D., Ph.D., a neurologist at Harvard, has a theory that the brain has a certain amount of auditory and visual processing resources that is dispersed when needed for completion of a task. Maybe Whitney's dispensing mechanism would flood and then he would need to replenish.

It took an unbelievable amount of work and energy to get him to attend the preschool, but I was determined to get him used to being with people other than our family. I knew that if we kept him isolated, he'd never be able to have a normal life. The hours of effort it took to get him dressed and inside that building and to calm him down afterward were worth it if he could be with others in a school setting for even an hour a day. So I continued the routine, hoping that Whitney would begin responding to the routine of the school and start behaving.

Battling my mother's optimism was the scientist's voice pointing out that Whitney seemed to be getting worse, not better. I pushed away the nagging voice that suggested that many of his behaviors were adding up to a diagnosis I didn't want to consider: autism. He had communication and language problems, he didn't like physical contact with others, he had "temper tantrums" for no reason, he perseverated, he didn't interact with others or make eye contact, and he didn't tolerate changes to routine. I told myself he was just having trouble adapting to a new school.

One morning, in the mayhem of kids piling out of the car at the bus stop, somehow someone closed the car door on Whitney's arm while he was outside the car. I let out a blood-curdling yell when I saw it happen. William and Vanessa started crying; the other kids got scared. Whitney just stood there, nonplussed. I opened the door, afraid his arm would be broken and I was amazed to see that his young, malleable bones appeared intact. Before I knew it, Whitney seized the opportunity to take off running down the road. I dashed after him to catch him and put him back in the car.

On the drive to preschool that day, I had to fight back a lot of emotion. Seeing his arm caught in the car was frightening enough. But what really shook me up was his lack of response to physical pain. On top of that, he had no fear or anxiety in reaction to all of us screaming and shouting. It was impossible to ignore that something was seriously amiss with him. I'd seen children with severe disorders and I knew the prognosis wasn't generally good. Many of the severe cases I saw were in, or on their way to, residential homes. The thought of Whitney being institutionalized made me sick to my stomach.

I was scared and lonely. I didn't know where to turn for help. I knew that my family's concern would only escalate my anxiety, and so I didn't share much of this with them. With no one to turn to, I felt I had no choice but to keep doing what I was doing: trying my best to keep Whitney in preschool, and hoping that all of the work we were doing with him would somehow break through.

One morning, after I'd gotten all the kids to school relatively uneventfully, I pulled into the hospital parking lot a half-hour earlier than usual. I thought I would have time to catch up on a few phone calls and paperwork before the day got away from me.

When I got to my office, one of my staff members greeted me with a grave look. "The hospital's in financial trouble. A decision's been made to sell to a for-profit company."

There was no time to determine how or why this had happened. The next day, my staff was at my door, wanting to know what would become of them. I had to get my therapists placed in new jobs. I had to start closing down my hospital-based contracts with people in a way that worked for all of the patients. Most frightening, how was I going to earn a living? I owned my clinic, but we'd been largely funded by contracts through the hospital that had allowed us to negotiate payment for many of our clients. I could have tried to associate myself with another hospital, but it had taken me twelve years to develop my current contracts, and I didn't have time to go through that process again. HMOs were popping up and I suspected major changes in the way medical care was administered and paid for; I knew that being paid via third-party contracts might no longer be viable.

I had to seriously consider if I needed to seek stable employment working for someone other than myself. While that might provide financial security, it created another problem: how would I care for the kids? Having my own business, I could be flexible. If I had to run out to deal with a Whitney crisis, I could. What if he needed me while I was teaching a university class or in a corporate meeting? Chances are I wouldn't be able to hold onto a job that required a set schedule.

I didn't know what to do. I had children and expenses. I couldn't sleep. At night I began to wander the house after the kids went to bed. I tried to numb myself out with chores: doing laundry, getting lunches ready for the next day. By two a.m., I would retreat to my soul-searching spot on the basement stairs of our house. While the laundry spun in the machine, I would sit at the bottom of the steps and cry. I didn't want my children to see my sadness. I wanted to help Whitney, raise William and Vanessa in a healthy environment, and save my business—I just didn't know how.

One night, I asked myself: *What do you want to do?* I got very quiet and listened for the answer. On those basement steps, in the predawn hours, the reply came to me. It was the recurring image of Whitney with his arm caught in that car door. On my death bed, I thought, I won't care about how many articles I've written, how many times I appeared on TV, how many corporate consulting contracts or awards I'd won. I'd already proven to myself that I could achieve those things. What I would regret was if Whitney was living in a residential home.

The core of any plan had to be staying close to Whitney.

I had an intense passion to be the best I could be at treating communication problems. Why not turn the energy I'd been spending trying to understand Whitney's visual mind into my professional work?

Was it possible? Could I start building a private practice exclusively for highly visual patients with communication problems? The scientist and researcher in me wanted to take some time and determine a way to tackle this problem beyond the current understanding. As a mother, I wanted Whitney to have a normal life and was willing to learn all I could to help him. The mother of three knew I needed to earn money to pay my family's expenses.

The voices of reason and passion battled in my head. But something deep inside said, *You cannot do the safe thing.* In every tragedy, there's change, and in change there's an opportunity to rethink something, maybe for the better. I thought of the parable where the master gave his three servants talents. One of them buried his talents because he didn't want anyone to steal them. One invested his talents conservatively, and the third invested in growing crops and helping the community. The first led a miserly, selfish life; the other lived the status quo but never soared. The third reaped what he sowed. Taking a traditional job felt as though I would be burying my talents. On that dark night, I asked to be shown a way.

A few days later I got a phone call from the pediatrician I knew who had urged me to test Whitney's hearing.

She was married to a doctor with whom I had worked on one of my research projects with stutterers, so she knew about the problems my practice was facing. She had recently moved her practice into a new medical complex in Dublin, an affluent suburb of Columbus. "We have another office available in our building, would you be interested?" she asked.

As she described the facility to me—five pediatricians, a nutrition center for weight management and stress management, healthy lifestyle, eating and exercise classes, physical and occupational therapy, and a group of adult and pediatric dentists—I could see a new kind of practice taking shape. With all of this support in the same building, I could create an outpatient communication practice, attracting highly visual children like Whitney. Maybe I could design a questionnaire for the pediatricians to give to their patients to try to identify young visual patients and start to study this issue.

I could feel a sense of excitement I hadn't felt in ages.

Of course, one patient at a time paying out of pocket rather than a company buying my services was very risky. The advantage of private practice was that I succeeded or failed based on my own abilities. While it was the least secure in the short run, it could provide the most security in the long run. Deep down, I believed that if I got a chance, clients would be happy. I just didn't know if I could get enough patients to give me that chance.

I took a deep breath and asked, "How soon can I see it?"

Within weeks, I signed a five-year lease at the medical complex, and prayed for the best.

It took about six months working with attorneys to untangle my relationship with the hospital, close down that practice, and get everything resettled. During that time, I commuted back and forth—spending a few days at the Dublin office, getting it set up and starting to recruit patients, and a few days at the hospital.

Somehow Whitney made it though a year at the Lutheran preschool. I was hoping to have him attend a second year of preschool, now that he was finally getting used to the routine. Unfortunately, at the end of the year, the principal got a puppeteer job in a theater in Atlanta. I was happy for her as she headed off to pursue her life's dream. She assured me that everything would be better than ever. The preschool had hired the director of a local special education school for autism to replace her.

I was giving a lot of thought to how to maximize these benefits for Whitney. Was he really handicapped and disabled? My preference was to get him into a regular school program. Mulling this over one evening on my way home, I pulled into our driveway as our neighbors, Dr. Richardson, our pediatrician, and his wife, Rhonda, a junior high school principal, hailed me from across the street.

"Could we talk to you for a minute?" they asked. "It's about Whitney."

Oh no, I thought. *Now what's he done?* They'd been incredibly supportive of my efforts with Whitney, and knew I was struggling mostly alone to raise my family. I was hoping Whitney hadn't done anything to alienate my allies and neighbors.

It was time for Tammi to leave, and I knew all too well how much she needed a break by the end of the day. I darted across the busy road and told them I only had a minute.

"We've been talking, and you know how much we care about you and the kids . . . ," she started but then trailed off awkwardly. Her husband stepped in. "I don't know how to say this, other than to just come out and say it: Whitney is autistic. I suspect that may be hard for you to accept. But you need to get some specialized autistic training for him. There's a school . . ."

This time it was my attention that trailed off. I couldn't hear any more. I excused myself as quickly as I could and crossed the street back to my house. It felt like things were starting to close in around me. Here I was struggling to help Whitney, to keep him in the mainstream, and his pediatrician was telling me he was autistic. They were right. Not only was it hard accept, I refused to accept it.

In the previous week, I'd spent a lot of time working to help institutionalized patients succeed at communicating. We were now involved in a special project for a specific nursing home that would teach aides, nurses, and administrators how to help the patients become more communicative and engaged in productive activities. From the moment I'd first started working with this group, it had struck me as odd that although they were living with nearly a hundred people of the same age, most of these patients never spoke. They'd usually been moved to the nursing home because they were sick and they had given up all their belongings. Often they became depressed and mute. We took a team of therapists into these homes and had the patients put on plays and write music, make art, or read classics and have book discussion groups. Soon they began interacting with each other. The key, it seemed, was to identify what they had loved to do in their former life and bring that skill out in the activities we did with them. What happened in the nursing homes was proof to me that when you isolated people with a disability, it only made their condition worse. I wanted to get Whitney as close to the mainstream as possible. I had been involved in legislative activity for the communicatively disabled since the 1970s, pushing to develop the least restrictive environment and assimilate the handicapped toward mainstream education and social activities as much as possible. I believed that children imitate what they see, and that if you placed handicapped children with normal developing children or younger children with older children, you create a situation with positive role models for the handicapped or younger children to learn behavior from. I set up many communication partners programs where older students taught younger students, spouses taught their stroke-victim partners, and parents taught children. Having capable communicators supporting and modeling behavior and skills for the less capable was a long-standing premise in my work. So the idea of putting all handicapped people together to serve their special needs did not fit my paradigm.

It was particularly upsetting to be told by everyone around me that Whitney needed a segregated autism program. I had served on state and national committees that addressed research or clinical issues pertinent to mainstreaming children in the least restrictive environment. So segregating him was against my beliefs.

I don't think specialized schools for autistic children are bad in any way. It's just not what I wanted for Whitney. I only wanted the chance to help Whitney so he could function like everyone else.

I began researching a new handicapped program that had been proposed for the Dublin school district that would teach autistic and language-delayed children in a small preschool group with the goal of mainstreaming them as fully and quickly as possible. There were several things about the program that seemed appealing. First, it was a new program and only had a few students enrolled. Second, my practice was in Dublin now, and there were aspects of this community that I thought could be a good fit. Dublin was a newly developing suburb, a high-tech training area where companies would send people to be trained before relocating them to regional offices. For this reason, many high-level international executives were temporarily assigned to the area, which meant lots of bilingual children having to adjust to new schools. Surely this meant that teachers would have to be sensitive to communication problems.

The problem was that in order to get into the school, we had to live in the Dublin school district. When I tried to find out if Whitney would be a candidate, they said that, in theory, he sounded appropriate for the program, but they'd have to test him. However, I couldn't get them to test him unless we lived in the district.

It was a frustrating catch-22, but something told me this was the best hope for him. I decided to move without knowing for sure that Whitney would be accepted. We picked a great house right across from the Dublin swimming pool and the Wyandot elementary school. Living in Dublin would be easier on my commute and would cut down on the several hours of driving each day to get the kids to their schools and me to my new office. It still meant that Vanessa and William had to travel to their private school, but they could take a bus from Dublin.

In July of that summer, we moved to our new home on a suburban cul de sac. It was totally different from our little urban Tudor house. Soon after we moved in, several of the wives in the neighborhood came over. "We just wanted to point out how we try to do our yards all the same," they said. I looked around the street and noticed that, in fact, all of the yards were pretty much identically landscaped. "We just think it looks nice to keep it that way," they said. I must have stared blankly, so they continued. "Oh and you'll love the holidays, we all do our Christmas decorations exactly alike so when people drive by, our cul de sac looks so pretty." If I ever felt like my old life was over forever, this move was it.

I felt as if I was being warned, or at least told how to decorate. None of them worked outside of the home, and they hadn't seemed pleased to learn that I worked full time. I couldn't help but worry as I continued unpacking boxes that night. *I hope I haven't made a terrible mistake,* I thought. *If I can't have a different flowerbed, how will they respond to Whitney?*

Because the Dublin handicapped program was new, it wasn't going to start until later in the fall. In the meantime, I had to get Whitney into some kind of program. There was a Montessori school in town, and I had always loved Maria Montessori's philosophy of teaching kids visually. I knew it wasn't going to be a sufficient solution for Whitney, but I thought it might work for a few months.

I made an appointment to talk to the school's teachers.

"I have a very visual child," I explained. "All of these visual mechanical toys you use would be perfect for him. He'll excel in this. But when you try to talk to him, or tell him things, he might not respond to you as you expect."

They assured me that the Montessori approach was to teach through experience, not verbally. "Bring him in," they said.

I was starting to realize that no one truly understood my explanations about Whitney, so I told them I would bring him for an hour and stay with him to see how it went.

Whitney couldn't have been happier. He ran around and played with everything. The teachers were thrilled with his visual skills. "He's so smart!" they exclaimed. "Leave him here, you can pick him up in an hour." I'm sure they thought I was being an overprotective mom. I left and went to my office, leaving my phone number and assuring them I was only minutes away.

Less than an hour later I got a call: "Could you please come get your son? This isn't working out."

Nap time had been his downfall. He had actually gone to his cot for a quick nap, but soon he was ready to return to playing with the toys across the room. When the teachers tried to get him to return to his cot, he started biting, throwing his hands around and twirling. "This kind of temper tantrum isn't acceptable," the teacher said.

"He doesn't understand your routine and he didn't understand what you were saying," I tried to explain.

"We're just not equipped to handle behavior like this. We're sorry."

I gathered him up and returned to our new house, more concerned than ever about his chances of getting into the Dublin school program.

Without the option of the Montessori school for the summer, I was desperate for ways to keep Whitney occupied without wearing myself out completely. Going to the movies was one of the few things that we could do that would keep Whitney's attention—which meant I could get some rest. I would often take the kids to the movies on Saturday afternoons, when theaters had matinees of children's films, and doze off in the chair while they were mesmerized by Disney.

One weekend afternoon, about the twentieth time we had seen *Snow White,* when the dwarfs were coming home from a hard day's work in the mines and washing up, Whitney suddenly burst out laughing at the sight of them lathering up their beards. William and Vanessa and I practically fell out of our seats. For four years he hadn't made a sound. He'd had his arm caught in a car door, thrown tantrums, but never uttered a cry. Here he was laughing at the dwarfs! We laughed along with him, joyfully. The people in the theater must have though we were crazy—it was a funny scene but not that funny. After this, he began making sounds. I was incredibly relieved to know his vocal cords worked; now I had hope that talking was possible.

I turned up all efforts to get Whitney into the Dublin handicapped program. They'd told me he sounded like a candidate for the school, but they'd never met him. I was worried about the testing, so I wrote up extensive reports based on the observations and work I and other therapists had done with Whitney at my clinic. But the school wouldn't accept this as sufficient for letting him in. When I reread these reports now, I see that they did have a mother's optimistic slant. I was insisting that Whitney's grunts and the sounds he was starting to make were words. Although the progress seemed miraculous to us at home, his communication skills appeared severely impaired to others, as I was about to find out.

The school administration was very polite about the situation and promised to take my reports into account, but insisted that for Whitney to be enrolled in this program, he had to be given the standard battery in the standard way. While I was not averse to his being tested, I knew that traditional tests wouldn't measure Whitney's visual intelligence because all tests were given with oral instructions. The instructions were explained verbally, and questions either had to be answered orally or the child was asked to copy geometric designs or write alphabet letters. Even when asked to build something or match block patterns, the child had to understand the directions to comply, and many of those tests were timed. The faster you understood the directions, the better you might perform. Measuring Whitney's visual skills was also complicated by the fact that he had inconsistent motor skills. He could take things apart and build things from Legos, but he did not have the motor control for using a pencil. I worried that Whitney would completely fail tests given in this way. The day of the exam, I packed a bag of Whitney's favorite toys—Legos and complex puzzle toys. If the traditional testing was a disaster, I hoped that if I could get the teachers to see how advanced Whitney's visual skills were, he might have a chance.

They wouldn't let me stay for the testing. I had to wait in another room down the hall. They gave me a series of questions to answer and I filled them out nervously while I waited. I have saved everything from these years, and when I re-read the checklists and test reports, I am amazed both at how bad his behavior appeared to others, and how consistently I attempted to put a good spin on it. Today I see how divergent our views were and why, based on their objective measures, Whitney seemed unteachable. But then, I was incredibly frustrated, feeling that no one was seeing the skills I saw—the intelligent child I knew was trapped inside this off-balance, silent boy.

For instance, one of the checklists I filled out that day, which was later included on Whitney's school report, reads as follows:

- Seems "deaf" to some sounds but hears others.   *yes*
- Engages in rhythmic or rocking activity for very long periods.
  not anymore
- Sometimes "looks through" or "walks through" people as though they weren't there.   *not anymore*
- Has unusual cravings for things to eat or chew on.
  not anymore
- Has certain eating oddities such as refusing to drink from a transparent container, eating only one or two foods, etc.
  not anymore
- Deliberately hits or pinches him/herself?   *rarely now*
- Sometimes whirls like a top?   *not anymore*
- Is skillful in doing fine work with fingers or playing with small objects.   *very*
- Likes to spin things like jar lids, coins, and coasters?   *yes*
- Is upset by certain things that are not "right" (like a crack in wall, broken rung on chair [etc.])   *yes*
- Has complicated rituals which make him upset if not followed? (taking exactly the same route between two places, dressing according to a precise pattern)   *yes, but much less*
- Gets upset if certain things he is used to are changed?   *yes*
- Is deliberately destructive?   *not anymore*

- Is hyperactive, constantly moving, changes quickly from one thing to another? *much better*
- Sits for long periods, staring into space or playing repetitively with objects, without apparent purpose? *not anymore*

I was writing "not anymore" so that they would see that although these abnormal behaviors existed, he was responding to our attempts to mold and shape his behavior—even though, in truth, he still did many of these things at times. When the testing session was over and I came to collect Whitney, the teachers said, "He's very low functioning. We adapted our procedures in every conceivable way and we got nowhere." They told me that Whitney had crawled around on the floor, tried to get out the door, and wouldn't pay attention to the testers.

The school year started before we knew whether Whitney would be accepted into this new preschool program. While I awaited his final test results and their report, I clung to the fact that the school still had not said no.

One day as I was getting ready to make my daily call to the Dublin school to see if they would take Whitney, the phone rang. I was surprised to find the new director of the Lutheran preschool Whitney had attended the previous year calling me.

She told me Whitney's case had come to her attention. She felt Whitney needed to be in a segregated school that specialized in handicapped children, not mainstreamed with normal children.

She had never met Whitney, or me, Whitney wasn't in her school at the moment, nor were we planning to return there in the fall. "Thank you for your concern," I said. "But I don't think a segregated program is the right thing for my son. I'm hoping to design a program where he can be in the least restrictive environment and eventually be mainstreamed."

"I don't think you understand," she continued. Something in her voice made me stop. She told me if I didn't enroll him in a special education program within twenty-four hours, she would report me for parental neglect. I didn't know on whose authority she could do this, and I had no idea what would prompt her to say such a thing.

I lowered myself into a chair. The room was spinning. I told myself to breathe. "Neglect?" It seemed unfathomable. I had spent almost every waking moment thinking about and working with Whitney from the moment he was born. "But you've never seen what I've done to work with him. He's been in a rehab center for most of his life. . . ." I spewed forth a defense. I was terrified, and certain my voice was shaking. "Please," I begged, "I am trying to get him into the Dublin school's handicapped program."

After I hung up the phone, I sat there in a daze. I was certain she would call back the next day to check on my decision. I had no idea what to do. I spent the next twenty-four hours going through the motions, my insides churning with anxiety. I didn't sleep that night, wandering the house trying to figure out how I could convince this woman not to report me. I knew that ultimately she could not take Whitney away and that I would have a chance to represent myself and my program for Whitney, but she was still an unwelcome threat.

All I'd ever wanted was to keep Whitney out of institutions, to keep him in as normal an environment as possible because I feared that once he became part of a certain kind of system, labeled in a certain way, it would become harder, not easier, to help him.

The next day the phone rang at the exact same time.

"I was checking in to see what you decided," she said, as if I was choosing a color for a new car.

"Whitney's been accepted into the Dublin program." The lie flew out of my mouth.

I got off the phone quickly and stood there ready to bang my head against the wall. How could I have lied like that? Why had I blurted that out? I knew that she could be calling the Dublin program that very minute to check up on my claim. I was mortified. Not only would she report that I was neglecting him, she would say I lied about help I was getting for him. What had made me say those words that I knew could only get me into deeper trouble?

Before I could figure out how to get myself out of the mess, the phone rang again. *Here it comes,* I thought. I took a deep breath and braced myself as I picked up the receiver.

"It's Cathy from the Dublin school administration. I think you'll be happy to hear that we met and we've decided to accept Whitney into our handicapped preschool program at Chapman elementary school." Whitney's IQ from the testing session was rated as 50 for verbal and 46 for performance, with 100 being average, well below one percentile. That meant that out of a hundred children of Whitney's age, he was worse than all one hundred. A score of 100 IQ is average; most people would score between 90 and 110.

Whitney had not answered any questions right, but they still scored the test to allow him to participate. The test scores were as low as I'd feared because of his inability to be tested, but ironically, these scores got him labeled as multihandicapped—which qualified him for the program. It was well into September, but Whitney could join as soon as we met to discuss his test results and go over an "individualized education plan" (IEP) for him.

When I look back, I again see that the summaries from those tests described a very low-functioning child. The school psychologist wrote that Whitney

had a great deal of difficulty attending for more than 15 or 30 seconds to any one of the tasks presented to him and it was often necessary to provide him primary reinforcers to redirect him back to the task at hand. . . . Whitney had difficulty persevering on a task which he found to be difficult, and he would tend instead to abandon the activity and attempt to leave the room. . . . Based upon information received from the child's mother, it is often very difficult for him to interact with individuals whom he does not know. This was clearly evidenced in spite of the great efforts which were taken to accommodate this child's needs.... Cognitively based upon the current intellectual assessment, Whitney is functioning within the "very low" classification.

The speech and language therapist found:

Standardized testing was attempted but Whitney did not look at the testing materials, did not respond to verbal directions and did not respond to any test items.... Whitney would not enter the assessment room.... He sat down outside the room and took out his belongings to share.... Whitney made several responses when sharing his belongings. These were one word, naming responses inconsistent to verbal or non-verbal stimuli. [meaning that they were babbling and not really naming the object]. Whitney made several echolalic responses [meaning he might say mickimackey mickeymackey mickeymakey over and over]. Whitney eventually (10 minutes later) came into the assessment room.... Whitney acted out functions of pictures from his books and could mimic sounds including a clock ticking, swallowing sounds, and blowing out a candle. He interacted with the tester non-verbally in a play situation using pictures as functional objects from his books. (Example, He drank tea, stirred the sugar, blew out candles on a birthday cake.)... Whitney inconsistently understood directions, followed directions and made verbal responses.

Today these reports sound grim. But at the time, I felt his being accepted to the program was a huge victory. I felt there was an angel shepherding me in my choices for Whitney. My rational, scientist's brain would never have allowed me to lie to the preschool director like that.

Something had made me blurt out a lie—and moments later made it the truth.

6

Juggling
(or: Where There's
a Will, There's a Way)

It seemed every time I thought I'd made it over a hill, I would open my eyes in the morning to a giant mountain to climb. Now Whitney was finally in the Dublin preschool program, and he had started vocalizing, but sometimes it seemed he was harder to control than ever. I found myself looking forward to the first day of school, so that he'd have a place to go every day. I prayed the structure would help him.

On Whitney's first day at the handicapped preschool program at Chapman elementary school, I was up extra early to make the kids a big breakfast and get them off to school—and to make sure I had built in plenty of time for any tantrums. Things went smoothly that morning—at least as far as Whitney was concerned. I almost threw a tantrum, though, when we arrived and there was a substitute teacher in charge of the small class of five students. She introduced herself as Mrs. Ludwizac, explaining that the regular teacher had broken her leg that morning and she'd be filling in. "Just call me Mrs. Lud—we will all learn together, OK?"

"How long will the teacher be out?" I asked, trying to maintain my composure.

Mrs. Lud didn't know, but she must have sensed my apprehension. She invited me to stay and see how Whitney did. We got to chatting and when I told her my profession, she urged me to improvise a few activities with the kids—I sat cross-legged on the floor and began to sing.

> *She'll be comin' round the mountain when she comes*
> *She'll be comin' round the mountain when she comes*

Four of the kids started to sing along. Whitney wandered around the room looking carefully at the cement bricks on the wall, exploring the texture of the bricks with his hands, examining how his shadow played on the wall by leaning forward and backward.

> *She'll be wearing ketchup and mustard when she comes*
> *She'll be wearing ketchup and mustard when she comes . . .*

The kids laughed. Whitney continued to move and watch his shadow on the bricks. Mrs. Lud said, "Whitney, come over and join us in our song."

Whitney ignored her.

We finished the song. "Time for snack!" Mrs. Lud went to Whitney to redirect his attention and he pushed her away. He was still exploring his shadow-brick examination. Of course this looked like random rocking back and forth to everyone, but I was sure Whitney was marveling at how his shadow changed as he moved.

The next day I found out from the head of the school that the regular teacher could be out for quite some time and it had been decided Mrs. Lud was to be the substitute. I was devastated. I'd worked so hard to get Whitney into this program to have special attention, and now we were back to square one. Mrs. Lud seemed great, but even she was concerned that she wasn't trained in special education.

In those first few weeks, I took Whitney to school and stayed until I could tell he was on the brink of becoming unmanageable. At first, we would last half an hour but gradually increased the time. Mrs. Lud and I formed a rapport, and as the Dublin city school district encouraged parents' volunteer participation in the schools, I was soon bringing some of my language gym materials to the classroom to work with Whitney and the other children in the class.

Each Wednesday morning I played guitar, sang songs, or read story-books to the small group. I left that week's activities with Mrs. Lud—a song to sing, stories to read, or art projects to do, and she'd do them with the kids until I returned the next week. Basically, I was modifying some of our Head Start activities for these students.

I had a working lab with this class. I could devise new art, music and story activities, and games to teach the verbal-visual brain once a week and have Mrs. Lud continue with the activities. In this way, I was able to partially design what Whitney's curriculum should be. Unfortunately, Whitney wasn't responding and the other children were. I tried to convince myself that seeing the other kids do these activities would "rub off" on Whitney.

Whitney's new class comprised children who had been identified as high risk and in need of preschool handicapped services. To be eligible, the children had to have obvious language development problems that would interfere with attending a class with regular kids. For instance, some of the children in Whitney's class had articulation problems that made them hard to understand or language delays which meant they had considerably less vocabulary or expressive language skills than children have by age four. Some had lags in the development of their attention-memory systems, which meant they were having trouble learning nursery rhymes, following directions, staying on task, or remembering the alphabet. Their prereading skills were behind, and they had limited interest in listening to stories or exploring books. This was all very similar to the Head Start children I had worked with. Spending time in Whitney's class was making it harder for me to ignore his limitations. I'd been working with him for five years, but this was really the first time I had other children to compare him to in a structured prekindergarten "academic" program—and they had many more skills than Whitney.

After several weeks, I was surprised to notice that one day as I entered the classroom with my guitar and a bag of "healthy snacks," Whitney's classmates moved toward me and gathered around as I placed my things down on the table. Maybe it was the expectation of snacks or maybe it was the music they'd come to enjoy, but I was touched that they seemed to be responding. A child's face lighting up as you enter a room is precious—it's hard to explain how extra special that look is when it comes from children who seldom respond to their environment.

Perhaps that's why it was so difficult when Whitney not only didn't seem to notice my entrance, but actually tried to bolt from the room when I opened the door. Mrs. Lud had to run after him and close the door before he could escape. In response to her stopping him, Whitney pulled down his pants and peed on her. When Whitney was acting out as a two- or three-year-old, we could usually grab him and hold him. Now that he was five, he was getting too big. It was much less acceptable to be peed on by a child who wasn't wearing diapers. When Whitney was younger, it was hard to discern any cause for his fits because there didn't seem to be anything obviously upsetting to link them to. But the older he got, the more purposeful his fits seemed. His outbursts these days tended to be destructive. When he would bite, kick, pee, rip up books, or tear down drawings from the wall, it certainly appeared to be a willful act, as opposed to a toddler's accident. No punishment was effective with him. All I could do was thank Mrs. Lud for being so patient.

On the ten-minute drive back to my office that day, I thought, *Why am I doing this? I'm helping everyone but Whitney.*

Meanwhile, life in our new home wasn't getting any easier. I'd played up the fact that, for the first time, all three of them would each have their own room. In our previous house, because Whitney had needed his own room, William and Vanessa had to share. I let the kids pick out their new beds. Vanessa had chosen a canopy bed and William a trundle bed so he could have friends sleep over. We chose a firetruck bed for Whitney because he enjoyed the fire engine jungle gym at the park across the street.

I made a big family project of assembling Whitney's firetruck bed. We put decals on it and decked it out in red sheets. Whitney was oblivious. In fact, he'd wandered off, uninterested in the whole thing. Then we heard a squawk and a thud from the next room. We ran to see Whitney lying in the middle of Vanessa's new bed, the delicate canopy hanging limply from the four posters. He'd climbed up onto the top and broke through the middle.

I was ready to wring his neck. We'd spent so many hours on his bed and all he'd done was ruin his sister's. But Vanessa and William just burst out laughing at the sight of their brother and his look of hapless confusion.

Whitney was into everything these days. William and a friend of his had discovered a crawl space in the attic of the garage and built a makeshift tower from a pile of boxes so that they could climb up and play in the little fort they'd created up there. Whitney must have observed them doing this because I came home from work one day to find him precariously balanced on a wobbly box, reaching for the crawl space. I made William disassemble the tower and closed up the crawl space.

It surprised me that William and Vanessa weren't throwing their own tantrums or getting angry at Whitney when he destroyed their rooms or ruined their fun. I don't know why they weren't upset. It must have been because it was now clear there was something wrong with their little brother and they couldn't get angry. But I was getting more and more worried about how to give them enough attention and not let Whitney's behavior ruin their childhood. William and Vanessa seldom brought friends over to play after school. If they did, I had to make sure Whitney had someone or something to keep him occupied. I tried to find things we could do that Whitney could tolerate, and when I did, we did that thing often. For instance, Whitney seemed to enjoy going to King's Island, a big theme park with rides and people dressed as giant cartoon characters. We had to keep an eye on him and chase after him at times, but this was an outing everyone enjoyed; I bought a season pass.

I was also struggling to find help so I didn't have to do it alone. We were between regular babysitters—Tammi married and moved away with her new husband to Minneapolis. I hadn't found a regular after-school sitter. I went through a parade of sitters, looking for someone who could handle Whitney, be flexible according to my schedule, and also provide William and Vanessa with support. I also wanted someone who could fit in at the office, because all three kids were still participating in therapy after school and doing their homework where I could keep an eye on them. By having them at the office, I felt like we were together when the school day was done but I was still able to work.

I had always looked for ways to provide special time for Vanessa and William so they would not resent the extra attention Whitney required. One of the main reasons I'd enrolled them in Columbus Academy was not only for a good education, but as a way to give them a break from the intensity at home. There were a wide variety of great after-school programs, and I signed them up for everything: drama, art, sports. Between after-school activities and coming to my office to "work" and play, I thought they got a respite from Whitney that helped them cope with him when we were all at home. One of the reasons that I decided to have a private practice after the hospital closed was that I knew most of my patients would want afternoon or early evening appointments. After work or school was finished, they could schedule appointments before going home for the evening. That would leave me the mornings free to prepare for their appointments or volunteer at all three of my children's schools.

This year, I signed up to be room mother for Vanessa's class. As part of my participation, I created the "mom in the classroom volunteer day." That allowed me to come into the school and teach in Vanessa's class every month. Her class was right next door to William's, so when I was there for Vanessa's room, I could observe or do activities in William's also. Working with other moms, I was able to concoct rather elaborate theme-events for various holidays and to plan special projects around what they were studying. For example, when they were reading Tommy Paola or William Steig books, I asked my art therapist to make masks of the books' characters or create a sequence of pictures the kids could color to create murals to augment the lesson.

The next year, I served as room mom for William's class. By becoming a room mother and parent volunteer in each of my kids' classes for all of their years in elementary school, I was able to share their school experience with them, developing relationships with their teachers and classmates, understanding the ecology of the classroom, and gaining the ability to intuit expectations.

In January, I invited all forty of the boys and girls from both Will and Vanessa's classes to our house for a slumber party. All went well and I was able to keep Whitney away from the fray. Then, as Vanessa and I started to serve breakfast, Whitney appeared wearing his favorite yellow T-shirt and nothing else.

Before I could try to get him to go upstairs, Vanessa's girlfriends spotted him and began giggling and pointing. Seeing a cute five-year-old boy walking around with no underwear was an event. As I ushered him upstairs I could hear the girls teasing Vanessa.

"That's weird!" the kids squealed.

I felt a wave of anger—all the work I'd done to prepare this big party and the only thing these kids could do was ridicule Vanessa for her brother's behavior. I wanted to yell at these girls for bad manners, but I stifled my initial reaction because I knew they didn't know what they were saying. They didn't even know there was anything wrong with Whitney. As far as Vanessa was concerned, there wasn't.

I could hear Vanessa shrugging it off. "That's just how my brother is." But my heart tightened with pain.

When she tells the story today, she laughs and says, "Whitney must have thought he only had to wear one item of clothing at a time when he was a kid—either underwear *or* a T-shirt."

Everyone had had fun—but I felt like next time I needed to plan things differently. By May, when it was time for William's school birthday, rather than cupcakes in the classroom, I organized a Brain Day field trip at my new Metro Medical Park office. It was as if I had to prove to myself that I could provide special experiences for Vanessa and William so that they wouldn't feel their childhoods were ruined by all of the attention Whitney required.

Columbus Academy allowed both Vanessa's and William's classes to take a 40-minute school bus ride to my office. I will never forget the look on Will's face as the buses drove up and he saw the big "Welcome to William's Brain Day Birthday" sign on the front of the building. He was thrilled and felt very special.

By this time, I'd finished building my language gym using computers, audio and visual equipment, and the arts to create different ways to work on language skills. We had fourteen simulation labs, including art lab and therapy stations, Computer Arcade, Reader's Theater, Writer's Workshop, Executive Excel Lab, Mental Workout Room, Parent Observation, and Simulation classrooms. These labs were the culmination of the "brain workouts" I'd been developing with Head Start kids and using with Whitney at home.

The kids rotated around the different stations, and each station had a handout in "kid talk" to explain how a part of the brain works. Mary, the head room mom, and some of the other moms ran stations, and some of my staff and parents volunteered to help. My best coup was that I'd conned my uncle Don, a Sandia Laboratories computer scientist visiting from Albuquerque, into running the computer station.

At the art lab, kids played visual memory games; in another area, Uncle Don showed them how computer games can strengthen speed of thinking. My administrative assistant, a trained opera singer, taught songs and asked the kids to predict lyrics to show them verbal memory and verbal recall. She was teaching them "Jelly Man Kelly" by James Taylor. They stood on a little stage with music stands like they were at Carnegie Hall.

The most popular activity was the Movie/Dance Theater. A friend of mine had designed the first big-screen TV used for sports bars and installed one in the ceiling of our office. We then put a floor-to-ceiling mirror on one of the walls. With this setup, we could play movies on the ceiling screen and aim it at the mirror. I ran this station, with a rock star and Brer Rabbit singing "Zip-A-Dee-Doo-Dah" on a Disney tape. The kids learned to do a break-dance, and by looking in the mirror it looked like they were actually in the movie.

I had each station timed so that the kids were in ten groups of four rotating around. The handouts explained visual memory or auditory memory or visual attention or whatever skill each lab was using. As they left the party, they each got a giant cookie from "Will's Grandma" (my mother) that had a huge "W" on it for William and a brain book on how the brain works. They left laughing and skipping. Mrs. Green, Vanessa's teacher who had moved through all of the labs with the children, said, "This was such fun and it was the most educational field trip we have ever had."

"I am a different teacher for having attended this party myself," I told her. "I always get something out of observing how the young brain learns."

I was quite pleased when Mrs. Green added, "I did not realize how some of us think in visual pictures and some of us think in words." Trying all of the labs and reading our handouts, she had experienced the difference between visual and verbal thinkers.

My ideas were coming across! It was just the affirmation I needed— the new practice was such a struggle that it was great to see all I believed in put to good use. I was pleased that the day seemed to have been a success and I was glad that both Vanessa's and William's classes were able to come so that I got to know all of the children better.

Vanessa, William, and I were now in the habit of nightly huddles before bedtime. We'd settle with blankets at the end of the upstairs hallway where I could keep an eye on Whitney roaming around, doing his own thing or occasionally sitting with us. I would review the day with each of them, and now that I knew about the classroom and class-mates, it was easier to cue them to discuss their days.

When I think back on that first year in Dublin—struggling to get Whit-ney adjusted to school, doing everything I could for William and Vanessa, not to mention trying to get my practice off the ground and basically trying to force some semblance of normalcy on our frenzied life—I felt like I was drowning. My friend, the pediatrician who had invited me to lease my new office space in Dublin, was one of the few people who glimpsed my frantic comings and goings enough to sense my despair. She had known me for years and she could see that I was becoming a shell of the former Cheri. The young scientist who made television appearances and was often invited to be keynote speaker was letting herself go, and struggling to keep a private practice afloat.

One afternoon, she came into my office and insisted I join her for lunch. We chatted about the office, our children, the weather, and I couldn't believe how odd it felt to be out with a friendly adult. I real-ized how rare social outings had become. My shoulders started to relax, and tension I wasn't aware of began to drain away.

Halfway through our salads, she leaned in and said. "Cheri, you know I care about you very much."

The tension rushed back. I knew that segue all too well. I braced myself.

"You need to put Whitney in a residential autism school. It is ruin-ing you, not to mention what it's doing to Vanessa and William."

I didn't respond.

"Your two other children have no life. They're doing everything to help their brother. It's not a normal childhood. You're going to take the whole family down. Your husband's not around, your kids are becoming therapists to their brother—they're too young for that kind of responsibility and you don't look like the healthy, bubbly, provocative, witty friend I have treasured for so many years. If you crumble, then all else fails."

The blood was rushing in my ears, drowning out the sound of her voice. I told myself that she was a friend and she meant well. But I couldn't imagine she knew what I was going through. She sat there, thin, in her beautiful designer clothes, her biggest worry whether or not to go with her surgeon husband to his conference in Hawaii. I sat there overweight, with wrinkled clothes that no longer fit quite right, hardly knowing what day it was, and worrying about my world caving in around me. My new career was barely supporting us, though I hoped it would take off. Whitney had a very poor prognosis for improving, and William and Vanessa needed parenting from two parents during their very critical formative school years. She was right. The amount of responsibility I had on my shoulders was too much for one person.

I knew she was trying to help. I plastered on a smile and tried to look like I was taking in her words.

"You're going to have two great kids—but only if you give up Whitney. If you don't, you could end up with three messes."

I didn't know what to say. Why was it bad to try to get Whitney to be part of our world? Why would that be scary and threatening to people? I knew that Vanessa and William were missing out on certain opportunities, but I was working hard to keep them at Columbus Academy so they'd have lives separate from Whitney as well. I believed helping their brother would make them into fabulous, caring people. Could I be wrong?

When I think back on incidents like this, I realize that though I may have wanted to shoot the person challenging me, these confrontations rather than dissuade me from my plan instead strengthened my resolve. At this particular time I was starting to doubt my own ability to continue. I was tempted to take the easy way out—my will to keep trekking on across the unknown rocky path was weakening. To have someone nudge me toward giving up was just the push I needed—but it didn't have the result she was looking for.

As we drove back to the office, my friend said, "You're upset, aren't you? I didn't mean to hurt your feelings. I am just trying to help."

I was so full of fury, I faced her and said, "If I can't fix him with my professional training, I am going to *will* this disorder out of him."

She turned to me in shock. "Don't you see what I mean? You're losing your mind. You can't *will* autism out of someone."

I stared hard right into her eyes and said, slowly, deliberately, and with conviction, "Wanna bet? You just watch me."

7

Fire Drills

I was now no longer talking about Whitney to anyone. Instead, I was getting up at about five a.m. and working out on my NordicTrack machine for one hour. For the first thirty minutes, I would have a mental board meeting. I'd read a biography of Charles Dickens written by his son that described how Dickens had debates and discussions with his characters about their behavior and actions. It was only once he had a firm sense of what his characters would or would not do—from debating with them—that he would proceed with his stories. Dickens felt that the books he wrote were not really his; they belonged to the characters that descended upon him. He was simply a conduit for the people in his stories.

My mental board meetings were taking on the same characteristics: the arguing in my head went on daily, and I felt as if the voices were coming from other people because many of the ideas for what to do next seemed like things I wouldn't have thought of myself. "Stay away from everyone." "Keep your children next to you." "Don't talk about Whitney to teachers or your patients." "Turn off the TV. Don't listen to the radio in your car. Don't go to the movies. Don't play a CD. Get very quiet." "Don't read a magazine or a newspaper. Sit in the bathtub and think . . . allow us to talk to you . . . we will tell you what to do to help Whitney . . . trust us—come to these board meetings and we will show you the way to the answer." I know this sounds weird, but I know these were not an auditory hallucination because I knew how to behave socially and harness the sounds in my brain. I knew that the different voices were a way to sort through various options and perceptions.

In spite of my attempts to "will" the autism out of Whitney, he was still biting and peeing on people. He was having fits where he'd bang his head and rock. He would take off all his clothes, rip up books, and throw things at the other children in his class. My cockeyed optimist approach wasn't working. There wasn't much positive to focus on.

I thought our time at Chapman was finished when I got a call to come get Whitney. "This isn't going to work," the administrator said, exasperated. I rushed over imagining the worst. But by the time I arrived, Whitney was sitting at the principal's desk, eating a hot dog and french fries and smiling.

The principal looked up at me proudly. "The storm has passed," he said. "He was having a tantrum in the cafeteria when we were trying to mainstream the class for lunch. I got this food on a tray and was able to get him to follow me. I think it was the cafeteria noise and chaos."

I had been wondering about noise and Whitney lately myself. How could it be the noise that bothered Whitney if he couldn't hear?

Meanwhile, the principal was so pleased they'd gotten him under control that they gave him a reprieve.

I was exhausted trying to figure out what would cause Whitney to have the majority of his fits. The only instances in which the cause was clear to me were the times he threw a tantrum when someone was trying to get him to do something he didn't "understand," meaning I didn't think he understood what was being requested or perhaps the request was in conflict with his mental image of what he was predicting would happen next. For example, if we had to get him to stop watching a film, or go somewhere on our time schedule that we couldn't explain, or put on shoes he didn't want to wear. Sometimes it seemed he was full steam ahead on a Whitney plan of some sort, and any interference with this undecodable plan would cause a commotion. However, I would say that for most of his tantrums, which occurred several times a day, there was no repeating logic that I could discern. I couldn't figure out how noise could be the trigger. After all, I could yell in his ear and he wouldn't budge. He would put his cheek up toward me for more—as if he wanted to feel the vibration on his head bones. During the board meetings in my mind, I explored what could be happening with his auditory system, but I wasn't getting any answers.

Right before Halloween, Whitney's school installed a new fire alarm system and started having regular fire drills. As soon as the alarm went off during the first drill, Whitney started tearing the room apart. He pulled toys out of their bins and emptied cubbies. When Mrs. Lud tried to subdue him, he flailed around, biting and kicking her and anyone who came near him. She had lined the other children to go outside, but didn't know what to do about Whitney. The firemen tried to get him outside, but not wanting to restrain him forcefully, they finally told Mrs. Lud to let him stay inside by himself and lock him in the room. I didn't find out about this until years later, when Mrs. Lud confided in me once Whitney was doing much better. She told me the story to remind me of how far we'd come and I had to agree. She didn't say how many times they'd actually had to resort to this, and I didn't want to think about it years later, when we were past that. It will always be a mystery what Whitney was thinking or feeling during these tantrums. To this day, he doesn't remember this school at all.

What Mrs. Lud did tell me at the time was that Whitney went berserk when the fire alarm came on. I have to admit, I was more fascinated than upset. I was used to stories of Whitney having tantrums and had certainly witnessed plenty myself. But he had never had a tantrum triggered by loud sounds. As it turned out, each time they had a fire drill he would go wild.

Was this more evidence that Whitney had a hypo-hyper brain—a sensory system that overworked and underworked in spurts? I'd been bombarding his auditory system so much. Could it be that his rocking and head-banging was the result of being overstimulated? When he sat in the corner and stared, comalike, was he shutting down in response to stimulation? Maybe this hypo-hyper functioning was why he was behaving in such extremes.

The theories were flying at my morning board meetings. My mind was churning out ideas for how to help Whitney. Now I was flooded with new ideas. In addition to postulating how this hypo- and hyper-functioning might be causing his fits, I started to think that he was allocating his brain processing resources entirely to his visual thinking pathway and allocating no resources to his auditory pathway. In other words, maybe his visual processing system was overworking and his auditory processing system was underworking. These two systems are supposed to work together to learn and process sound-symbol relationships for listening, reading, speaking, writing, and thinking. If they were out of balance, could that be causing his problem with language development?

By February 1991, I thought Whitney's skill had improved enough that he might be able to be retested. I was eager to test my theory about his high-visual and low-auditory skills.

We decided to use the Illinois Test of Psycholinguistic Abilities (ITPA). The ITPA was used as a predictor for determining which children might respond to better: the sounds of language or the symbols of language. I was trained to administer it while a research scholar at the University of Memphis working on a project funded by the U.S. Office of Education using rebus characters in teaching reading skills to underprivileged children in Tennessee, Arkansas, and Mississippi.

The authors of the ITPA, John Paraskevopoulos and Samuel Kirk, developed the test because they held a view contrary to the mainstream view—still widespread today—that overall intelligence was the sum of the parts, which was the philosophy when Whitney was tested by the Dublin School District.

I think Paraskevopoulos and Kirk state the case quite well for a different view of testing. They explain that testing of intelligence began with a Frenchman named Alfred Binet who created a test to measure the neuro-cogitive functions he observed in mentally retarded children. Binet was working on the theory that once you identified areas of weakness in thinking, vocabulary, attention, memory, or problem-solving, then you could create school experiences to train the skills and improve IQ. Binet created a school for "mental orthopedics" in the early 1900s to help children increase their brain functioning. However, when American psychologists imported Binet's test instruments to the United States, they didn't look at the individual scores, but rather viewed intelligence as the sum score of all the tests. Their idea was that people are born with a certain level of "smartness," and that this score reflected that inherited ability. Further, they believed that IQ cannot be changed through education and training—an idea that persists to this day. American psychologists combined the subtest scores to obtain a composite score, and this was used to place people into categories such as average, superior, or low-functioning.

However, according to Kirk and Paraskevopoulos, using the tests in this way was not helpful to a teacher or a therapist. These two psychologists felt dissatisfied with the use of composite scores because they had found that many children classified as mentally retarded displayed wide discrepancies among their abilities. Many of the children had very specific weaknesses in some areas, while other areas were normal or strong. They devised the ITPA to measure the psycholinguistic processes needed to move information into memory for thinking and learning. They refer to these processes as "communication routes," explaining that it is best to measure each of them as distinct processing systems. The communication routes include receptive language processing, expressive language processing, and the internal thought process of organizing and intepreting.*

The authors of the ITPA would not have seen Whitney's baseline testing at the Dublin school as optimal because those tests were scored by adding all the scores together and using the composite score to represent a static and unitary IQ My training was to look for strengths and weakness within subtests and across subtests to determine a target for training, just as Binet had done with his original IQ test over a hundred years ago.

I had my therapists administer some of the subtests of the ITPA to Whitney while I observed from our video monitoring center. He was now 5 years, 4 months old, and he scored as follows:

SUBTEST	PURPOSE	WHITNEY'S AGE LEVEL (IN YEARS. MONTHS)
AUDITORY SEQUENTIAL MEMORY	Measures the ability to store information in the brains verbal working memory when there is minimal meaning involved by asking the child to remember a string of numbers(instead of words).	3.5
AUDITORY RECEPTION	Measures the ability to decode sentences with increasingly difficult vocabulary while grammatic difficulty is not increased, using yes or no questions. Sample questions are "Do dogs eat?""Do dials yawn?" "Do carpenters kneel?" "Do wingless birds soar?"	3.5
AUDITORY ASSOCIATION	Measures the ability to see relationships in verbal analogies; this test requires auditory attention to detail. For example: "Grass is green. Sugar is _____ (sweet)."	3.3
		(continued)

*From *Technical Manual: The Development and Psychometric Characteristics of the Illinois Test of Psycholinguistic Abilities* by John N. Paraskevopoulos and Samuel A. Kirk. University of Illinois Press, Urbana & Chicago, © 1969, 1985.

SUBTEST	PURPOSE	WHITNEY'S AGE LEVEL (IN YEARS. MONTHS)
GRAMMATIC CLOSURE	Measures the ability to use language universals to predict grammatic form. Example: Here is a dog. Here are 2 _____ (barking) dogs. The dog likes to bark. Here he is, _____ (barking).	2.6
VISUAL SEQUENTIAL MEMORY	Measures the ability to store information in the brain's visual working memory by reproducing strings of symbol tiles in a sequential order from memory, after being shown the sequence.	6.2
VISUAL RECEPTION	Measures the ability to gain meaning from pictures. For example the child is shown a picture of a lamp and then a picture with four objects: one lamp (different from the first one shown) and three other objects, and the child has to point to the right answer (the different lamp).	5.0
VISUAL CLOSURE	Measures the ability to identify objects such as different types of fish or dogs in a hidden picture under time constraints.	4.6
VISUAL ASSOCIATION	Measures the ability to see relationships in visual analogies such as: A tennis racket goes with a tennis ball, so a baseball bat would go with a _____, and the child has four choices.	5.6

When subjects exhibit big differences between their auditory and visual processing scores, the theory is that it will be hard for them to have auditory-visual integration. That is, it will be hard for these two systems to work well together, as they are supposed to. For a child to read efficiently, the child must convert graphics (the symbols of print) into phonics (the sounds of language) to gain meaning. To make this conversion, the visual system (which decodes the graphic symbols) must be working in step with the auditory system (which decodes the sounds of language).

For most of us, the meaning of a word comes from what the word *sounds* like rather than what it *looks* like. Take the following sets of words, for example:

Cheri
Chair
Cat
Kitten

"Cheri" starts with the letter C, but represents the "sh" sound. "Chair" also starts with the letter C, but represents the "ch" sound. "Cat," too, starts with the letter C, but like "kitten," represents a "k" sound. So until we convert the symbol to a sound, we can't pronounce the word or decode it into meaning. Most of us automatically convert a word into its auditory correlate (what it sounds like) to be able to say it and know what it means. We "say it to ourselves." At least that is what verbal people or people with an integrated auditory-visual system tend to do. Try to read without "hearing" the words in your head.

The fact that Whitney did so well in visual sequential memory was thrilling to me. At least I could see from this testing that he had the visual skills to code and decode information. I knew that this was an important function for reading. So even though he was barely testable, it seemed very significant to me that he could do this well. The fact that he could do any of these tests at all showed that he was not retarded, but developing in a very interesting way. His visual memory was working, and this was the key to teaching him things. Evidence of his visual skills weren't based solely on my anecdotal reports anymore. This testing gave me the beginnings of the support that I needed to develop an understanding of Whitney's thinking system, a system that was totally devoid of words. If I could groom that system of thinking and problem-solving, maybe he could find a pathway out of his silent world.

When I was trying so desperately to get Whitney into this handicapped program, I'd made much of his "talking" in my reports to the school. Ever since the day he'd laughed at *Snow White,* he'd started making sounds. Vanessa and William and I tried to convince ourselves that he was saying words when he mimicked our playing. To be honest, they weren't words that anyone would recognize. They were sounds that he made when we were working to engage him in productive play with Playmobile characters. We felt he was communicating—unfortunately, it seemed as if it was more to himself than to us. I felt it wasn't the sounds that indicated the meaning, it was the context. For instance, if we were playing one of our Disney-related games and he held up Donald and made a sound, we were sure he meant "duck," or if he pointed to the firetruck, we thought it meant "truck." However if he wasn't playing these games, these "words" weren't recognizable; they weren't clear to his teacher or anyone else. It sounded like grunts or babble.

I sometimes think that one of the things that made me pursue language and speech therapy as a profession was my early obsession with the story of Helen Keller. I was so taken with the story of how Annie Sullivan worked day in, day out, never giving up, convinced that she could find a way to break through to Helen. The moment when Annie was first able to teach Helen the word for "water" sent chills along my spine. And here I was, now trying to do the same with Whitney— searching for a way to teach my son words.

While I might be convinced that when Whitney made a sound holding Mickey, he was saying "Mickey," I had to find a way to get him to use language to communicate. So in addition to working on his speech, since he was so visual, I decided to look for ways to get him to recognize the names of things visually. In other words, I had to find a way to get him to recognize the words for things using visual cues.

I decided to start with things I was sure he knew. He got excited when he saw Wendy's or McDonald's, for instance, because he knew he'd get to eat french fries—one of his favorite foods. I thought that maybe I could get him to associate a picture of Wendy's with the logo for Wendy's that appeared on the french-fry wrapper.

I began creating "Whitney books"—flip charts, photo albums, and binders full of pictures and associated words or logos. I collected logos and pictures of everything that Whitney was familiar with in his everyday life: pictures of everyone in our family next to their names; photos of the grocery stores next to the logos for Kroger's and Big Bear; Cheerios labels, milk cartons. Every item had both a picture and a word. Whenever possible, I used logos because I thought he would have an easier time recognizing visual images, not just typed words.

I also put a word label on everything in the house, the way I had with other patients in the past. Vanessa and William and I would play word games with these books with Whitney every chance we got. We'd try to get him to name each image in the book; we'd try to get him to say each item he came into contact with in his everyday life: Whitney's bed, shoes, pants, cup. At breakfast we'd have him choose between Cheerios and Cap'n Crunch. We did it so he thought it was a game. He was making sounds, but the words were still unintelligible. He would vocalize during these "games" more than at other times during the day; most of his other vocalizations were random and infrequent.

One day I was in the kitchen, trying to decide what to make for dinner, when Whitney came up to me and handed me the card for the Wendy's french fries box. I stared at the card in amazement.

"William! Vanessa!" I shouted to the kids and they came running.

"Whitney wants french fries!" I was laughing with manic glee. William and Vanessa looked at me with concern. Then they saw the card with the Wendy's logo in my hand and they understood. We piled into the car and drove straight to Wendy's and ordered up lots of french fries and hamburgers. As we sat at the table, happily munching our fries, I thought that I had never tasted anything quite so delicious.

I couldn't wait to see how far we could take Whitney with this skill. It reminded me of the turning point in some early researchers' attempts to teach chimps to talk. After working with the chimps in sign language, one day when the researchers entered the lab, a chimp signed "tickle me." At that moment, they knew the chimp was using language to request a need; she was engaging in purposeful communication, not just parroting or imitating the people training her.

Whitney was pleased to be eating his favorite food, but he wasn't nearly as excited I was: Whitney had asked for something. He knew that he could get something from us using his logos. I thought, *I know how to teach him now.*

One of my Wednesdays to teach at Whitney's school began badly. It took me longer than usual to coax Whitney into the car and my nerves were frayed. We pulled into the school parking lot at the exact moment that Mrs. Lynch, the director of special education for Dublin schools, was getting out of her car.

Please no, not today, I thought. I knew that Whitney was due for his evaluation for next year, and I guessed this was the day. I had been begging Mrs. Lynch to allow him to stay in the same program to maintain some continuity. I was trying to convince her that after a year, he was finally starting to grasp the classroom routine. I thought that if he stayed in the same preschool class for one more year, it could really help him. I knew she was skeptical. I also knew that on this particular day, I happened to look like I hadn't slept in months, and my clothes felt even more mismatched and disheveled than usual as I looked at this well-coiffed, very put-together woman who could have been on the cover of *Dress for Success.*

"Hello, Dr. Florance," she called out.

I smiled and waved, took a deep breath, and prayed Whitney would get out of the car and follow me inside with no resistance. I was driving my dad's old minivan at the time, and one way I was able to get Whitney into the car was to play a game with him. I would put him in the car, drive down the driveway with the door of the minivan open, then swing around so it would fly shut. Whitney loved it. Unfortunately, this was not good for the minivan, and before long, the door was falling off the car on the highway or when we stopped at a traffic light. I took the car back to the dealership and eventually back to the factory. "No longer under warranty," they said. "We have never seen a door fall off like this, but we tried to fix it." In a couple of weeks, the door would fall off again. So I gave Vanessa the job of holding the door on the car while we were driving to the gas station to get it put back on.

In the meantime, if you didn't open the door just right, it would fall off. When I opened it to let Whitney out, sure enough, the door clattered to the ground.

I turned to Mrs. Lynch and laughed sheepishly. "I'll see you in there," I said. She nodded.

It was another forty-five minutes before Whitney and I made it inside. He was big enough now that if he didn't want to do something, I couldn't physically make him. He bit me. Shook his head. He did not want to go to school. The more he resisted, the more anxious I became. And the more anxious I got, the more he resisted. I knew very well that in these situations I should make myself very calm in order to calm him down. But there were moments when the anxious and frustrated mother shut out the reasoning scientist, and this was one of those moments. All I could think of was that the longer it took us to get inside, the worse the impression we would make.

When we finally got to the classroom, Mrs. Lynch was perched on a small school chair in the back of classroom, clipboard on her lap, observing. School had started at eight a.m. and it was now ten-thirty. Whitney ran to the corner and started banging his head on the floor until I thought it would bleed. When Mrs. Lud tried to redirect him, he tried to run out the door. When we got him back into the room, he started grabbing books from the bookshelf, tearing pages out of the books and eating them.

After about thirty minutes, Mrs. Lynch rose, smiled, bid us a cheerful goodbye, and left. I looked at Mrs. Lud and she shook her head in empathy.

A few days later, Mrs. Lynch asked me to come visit a class that she thought would be "the right solution for Whitney."

"Oh, I think we already have a great solution for Whitney," I said. "He just loves his class at Chapman. And he's doing great." I hoped that my flattery would win her over.

"I think I have a better idea," was all she said, and directed me to meet her at a class at Indian Run elementary school—still in the Dublin school district, but a Franklin County MRDD (mentally retarded and developmentally delayed) funded program.

When we walked into the classroom, I was dismayed. It was full of ten- and eleven-year-olds who were highly medicated and severely retarded.

"How will this help Whitney?" I asked, incredulous.

"We think this is best," she insisted.

"Best?" I tried to maintain my calm. I turned to the classroom teacher. "What are your goals for your students this year?" I challenged her.

"To recognize a street sign, toilet themselves," she replied.

I had them here. "Well, Whitney can already do that," I said to Mrs. Lynch. Aside from the fact that Whitney could recognize a Wendy's logo, these just weren't the kind of long-term goals I wanted for him. I had higher aims. "I don't want him to regress, I want him to read and talk."

"Read and talk?" Mrs. Lynch could barely contain her incredulity. "This program will be much better for him," she insisted. "These teachers have special training. It will help."

I knew that if I stirred up too much trouble, they could try to have him taken away to a school that would require a long bus ride and where I could not participate. So I didn't throw the fit I felt boiling inside of me. Instead, I once again appealed to her to reconsider and to let Whitney stay another year in the Chapman program.

———

Weeks later, before the end of the school year, there was a new regulation put into effect at the school. If a child's sixth birthday was September 30 or later, he couldn't be in the Chapman preschool program. Of the five children currently in the program, only Whitney could not stay in the program.

Now there was no choice. Whitney had to go to Indian Run. He would have to change schools again, and go into a class for even more severely handicapped students.

I feared that going to Indian Run would be a major step backward. Being around older children who were worse off than the kids in his preschool would only make Whitney worse. *Now they're just warehousing him,* I thought in a panic. They had to place him somewhere; federal law required it. But that room had felt so hopeless—just like locking him inside during a fire drill. They were giving up on trying to save him. I wasn't, but I was running out of time. I knew that if I didn't keep his progress up in these crucial years—didn't build on his ability to recognize logos and find a way to teach him language by the time he was seven—he would have very limited hopes for a normal life. The alarm was ringing loud and clear, and I felt like I understood Whitney's frustration—I wanted to lash out, to tear things apart. I didn't know what to do with all these feelings, so like the fireman, I just told myself to lock them inside.

8

Me and

Mrs. Jones

During the summer between Whitney's year at Chapman and the MRDD class at Indian Run elementary, we hired a new home-office assistant. Lee was tall, blond, lanky—and determined to be the next drum major for the Ohio State University marching band. The kids loved him.

Soon after Lee started with us, he was out on the front lawn of our house, practicing with his baton and using the kids as his judges. He would march around the yard with OSU fight songs blaring from a boom box, do flips and twirls, throw the baton to the sky, and twirl around and catch it. The kids were enthralled. Lee told Vanessa and William that they were helping him get ready for tryouts and that the competition would be so harsh that he had to work hard to be the best ever. They were honored at the importance of their roles and took their jobs very seriously.

One day, while Will and Vanessa studied Lee's routine with their critical eyes, Whitney's own inner adventures drew him elsewhere without anyone noticing. Whitney never seemed bored; he just always seemed to be drawn upstream while we were all headed down.

Suddenly, a row of firetrucks and police cars came screeching into our cul de sac, sirens blaring. As the firemen and police came bounding into the yard, they asked where the emergency was.

Lee, with baton in hand and the OSU alma mater blaring in the background on the boom box, said, "I don't know what you're talking about."

"We got a 911 call from this address," the captain explained. After taking a look at Lee and the baton twirling setup in our front yard, the captain became a bit leery—this was not a typical yuppie Dublin scenario. They insisted on looking around. Lee was upset that his integrity was being questioned, but the police headed inside, with Lee and William and Vanessa on their heels.

There was Whitney, innocently playing with the phone.

"Why did the child try to get us? What's going on?" they questioned Lee. Whitney was in first grade now and looked old enough to know what he was doing.

Lee explained that Whitney had developmental problems and must have punched in the numbers by mistake. "He doesn't know what he's doing," he said.

When I got home that night, Lee was mortified. "I'm so sorry, I didn't realize he'd gone inside."

I was too tired to get upset. But when it happened again a week later, the police told me we had to do something about this "crying wolf situation."

It was also pretty upsetting to William and Vanessa. There they were, outside having a good time, and suddenly police show up and the neighbors come running. Mom wasn't home and it was embarrassing and scary. We still couldn't reason with Whitney, and I couldn't explain to him that he couldn't dial the phone. Aside from his limited language, there was no logic to it for him: We all used the phone—why couldn't he? Some people might have fired Lee, but I was afraid he would quit. This situation was very stressful for him and the tryout he'd been working toward for ten years was only a few weeks away. The kids and I loved him and he was perfect for our seemingly gypsy lifestyle—flexible enough to roam between home and office to help me.

I simply unplugged the phones and we plugged them in when we needed them.

Today, I think that Whitney must have memorized 911 from TV. This was not a random act. He wanted the police and firetrucks to come to visit him. He has done many things since that show his visual memory of numbers to be quite advanced. But we did not understand that then.

In spite of all the "fine messes" Whitney got himself into, we were starting to feel more like a family.

It was heartbreaking when I had to leave Whitney at Indian Run on his first day of school in his new class. There were only four students: Whitney and three ten- to twelve-year-olds who were heavily medicated and severely autistic, mostly staring straight ahead and rocking in their seats. It felt wrong. The room wasn't right; it was set up for older children, and yet there was my six-year-old, legs dangling at a desk that was too big for him.

I'd been feeling like we were making progress, but it wasn't the kind of progress the schools were looking for. We were back in reality, big time.

I realized the teachers and administrators were concerned about Whitney's inability to follow directions or adhere to classroom routines and perceived him to be mentally retarded. Whitney had moved from the teachable to the unteachable. They felt he couldn't pay attention and couldn't follow directions; they wanted him to sit in the circle for story time, he wanted to get back to his Legos.

Although this class was housed in a Dublin school building, it was
part of the Franklin County program for mentally retarded and developmentally delayed, so he had to be retested and evaluated by Franklin
County in early September to secure his placement and set goals for
the year. After this evaluation, in addition to his placement in the
MRDD classroom, they assigned him to PT (physical therapy), OT
(occupational therapy), and speech therapy. The school labeled him
"multihandicapped." They saw a severely retarded child with multiple
handicaps in his physical abilities and his communication and his intelligence: a kid who could barely ride a tricycle at age six, someone who
could not hold a pencil or erase without tearing the paper, who had all
strikes against him. The mother in me saw a future engineer en route to
MIT. The scientist saw not only the high visual scores on the tests, but
also a thinking system that was very powerful for solving problems. I
only needed to figure out how to get the visual thinking pathway to
activate the auditory one.

I was not interested in arguing about labels such as autistic or mentally retarded at this point, I was interested in trainable target behaviors. I wanted to figure out what I could teach Whitney to do reliably
and how I could increase the probability that he would retain these
newly learned behaviors.

I believed he had trouble following directions because the routine
just didn't make sense to him. Most kindergarten and first grade children learn their school routines within the first six weeks. The schedule
is usually on a storyboard with great big graphics: *First we have calen-
dar time, then we do our reading groups, then we have art class.* The
children are trained easily to follow the routine, and by the third week
of school most children remember the pattern of events.

I imagined that to Whitney, because he couldn't sequence verbal
information, the routine felt arbitrary, maybe he felt as though he was
being singled out because he wasn't understanding their verbal explanations. If he could get to the point where he learned the classroom routine without the need for verbal cueing, I thought he might do better.

As for his being inattentive, this wasn't the exact problem for Whitney, either. When Whitney got involved in something visual—whether it was building Legos, or playing with his Playmobile sets, or examining how his mouth moved in the mirror as though he was trying to figure out the underlying muscle movements—he could do these things for hours.

Whitney would totally overengage in these visual activities. Einstein was said to sit in his father's plant and watch the machines work for hours on end. He would stare at the machines, thinking about how they worked and what the moving parts were accomplishing. One of my patients, an anesthesiologist, says that he visualizes the internal organs of the patient and how the drugs he is administering are working in these organs during operations. As the machines he uses change, he visualizes what changes are occurring in the organs involved. When Whitney was building Legos, he would often glance at the picture on the box once and then build what he remembered without much of a review of what he had seen. He never followed the directions. He worked from the gestalt, or the whole, and he intuited the component parts. He would sometimes make precisely what he had seen and other times he would make creations of his own invention. He would spread out his Legos on the kitchen table or on the floor and work away. If he was interrupted to do something else, he became quite distressed. It was as if until he could finish the thought, he could not stop.

But classroom learning occurred in short intervals, and most activities tended to last fifteen to thirty minutes in the early grades. I believed that short activities worked best with this age group—after all, I'd set up the early language gyms for Whitney in this way. But while these had been fine when Whitney only had to passively observe some of the more verbal activities, we'd never been able to get him to change his own activities quickly. Once he got involved in something, he wanted to finish it. There was always trouble if Whitney got caught up in a visual project and someone made him stop. If his thoughts got interrupted, he could barely cope. It was as if his mind was untangling a puzzle, and if interrupted before he solved it, he would react with the frustration of someone whose TV has been turned off right before the end of a "who-dunnit" mystery show.

I thought mastering a classroom routine might help organize the sea of time Whitney apparently lived in. His sense of time didn't seem to be developing normally. Many two-year-olds have separation anxiety because they have no sense of time. They don't know what "I'll be right back" means, but they learn this as they mature. Certainly by age six, you can develop a bedtime routine for most children. Often after dinner, a first grader might do some reading homework, share a story with Mom or Dad, play a game, take a bath, have a good-night song or story, and go to bed. During the school year, most children do this on a fairly reliable basis. They might have some trouble falling asleep but most would be tired by nine p.m. But at age six, Whitney hadn't developed a temporal sense. He didn't seem to have an internal clock that signaled night and day, morning or evening. Once in a while, he would still stay up or get up at night and wander around the house. His brain wasn't experiencing time the way most children his age did.

I knew that Whitney would have to be able to stick to a routine and follow directions if he was to be allowed in a regular class again. Richard D. Lavoie, an expert in children with learning disabilities, reported on his videotape entitled "Learning Disabilities and Social Skills with Richard D. Lavoie: A Parent's Guide" that,

> *When fifteen hundred teachers were surveyed about what a handicapped child needs for successful mainstreaming, they answered the following:*
>
> *1. Good listening skills*
> *2. Good ability to follow auditory instructions*
> *3. Good ability to follow written instructions and stay on task for verbal work*
> *4. Good ability to speak and ask for help*

5. *Good ability to get started*
6. *Good ability to finish on time*
7. *Word attack skills*

Mr. Lavoie notes that the first academic skill listed is number seven. The first six are related to listening and speaking—skills that are not taught in the classroom but are expected to be acquired intuitively and used within a tight range of age-appropriate conformity. The Ohio Department of Education states that 76 percent of a child's school day is spent listening. My long-time friend and mentor Dr. Ronald Goldman, who authored many of the widely used auditory processing tests, served on the President's Committee for Education that added "listening" to reading, writing, and arithmetic as the fourth basic skills that every U.S. student must master. And I have given talks and written articles about the fact that the primary reason someone is institutionalized in a nursing home is communication disability, not illness.

I believed Whitney's proficiency in following directions would improve under a structured situation. So I was concerned when, after a few weeks in his new class, I saw that the time requirements in this MRDD class were less stringent than traditional kindergarten classes. There were no organized activities. How could there be? What was the teacher supposed to do with these highly medicated, nonfunctional preadolescents, and six-year-old Whitney?

When I first met his teacher for the MRDD class, Mrs. Jones, she seemed like a laid back, go-with-the-flow person. I thought, *How will she help Whitney? He needs a bubbly, aggressive, let's-get-this-fixed person.* My heart was torn in two looking around Whitney's classroom. What was she doing other than babysitting hopeless, severely impaired people? Whitney could do things, make things, build things—why did he have to be here?

I considered appealing to Mrs. Lynch, the special ed director, again but a friend of mine who worked in the district warned me that she could recommend that he go to another school district or into a residential program. So while I hated to accept the situation, I decided that, at least for the moment, I had to make the best of things.

I appointed myself "room mom" for Whitney's class. Room mothers didn't formally exist in this MRDD classroom, although they were very prominent in all other classes in the school, but Mrs. Jones was thrilled that I wanted to help. Mrs. Jones was the ultimate schoolteacher in appearance. Wearing a denim dress and comfortable shoes, she was tall and thin with well-groomed hair and a pencil tucked behind her ear. Her room was organized, with materials neatly arranged.

I was soon to discover that she was a take-charge but gentle, warm woman who was dedicated to the hard to teach.

In Chapman, Whitney had been the worst off in the class. Here, he was the best—and somehow he rose to the occasion. He began to notice his surroundings more—and recognize people. One of his classmates was Terry, a Japanese boy of about thirteen. His family was transplanted to Dublin to work in the new Honda plant; no one in the family spoke English. Terry had a physical disorder that resulted in his having an abnormal appearance. Nevertheless, he was the most alert of the other students. When I came to the class, Terry and Whitney were the only ones who would react to me walking in and out of the room. I was happy to see that Whitney was recognizing me and was acting excited to see me.

I began coming twice a week, showing Mrs. Jones my method of trying to teach Whitney to read. We were moving from simply showing him individual logos to writing strings of words to describe events in Whitney's life. We would cut up the word strings and put the individual words out for him to put in order to re-create the story. For example, for the sentence "Whitney ate french fries at McDonald's," the string would be the word "Whitney," then a picture of fries with the word "french fries" written below it and then the McDonald's logo with the word in block letters below it. He wasn't attempting to say the words at this point. We were just trying to get him to create a thought sequence with the visually cued words.

Mrs. Jones was not only very eager to help me, she seemed very pleased to have me in the classroom as much as possible. She really wanted to teach Whitney in whatever way would benefit him. Each time I came to the class, Mrs. Jones was trying my exercises, or putting her own spin on them. I brought her more activities from the office. I was delighted—Mrs. Jones was doing anything I suggested and doing it well.

I knew that, ultimately, to go to regular first grade Whitney would have to be listening and reading. And I felt strongly that reading was the crucial skill he needed to have any hope of a mainstreamed education. Although inability to listen is the primary reason kids fail, reading was the big marker of intellectual ability at this age. Talking and writing weren't as important right now. If a child couldn't read by the end of second grade, his academic program would be quite different from the mainstream child. It would also create a bigger risk of future educational jeopardy. Once the building blocks of reading are mastered, the child moves on to learning history, English, math, and so on. This advancement depends on a standard class-wide level of language competency.

Furthermore, the brain is more plastic at younger ages and it is easier to teach these skills to a developing brain than to reteach them to a brain that has already crystallized basic learning formats. In my practice, I have worked with all ages and know it is possible to help most people learn language skills at nearly any age. Whitney was in a period of growth and development, when language is most easily facilitated.

After the fire drill episodes at Chapman, I'd started to suspect that maybe whatever was happening with Whitney's auditory system was getting in the way of his learning—that was why I decided to use logos to teach him words, rather than orally repeat everything all of the time. I still wasn't sure what was going on with his hearing. He would not reliably react to noise—sometimes he seemed very sensitive to noise, almost oversensitive. He would startle as if a thunderclap was ten times louder than it was, as if it hurt his ears. At other times he appeared deaf, oblivious to all sounds around him. He was unable to tolerate audiometric testing for further testing of his hearing because he would not reliably react to noise. In hearing tests, the subject wears headphones and beeps are made at different volumes and pitches, to different ears. The subject is supposed to raise his right hand if he hears a beep in his right ear and his left hand if he hears a beep in his left ear. We had no way to explain this testing procedure to Whitney.

If his auditory sense was waxing and waning, maybe he couldn't make sense of the racket. Stroke patients, particularly those with Wernicke's aphasia, appear to wax and wane in alertness and auditory processing. Certainly, trying to teach him to say words wasn't getting us anywhere. So I'd decided to extend the logic of using the logos to teach him words and use a new approach: to be quiet, to reduce all the noise that might be distracting Whitney, and continue using only the visuals to teach the auditory.

Mrs. Jones was willing to try this approach, and we experimented in the classroom. At my office, I had hired a specialist who was trained in programs that break down the reading process into trainable chunks while maintaining the pragmatics of language. The children learn to understand print in user-friendly ways that build on their own life experiences and interests, and build on semantic units rather than memorizing rules. This specialist was an excellent third grade teacher and was looking for some added income after school. I had Whitney work with her after school along with Vanessa and William.

We used the same visual games with Whitney, but we stopped talking. We no longer repeated every word, or asked questions out loud.

During his reading instruction, we tried to do everything by pointing or indicating the visual logos and words and pictures from the books and cards I'd assembled.

Reading begins by understanding that a symbol stands for a meaningful sound unit. For Whitney, we built the symbol to stand for the meaning without the accompanying sound units. He remembered the words as whole units. We were using the visual code of reading to teach Whitney that words were words, much like teaching Helen Keller through her hands. We stayed with whole words, avoiding breaking the words down into smaller units (letters or syllables) or the linguistic rules that seem to govern the way children learn language. For instance, the semantic units of agents, actions, and objects can describe most of what children say when they are first learning to speak. They move from labeling things to making short thought connections. Agent action could be "Mommy drinks," for example; action object would be "drinks juice"; and agent object would be "Mommy juice."

I took tons of materials to Mrs. Jones—enough for a six-hour day. Many teachers would have told me to get lost, or at least ignored or adjusted my demanding schedule. Mrs. Jones quietly supervised the other students while having Whitney do these exercises and adding her own ideas for me to see when I returned. It turned out that my initial concern that there was no rigid requirement in the MRDD class for completing work in a timely fashion was actually working to our advantage; Whitney could take as long as he wanted to work on his visual games and reading lessons.

Because these students were too hard to control, they weren't allowed out; they couldn't go to the cafeteria at lunch like Whitney had been able to at Chapman. They brought their lunches to school and ate in the classroom. They were not permitted to go out with the other children for recess. So Mrs. Jones's classroom became our cocoon—a sheltered workshop. For the first part of the year, Whitney was not allowed out of his classroom at all. As the year progressed, however, he was able to leave more and more often.

———

In only two months' time, I'd become Mrs. Jones's biggest fan. The laid-back teacher whom I'd thought I wasn't going to like had become our best friend—now she was part of the team trying to teach Whitney that included me, William, and Vanessa.

For Halloween, I stayed up late making chocolate cake that I crumbled into paper cups and stuffed with gummy worms to create worms in dirt. Yuck. Maybe it would make Whitney laugh. My mother, who could whip up costumes in no time on her sewing machine, made Whitney a Superman costume. He was very into Superman toys at the time, so I had no trouble getting him to put it on.

I loved holidays as a child, and as a mother, I loved to make a big deal over things like Halloween costumes, Easter egg hunts, and Christmas traditions. I had always been disappointed that Whitney didn't enjoy dressing up or trick-or-treating for Halloween. Even his first Halloween, just weeks after he was born, I had a sense that things were going to be different with Whitney. In order to take Vanessa and William trick-or-treating, I dressed Whitney warmly and put him in a cloth trick-or-treat bag with his head poking out of the top and carried him in my arms as my bundle of sweets. We weren't supposed to be going out for the first six weeks, but our pediatrician had given me the OK to walk down to the corner with him. Usually, I loved how excited kids always got about their costumes. That year, William was a devil, Vanessa was a black cat, but rather than enjoying their glee, I remember thinking it felt as if I had a doll in the trick-or-treat bag instead of a baby, and it made me very sad. Not that Whitney could be expected to be enjoying the holiday at this age, but I already knew that something was different from the way he didn't snuggle or cling or coo.

The next few years were worse. Vanessa and William would ring the doorbell, and people would put candy in their bags, per the routine. My mother always made them the best costumes so neighbors would take the kids' pictures and ooh and aah over how cute they were. Whitney couldn't understand what we were doing. He didn't want to go up to the doors; he did not like it at all. At the Chapman preschool the year before, Whitney had experienced his first Halloween parade, which fit no routine he was familiar with and he refused to follow along. It made me sad that he didn't get to enjoy this kid holiday.

So I wasn't exactly sure why I was hauling a box of edible worms in dirt to this class for the unteachable. If there was ever to be a less receptive group for my theme treats, this was it. But this was the first year that Whitney seemed to like the idea of his costume. He was getting so good at playing pretend, and he seemed to understand that he was dressing up like Superman. Worms in dirt it was.

Indian Run had school-wide trick-or-treating, where the kids could go and trick-or-treat at other classrooms. Mrs. Jones took Whitney and Terry to make the rounds.

I stayed behind and watched the other kids in the classroom. I sat at the head of the class with my guitar as I had twice a week for the past two months. The kids wouldn't sing—some wouldn't even wake up—despite my most rousing efforts.

Discouraged, I set my guitar down when suddenly a voice I didn't recognize yelled, "Dr. Florance!" I looked up, and standing in the doorway was Mrs. Jones, staring in shock. It was Whitney who had yelled. There in his Superman costume, a big smile on his face, he called out again: "Dr. Florance!"

When I'd first met with Mrs. Jones during my visit the previous spring, I'd asked what her expectations would be for Whitney and her students for the year. Her goals were all functional: recognize a stop sign; find a bathroom by themselves; go to recess and come back to the classroom; eat lunch with others without creating a disturbance. No school learning—just practical skills that had struck me as depressingly unambitious.

Now, Mrs. Jones and I looked at each other. Had he really spoken?

"Dr. Florance," Whitney said again and gave me a big hug.

Here it was, only eight weeks into the year, and I knew we were going to speed to a place well beyond what I'd imagined.

"Dr. Florance!" Whitney demanded. I looked down and he thrust a gummy worm toward me as he put one in his own mouth and chewed happily.

I popped my gummy worm in my mouth and joined him. He handed one to Mrs. Jones as well, and as we all chewed away blissfully, Mrs. Jones and I started laughing and crying at the same time.

Then Mrs. Jones paused and asked, "Why didn't he call you Mom?"

I started to mull this over but suddenly I didn't care. If "Dr. Florance" was to Whitney what "water" was to Helen, that was fine with me. A door had been unlocked.

9

Reengineering Whitney's Brain

There is an age-old debate about how complex your thoughts can be if you don't have language. Whitney was teaching me that you could engage in complex problem-solving and thinking and never use words. He was doing visual activities that were more complex than other children his age and even at a higher level than his older brother or sister. The models he could put together easily were well above his age level. (Even now he can run circles around his peers playing computer or video games, and there is no learning curve for him with these games; he seems to have an intuitive ability in this area.)

But even if Whitney was seeing the world through a visual thinking system that didn't require words, the lack of language was causing him frustration. School was hammering the word code all day long. He had to have verbal language to succeed in school and to lead a normal life. How could we get his verbal system caught up?

Mrs. Jones and I felt that Whitney was improving. He was developing more of a relationship with me, he wanted to hold my hand. Although having Whitney say "Dr. Florance" was a big marker for me in terms of feeling that he recognized and connected to me as a person, it wasn't as if this event opened the floodgates to speaking. He still wasn't speaking much. He would attempt words here and there, but much of what he said was unintelligible. It still sounded like gibberish—sounds and babble that didn't mean anything discernable.

So I started a huge push to build his word bank and increase his core lexicon.

We have a team, I thought to myself. I am the CEO, Mrs. Jones is the manager, and Vanessa and William are the therapists. Who better to be Whitney's teachers? They were in the second and third grades now, so they were intimately aware of every skill a competent first grader needed.

I sat down and thought about how Vanessa and William could help. First, I realized that how they talked to Whitney and what they said was critical. We all had learned early on that verbal reasoning did not work with Whitney. Normally, you can start to reason with a child starting at around age three or four, when they are able to do things like wait in line, take turns, share, play games—all of this requires the ability to understand instructions from others and behave accordingly. Explaining the whys and wherefores was just a sea of words that confused and frustrated Whitney. I realized this was one of the obstacles that teachers and therapists in my office faced when they tried to help Whitney: they would instinctively talk faster, longer, and louder when he did not understand. Having had five years of training at the NIH on how to use interviewing tactics to create a therapeutic relationship, I had learned to paraphrase content, reflect feelings, interpret, share, and summarize rather than use sentences that imply "shoulds" and "oughts." Parenting and teaching is full of "shoulds and oughts": "Clean up your room," "Eat your vegetables," "You should do your homework." I have a theory that most highly visual people feel that they are bad when they hear a "should" or "ought." To a visual, intuitive person who doesn't live in the world of language, the implied judgment is, "You don't like me, I did wrong." Visual people usually don't respond to these kinds of statements and so don't do what is being asked. As a result, they then get a further verbal harangue about why they should eat their vegetables or do their homework. So instead we used open invitations to talk, and set up sentences so he could fill in the blanks. For instance, if he was painting and spilled water the kids would say, "Oops, the water spilled, I'll get a paper towel, you get a paper towel." Or they'd paraphrase something that happened and put words around it with no judgment implied: "You're unhappy because the water spilled."

Vanessa and William had learned to talk in a supportive way by watching me at the office and working with Whitney. As a result, they rarely used verbal reasoning to interact with Whitney. They used their words to create blankets of support around his emerging skills. How they were talking to their brother became a critical part of our program.

His visual skills showed me that he was thinking outside the word code. My goal was to get him to know there was a code of thinking that depended on words. I wanted to re-engineer his thinking system so that he could process information using the word code. To most people, the best way to explain this is to say that I wanted to teach him language— I wanted to teach him to be able to recognize and use words, to read and speak and write. But really, what I was doing was searching for a way to use the visual processing that I knew was working in his brain in order to teach him auditory processing. *I wanted to re-engineer how his brain processed information.*

I decided that we needed to build an architecture of learning in Mrs. Jones's classroom that would teach Whitney all of the skills needed for first grade. Because no other student in the classroom was talking and their goals centered around self-care and recognition of common signs, we were left a lot of time to develop a plan in which Vanessa, William, and I could work to reengineer Whitney's brain. Mrs. Jones could provide the practice lab, drilling him in all of the skills we were working on.

We knew we had a long way to go before Whitney could read chapter books, but I was convinced we could use some of the visual games he played with his brother and sister to teach him words. From watching Whitney, we knew he was easily decoding the problems and giving us the answers if he could use his visual system to problem-solve. But he was muddled, confused, and incompetent when he was attempting to encode and decode with words, unless we took the task down to a very easy two- or three-year-old level.

By now I was convinced that Whitney was understanding and recognizing the words we were teaching him. Even though he wasn't saying the words out loud, I was confident that we were building his agent and object vocabulary with the logos. If I said "Find Wendy's" or "Find Cheerios," he could pick out the logos. When we had him put words together to make sentences, we did not get him to try to sound out the words or use phonics to decode the words in parts. We did not talk while he was thinking. If you are talking while someone is thinking in pictures or words, it can become very distracting. This seemed to be especially true for Whitney. So we gave him a large margin of quiet so he could think his problems through.

The next hurdle was to get him to recognize actions—that is, verbs. He needed to understand verbs to be able to form sentences. He loved the Disney and Sesame Street characters, so we got dollhouses with these characters in them. That way we could make all of the characters do the action. We also used his Playmobile sets, saying, for instance, "Cowboy rides horse."

Understanding verbs meant understanding sequencing, or time. To be able to understand "Whitney drives car," or tell a story of any kind about what he did in his everyday life, he had to have a sense of time, a sense of one thing following another. I wasn't sure he was able to do this. He still didn't seem to sequence his thoughts the way verbal children did. By six years old, most children have learned all of the grammatical structures needed for adult language. They are talking in paragraphs, taking turns in conversations, and are able to express their needs, feelings, and opinions. For most of us, these skills develop automatically; we had to build all of these skills in Whitney.

Once you can link words together to make a story, you can predict missing parts of something from the context. That is, you learn to predict what will happen next, an ability called "closure." Closure is part of the brain's organizing system for processing information. It helps us formulate thoughts before we have all the pieces or understand all aspects when we are learning something new. Auditory closure is an automatic function that occurs in everyday life in situations such as understanding speech in a noisy room, foreign accents, articulation disorders, or poor phone connections. Visual closure allows you to recognize an object when you can only see parts of the shape. Your brain fills in the missing parts. Your ability to do this allows you to predict the whole from the parts. Whitney was very good at predicting the visual whole big picture but not the auditory. We were working on developing these underlying brain skills of visual closure—visual predicting—and then getting ready to move into auditory organization of brain processing.

One snow day when school was cancelled, Whitney got Will and Vanessa to play outside and they built a snowman. A TV van was driving around shooting footage for a story about the snowfall, and they stopped and filmed the kids. The TV crew told them they'd be on TV that night and the kids came tumbling into the house to report their pending fame.

When we watched it on the news that night, Whitney seemed especially excited to see himself on TV. We habitually made word cards of things Whitney would recognize from his daily life, so we made a card of "snowman" and "news van" and "camera" and "TV." We made the letters look like the word: "snow" had a snowball on the "s" and "man" had eyes in the "a" like a man's face.

Later that week we were working after school in the office and I was leading a group of kids through a dance routine to James Taylor's "Jelly Man Kelly" in the dance studio lab. William and Vanessa, along with one of the therapists in my office, were working with Whitney in the room across the hall, trying to teach him reading by the visual look of the letters, not by pushing auditory sounds the way their teachers had taught them. In other words, we wanted Whitney to recognize the words visually, not by sounding them out phonetically.

The therapists in my office and I were trying to build on Whitney's language skills by using examples from his daily life. Whitney would say a word or phrase, and we would build on it by adding more words. So on this day, Whitney told the story of the snowman in his telegram way of talking: "Snowman TV." This telegraphic speech (using agents and objects) that is typical of early language was odd coming from a six-and-a-half-year-old—usually this is the kind of speech one hears from a one- to two-year-old. But it was a huge advance for Whitney.

Vanessa and William used Whitney's words but added a few other words that we had been working on to make the grammar correct: *We made a snowman with a red hat, a carrot nose, and candy eyes. The TV made a show. We saw it on TV. We are happy.*

Now we had a complete story that we knew Whitney was familiar with, and we could create visual images to help him learn more words. To do this, Vanessa would write out the story of the snowman and William would then cut the story into rectangular word units. Then they would illustrate the words. For instance, Vanessa colored the word red with a red crayon; William drew a carrot on the card that said carrot. They would put the words of the story in order, then jumble the words up and see if Whitney could put it in the right order. By this time, we were pretty sure he could recognize individual words, but we were trying to see if he could recognize a sequence. "Don't talk or try to have him think of the sounds," I had told them. "Just see if he can remember what the word looks like."

After a while, I heard William shriek from across the hall, "Hurray!"

When I came into the room, William and Vanessa excitedly pointed at the table. "He did it. Whitney 'wrote' the story!"

There on the table were the words: SNOWMAN RED HAT, A CARROT NOSE, CANDY EYES.

I turned to the kids and asked, "Did Whitney do that by himself?"

"Yes!" they said, calming down. They could see this was serious. "We mixed the words up and he put them in that order."

I looked at Whitney, who was beaming—happy that we were all happy but oblivious to the import of what he'd done. Whitney had tied the ideas together and placed them in a thought unit. He had the snowman grouped with the major ideas that went with it. We were hoping that this could be the beginning of teaching him to organize verbal thoughts.

Did Whitney understand syntax? Whitney demonstrated on the ITPA that he could put shapes in order to match a pattern from memory. He was able to do this at well above his age level. What we were doing was using these advanced pattern recognition skills to teach syntax, grammar, and semantics. He had been doing this visually now for about a year. We were converting his visual pattern recognition to words and from words to meaning by making the story about his real life—and using the power of his visual thinking to help shape his verbal brain.

Perhaps his receptive knowledge was better than the tests showed. My mind raced ahead—if this was so, we could get him ready for first grade by cueing words through his visual processing systems. Was it really working? I decided to let myself have a moment of celebration. "Hallelujah!" I said and grabbed the kids for a big hug.

Whitney called out, "*Hawauya Mom!*"

We started laughing. The kids from the dance room had gathered around the door drawn by all the commotion.

"OK, OK, back to work," I said in my most professional voice. We all resumed our workstations.

When our workday was done, I whisked the kids off to Max and Erma's, our favorite spot for dinner. They loved it because they could make their own ice cream sundaes from the big bathtub of treats.

As I watched the kids making their desserts and debating over which toppings to use, my thoughts churned. If Whitney could arrange words to tell the story, I knew that even though he couldn't talk in the full sentence he assembled, he understood receptively enough that he could arrange the words properly. The words were not units of sound to Whitney—they were symbols. But the symbols stood for meanings that were correct.

We were using the kind of skills Whitney had when he built a Lego or a model to build an architecture for using words. We were following how a visual thinking pathway would work to solve a visual problem and using that to cue up sorting and organizing words. We were using Whitney's strength to develop his weak verbal brain.

He was recognizing groups of words from logos, or the print from sight-memory and we had attached them to meaningful objects long enough that he had constructed a memory that was meaningful. The words were symbols of meaning. He had a master lexicon, a mental dictionary now.

We made games where he would sort picture-and-word cards, for toys or for food. Next we would attempt to phase out the picture cue.

In short, he was learning reading purely as pattern recognition. We were skipping the rules of language and making the words stand as visual symbols of meaning. As he learned a group of very familiar word logos, such as Wendy's or Kroger's, we would use the print card only. He was learning about twenty-five new words a week.

He couldn't walk or run properly. He couldn't hear correctly. He couldn't talk clearly. He could barely hold a pencil, and his writing looked like chicken scratches. But he could think! And think powerfully enough to override all of these huge disabilities and process the code of language.

After his success with the snowman cards, we began creating strings of sentences from our rebus cards. Rebuses are picture cues that help you decode a word. For example, if you had the word "fire" written on a card, the dot of the "i" could be a drawing of a red flame. He was re-creating sentences he had been shown before that told stories about his life. Each story he learned, we would then put in an envelope for him to come back to and practice reassembling again. These envelopes were like the mental files that most verbal children store their memories or stories in; for Whitney they were files that we had to have him practice.

This is how we were teaching Whitney to *read*.

Despite our success, I was dreading meeting with the school officials about Whitney's plans for first grade. Without his ability to speak and write well, to outsiders this progress sounded hypothetical. If they sat down and asked him, "Sugar is white, grass is ___" his response was unintelligible. If they asked him to write the alphabet, they couldn't read what he wrote; it looked like a bunch of random lines. He couldn't copy a square or a triangle because he didn't have adequate fine-motor control to make the pencil do what he wanted it to do. He couldn't count or put the alphabet in order. The letters or numbers as isolated units did not mean anything to him because we were teaching him whole words with visual cues.

Without picture cues, he seemed very impaired. He couldn't do the things normal children do like read *Hop on Pop* out loud or sing along to "Eensy Weensy Spider" or "Happy Birthday." He played on his own more than with others. He liked to play outside, swing on the swing set, or ride on his tricycle. Because of his poor fine-motor skills, he would squeeze things too tightly and couldn't color or draw. He preferred to watch Disney videos rather than look at pictures in books. He liked puppets and stuffed animals and little manipulatable toys of Winnie the Pooh or Disney or Sesame Street characters. He would sit still and stare at things for extended periods. He liked to examine things like pinwheels, and as he stared at them, I imagined he was organizing in his mind how the pinwheel worked to change color and rotate around. He would walk up to things or people and stare at them.

Most of the preschool skills that are considered necessary for first-grade readiness were missing. So my insistence that he could read wasn't apparent to those who hadn't worked with him day in and day out like Mrs. Jones had. And even Mrs. Jones was seeing a child who was severely impaired.

When I look back now at the goals set for Whitney's IEP (individualized education plan) for his year with Mrs. Jones, and what he did and didn't achieve, I am amazed at how delayed he was in so many areas. I am surprised to be reminded of how poor his motor skills were, especially when he was so adept at building with Legos.

By April of that school year, when Whitney was six years, seven months, his physical therapy progress report stated the following:

Whitney has made excellent gains in his gross motor skills development. Goals for next school year will continue to address static and dynamic balance skills as well as address activities that stress proprioception development.

He was still at a very low age level in most motor skills:

SKILL	FALL (AGE LEVEL IN YEARS.MONTHS)	SPRING
STANDING	3.5	4.0
WALKING	4.5	5.0
STAIRS	4.0	5.5
RUNNING	4.0	5.0
JUMPING	3.0	5.0
HOPPING	2.6	3.6
KICKING	5.0	5.0
BALANCE BEAM	0	4.0
CATCHING	4.0	5.5
THROWING	2.6	3.0
BOUNCING	0	2.0

When I look back now, I see even more clearly why so many of the school teachers and administrators I crossed paths with over the years felt I was being overly optimistic.

Here are some of the goals Mrs. Jones had set for Whitney in late October. The goals were reviewed again in January and March of that school year.

- Whitney will name upper and lower case letters—*Achieved by January, maintained in March*
- Whitney will recognize 20 words with 75 percent accuracy—*Achieved by March*
- Whitney will demonstrate understanding of functions of common objects 75 percent of the time—*Not achieved*
- Whitney will follow daily routine with 90 percent reliability—*Still needs encouragement to follow the routine upon entering the room but once settled in, he does better; progress made by January, met goal by March*
- Whitney will count to 50—*By March, Whitney can count to 12 and then gets confused with the teens.*
- Whitney will engage in appropriate interaction including sharing and turn-taking—*By March, progress was made but still a major problem area.*

His speech therapy IEP included these goals:

- Whitney will increase his conversational relevancy to 50 percent of the time—*Not met*
- Whitney will decrease gibberish or nonsense speech 50 percent of the time—*Not met*
- Whitney will maintain eye contact 50 percent—*Not met*
- Whitney will increase sentence length to 5–8 words—*Not met*
- Whitney will increase spontaneous speech—*Met* [He was talking more but you couldn't really understand it.]

The report ended with this summary:

Whitney has difficulty with articulation, language, and auditory memory. He can't answer more than a simple question and has difficulty conversing with any relevant words. He can name some objects.

For all that I felt he was communicating, it was still not evident, or understandable, to others. Even Mrs. Jones was not convinced that Whitney was as capable as I thought he was—and she had some valid concerns. After all, there were still times that his behavior was very autistic. He would wander away. He couldn't tolerate the noise on the playground or in the cafeteria without reverting to holding his ears or sometimes banging his head. He never tried to bite Mrs. Jones—but she knew when he had reached his frustration level and allowed him to have some solitary time.

When I spoke to her about Whitney's chances for getting into mainstream first grade the following year based on his visual thinking skills, Mrs. Jones kindly said, "Why don't we have Mrs. Fletcher, the occupational therapist, give some visual tests and see what happens?"

In April, Mrs. Fletcher tested Whitney's visual perceptual skills. You don't need to talk or listen to take this series of tests, you have to figure out a series of visual problems. At age 6 years 7 months, he got the following results:

Visual discrimination—7 years 5 months, 75th percentile

Visual memory—5 years 1 month, 25th percentile

Visual spatial relations—below 4 years, 1st percentile

Visual form constancy—7 years 6 months, 84th percentile

Visual sequential memory—5 years 7 months, 25th percentile

Visual figure ground—5 years 8 months, 37th percentile

Visual closure—4 years 4 months, 16th percentile.

I was thrilled. Whitney was a year and five months ahead on two visual tests and catching up in nearly all of the others. For a child who had a performance IQ of 46 with all scores well below the one percentile a year before, I thought this was a miraculous improvement. Plus, he had tolerated being tested by someone who did not know how to reach into his mind to illustrate the directions, which I found magnificent. Normal is the fiftieth percentile and nearly everyone scores between 40 and 60. He had genius scores in hard areas—I knew he could do this, but now I felt the school would have to believe me from their own testing.

Mrs. Fletcher wrote in her report: *Whitney is in the 25th percentile in visual perception.* The standard way for scoring such tests is to add the raw scores together and look up the composite score for the chronological age of the child to obtain the composite statistical score used for a summary score. *He is essentially normal in visual perceptual abilities and at age level,* she wrote. Viewing the scores this way did not illustrate his high and low scores. There are a couple points of view regarding composite scores. Binet did not want composite scores used in this way, nor did the authors of the ITPA because they wanted to use the subtest scores as a basis for designing intervention. "Average" did not describe an eighty-fourth percentile score, nor did it describe a sixteenth percentile score. Using composite scores would possibly work when all the scores were similar—if they were all at the thirty-seventh percentile or between 35 and 45, for example, then the composite scores would describe the performance. But when they ranged from 16 to 84, it could be very misleading to rely on the composite score. Whitney did not have a unitary intelligence, but he was learning to become verbally and visually intelligent.

In my clinical research on stroke patients, I used a model that required examination of variability within each subtest. This method, proposed by Dr. Bruce Porch when he developed the Porch Index of Communication Ability, requires the examiner to evaluate brain-communication function in auditory and visual processing, listening, speaking, reading, and writing. There are ten items per subtest. In order to predict who has the best prognosis, the therapist uses a method called the HOPE slope: First, you examine the scores on each item, variability within each subtest, and variability across modalities. You look at the highest and lowest scores with the premise that if the patient can do the task correctly once, then he has a better chance of doing it again than if he can't do it at all. Having been trained by Dr. Porch in these procedures and having been the director of a major stroke rehab program for many years, I thought a lot more expansively about test scores than just the composite score. Seeing that some of Whitney's scores were very high was very important to planning therapy and to predicting prognosis.

I tried to point out how important visual skills are in brain functioning. "The test shows how the brain processes visual thinking. And these visual processors need to partner with the auditory counterparts," I explained. "We are training his visual thinking every day at home and at school—that is why he is getting better. We are using it to help him learn to read."

"He is still in the bottom twenty-five percent of the population," she said. "Twenty-fifth percentile means low average."

He was not normal or low average at all. He was a genius with potholes, I wanted to shout.

Certainly Whitney had multiple handicaps. He qualified for speech therapy, occupational therapy, physical therapy, and adaptive physical education from both the Franklin County MRDD program and Dublin, so he had eight therapists—two for each service many times each week. These special education programs were working—he was dramatically better month by month. But I felt the school staff was missing out on understanding why he was progressing so well—*it was because he was learning to harness and maximize his visual thinking system.* I began trying to make the point to various school therapists and administrators (and anyone else who was around) that Whitney was a total visual thinker like Albert Einstein, citing examples of all of the visual things he could do.

Everyone must have thought I was just a mother in denial. At times, I felt like only the three of us—Will, Vanessa and I—believed in Whitney, giving him the space to explore his mind and then having discussions about his thinking as I took them to the bus stop every morning at six thirty.

For Will's birthday that year, we had a circus party. Ann, my secretary, was an opera singer and she and her husband, also a singer, put on an operetta about William and performed it in front of the fireplace. Dr. Cindy, one of the pediatricians in my office building, drew caricature portraits at the art station in the garage, Lee cooked hot dogs, hamburgers, and s'mores on the grill. We had face-painting, games, and lots more. I hired a couple of ponies that the kids could ride around the cul de sac.

I was not sure how this big event would go for Whitney, because with this much excitement, we could easily lose him to rocking and head banging. But to my surprise, for nearly the entire party Whitney stood by one of the ponies staring at his nostril and his teeth as if he was a sculptor trying to figure out the exact physiology of the pony's head. After the party, one of the moms came to pick up her son and stayed to chat for about an hour. She had an infant in a baby seat, and for that entire hour, Whitney sat by the infant and stared at her face. My friend Dr. Cindy, who'd drawn the caricatures and was very visual, said, "Baby faces are not proportionate to their bodies . . . they are too big. Whitney is probably evaluating that."

I began to see more clearly than ever that Whitney's fascination with visual tasks, his model building, his heightened sense of direction, his progress in learning language visually, his high visual scores—and this fascination with staring at things for hours on end—were all linked. I

began to suspect that I was discovering a new syndrome that no one
had ever heard of—one in which high visuals and low auditory created
a certain set of autistic-like symptoms, but symptoms that could be
corrected with the right kind of therapy: a therapy that used the high
visual skills to bring up the low auditory skills. I was too excited to
put the idea into words, but if I was right, there really was hope for
Whitney.

I continued to test this theory in our work with Whitney. Now that he
was able to read and form sentences visually and say a few words, it
was time to start bombarding his auditory system again.

William and Vanessa were able to help. They knew how to read, so
they would read stories to their brother both at home and after school
at my office. Meanwhile, we returned to the world of sound, and I
bought every video and audiotape of every Broadway show and Disney
movie I could find. We played them at home and in the car, memorizing
all of the tunes. We played Name That Tune so often that I could sing
"We're off to see . . ." and Vanessa would shout, *"The Wizard of Oz,"*
"Bloody" and William would beat her to the answer with *"South
Pacific!"* These second- and third-graders knew the entire score to tons
of musicals like *Oklahoma, Gigi, My Fair Lady,* and any Disney movie.

Whitney loved the videos but he was not going along with a lot of
our singing and dancing. William and Vanessa would play-act and
sing, but Whitney was not reliably engaged in these games. He would
play with us for a while but then go off by himself and stare at things
or play with his toys. He did not seem to get overwhelmed or bothered
by the music, he just had a tune-us-out mechanism and he could still
self-isolate.

We had the films like *Snow White* they'd seen for years. So quizzing
them on these songs was testing their "crystallized" knowledge—the
term for the things learned and stored in memory. Had Whitney stored

this information? Did he know it? To see if he could build new memo-ries, I could use the new films like *The Little Mermaid*. Could the kids remember the words? I'd drive around with my right hand on the volume knob of the tape recorder and when Sebastian sang, "Under the—" I'd turn down the volume and the kids would shout, "Sea!" Sometimes Whitney seemed to be listening to us and other times he attempted to guess the words. When we listened to *The Wizard of Oz* and got to "Lions, and tigers and bears, oh my," we made a big deal out of the "oh my" and stretched it out—Ohhhhhhhhhhhhhhhh Myyyyyyyy—and he liked to try to sing along with that. But often Whitney would stare out the window as if examining every visual detail passing by. (Even now he notices things as we drive along that I would never pick up on.)

We also used tapes that came with read-along books that would tell the story and then have snippets of songs. On the audiotape, a beep or gong signaled that the child should turn the page. Whitney would look at the pictures and wait for the signal to turn the page, so I knew his auditory system was starting to respond.

I felt a huge sense of hope and relief now that I was beginning to get into my therapy comfort zone. Teaching nonverbal kids to talk and teaching children with weak auditory systems was a much more famil-iar place than trying to get Whitney to know I was a human being and to stop his perseverating. Where we were now felt much better. Now there was hope, and direction to where we needed to go.

It was time to place Whitney for next year. Will, Vanessa, and I felt pretty sure Whitney could manage at least part of first grade as a full participant—the reading part. I was beginning to see how the steps would fall into place—use his knowledge of words to build his reading skills, then from reading, teach listening—then from listening, teach talking, and from talking, teach writing. I was also beginning to understand the great power of the visual thinking system in a way I had never imagined. I was convinced this great thinking engine could help fuel his verbal thinking—I was not sure *how* yet, but I was working on that.

By my definition, he was reading because he could attach meaning to the word units by grouping them in like categories or matching them to the real item. He could string them together to represent thoughts that incorporated agents, actions, and objects. But I realized it would be a major mental stretch to make these fragments of "first grade" capability appear logical to anyone else.

So I knew we had to get past the testing hurdle. In the hospital, the patient must be given informed consent before any procedures are performed. Everything I did when I tested a patient was explained, and in fact the patient, the family, and I created the testing battery together so it made sense to all of us. School testing was nothing like that. The battery was established according to some protocol that I did not understand nor did there seem to be a written explanation anywhere. This made me feel like I had no ability to prepare him for the specific testing they required—we were at the mercy of a testing system that I felt didn't fairly reveal what Whitney *could* do, but only revealed his limitations.

I asked Mrs. Jones if we could work around the testing with classroom examples of all he could do, and she went to the administration on his behalf. "How do you know he can read if he can't read it out loud?" they asked. "He has to be able to either write the answers to questions or say the answers in order for us to give him tests."

She and I met to discuss her appeal.

Mrs. Jones had explained that Whitney could put sentences in the right order. But they argued that just because he can put words in a string, it doesn't mean he knows what it means.

"Did you tell them I have been training him for nearly seven years? And I have been working on building his brain architecture for language? I know how his brain works inside out," I asked her.

"I told them you believe he understands," Mrs. Jones explained, adding apologetically, "but, you know, it is hard for anyone else to know for sure."

"Look," I appealed to her. "If they test him the wrong way, they will still think he has an IQ of 46. I think if you test him correctly, you will find that he can go to normal first grade and he won't have to be segregated from all the other children like he has been this year."

She explained that the administrators didn't think he'd be safe in a regular first-grade class.

"Safe? What would endanger him? Trust me, I know he's reading and thinking. He'll be fine. Most of first grade is reading."

She sighed. She really was caught in the middle and I felt bad—but it didn't stop me from arguing my point of view.

She knew I wasn't going to like the decision, as she explained that they planned to graduate him from the program for the mentally retarded up to the higher functioning autism class at Riverside. They agreed he was much more teachable now. So they were going to put him with kids his own age and mainstream him for gym. There would only be four or five kids in his class, with a special education teacher and a full-time aide.

I looked at her, angry that this was the result. I knew it wasn't her fault, but my powerlessness over the school system infuriated me.

She tried to convince me that this was lucky that Whitney would have another year with two teachers for five kids.

I was disappointed. I'd worked so hard to get him ready for normal first grade. And they still wanted him in special education class.

It wasn't that I couldn't see their point of view. I, too, was worried that Whitney would relapse. I understood that the school administrators wanted a situation that was manageable. I understood that it did not seem like good planning to take a labor-intensive special-education child like Whitney and put him in a group of twenty-five kids with one teacher. As a plain matter of fact, Whitney did not have any of the skills he needed to be in the normal first grade. He could barely speak or write. He had hearing problems. That all made sense to me. So why was I being so stubborn? Was I acting like a fool? The overzealous mom who had lost all objectivity?

I went home that night and couldn't sleep. After getting all the kids in bed, I poured myself a glass of wine and sat by the fireplace at midnight. I cleaned the kitchen, rearranging drawers at one a.m. I made lunches at one thirty—my mind whirling around, not really thinking in clear sequencing, but bopping from thought to thought. Then I sat again by the fireplace and tried to focus my thoughts. I felt like I was being pulled along to train Whitney's visual brain against all odds, against all evidence to the contrary. If Whitney were a patient, I would have given up long ago. If I was a mother without any science background, I would see what everyone else saw: an unteachable child. But I had glimpsed the power of the visual mind, and it had captured my attention.

I am still just beginning to realize how strong an engine the visual mind is. I can say that over and over again and still not completely understand what I am saying. I don't have a strong visual brain—to the contrary—my visual-thinking pathway is very weak and my verbal extremely strong. Even at the eye doctor's, my visual perceptual skills are below the first percentile. But I had witnessed it. At his young age, Whitney could do things I can't do as an adult. He could see how to turn on the VCR in a hotel room, how to put together puzzles intuitively that I couldn't understand logically. It was his powerful visual thinking system that made me think he could understand and succeed in first grade. I knew that first grade was primarily a verbal experience of listening, reading, writing, and speaking. I knew that this could be a problem. My intuition, however, said no, keep trying. Helen Keller only had finger spelling and Braille, and she learned four languages. Once the code reached her brain in a usable format, she could think. What I had to do for Whitney was make sure the code reached his brain in a user-friendly format; then his visual thinking engine could do the thinking part. The visual brain could handle first grade if we could get the thoughts there intelligibly. I had to keep trying.

It was the last day of the school year. And what a year it had been. Whitney's advances convinced me that I was right in the work I was doing. He was living proof that my visual and auditory processing therapy worked.

He seemed to be learning new receptive words every day, and we were working on this in his reading and sight vocabulary—building his "word bank," his master lexicon. His expressive language was still very minimal, but I was sure we could improve that.

I pulled up to the school to drop Whitney off for his last day of Mrs. Jones's class. I watched with awe as he got out of the car and walked into the school on his own. I couldn't believe the progress we'd made in this class that I'd assumed would be hopeless. Yet Whitney wasn't getting mainstreamed and had to go to his new class at Riverside School. I just couldn't accept that I was playing beat-the-clock and losing. I thought the strides we'd made in getting Whitney to read, follow directions, and adhere to routine were phenomenal. But school administrators were telling me these weren't enough for normal first grade.

I leaned over and shut the car door—Whitney still never closed a door behind him, no matter how many times I told him to.

With William and Vanessa, the day they first stepped on the bus by themselves to go to school, or walked into their school on their own, had always wrenched my heart. I could feel the maternal ties pulling, wanting them to stay a little longer, agonizing that they were growing up so quickly and becoming independent. Because they knew I hated to see them go, they would also say, "I love you, Mom" as they popped out of the car, and I would say, "I love you too, girlie," to Vanessa, or "I love you too, poobear" to Willie the Poo.

As I watched Whitney walk into his school on his own, my heart wrenched, but in another way: though I'd insisted he'd be able to do this one day, I couldn't believe the miracle. With his backpack on his back and his lunch bag in his hand, he waved at the other children as he approached the front door. Just as he reached the building, he turned to me and called out, "I whuhve ooouuu, Mom!" and I called back, "I love you too Whitney-Pitney!"

I drove away through the turn-around laughing and crying at the same time. So much of life with Whitney was a complex whirl of heartbreak and joy.

10

The Triangle

Over the summer before Whitney was to attend Riverside School, we made enormous progress. He still had many lapses into dense autistic behavior, but there were many things we could now do as a family.

After a bumpy start, Whitney had made great strides participating in the Dublin Parks and Recreation program. We'd started with twenty minutes of camp per day. By August, we were up to eight hours of social play per day, including swimming lessons. Whitney really took to swimming. After I got home from work, we would pack up for an evening swim at the pool—often we would take a picnic to eat and play cards during rest period. Whitney was always eager to go to the pool and paddle around the shallow end. He had a bunch of water toys and flotation devices that he loved to play with. I could sit on the steps at the end of the pool, all the kids within my view.

On August sixth, my birthday, the parents of the campers were invited to a swim demonstration, and I rearranged my work schedule to attend. I'd been to countless school recitals for Vanessa and William individually, but this was the first event that the kids were participating in together. I was excited and nervous.

The kids' camp was housed at Wyandotte elementary school, which was just across the parking lot from the pool. When their swimming demonstrations were over, the children could return to their day camp across the street.

The oldest children started first, demonstrating the swim strokes they'd learned. When Vanessa (who is now on her college swim team) dove in and swam back and forth across the pool—backstroke, breast stroke, freestyle, sidestroke—I couldn't have been more proud than if she were Esther Williams leading the most complex synchronized swimming routine.

Next was Will, racing his age group. When Will pulled out ahead, I stood and shouted, losing my sense of decorum in the stands with the other parents. My father had been a competitive swimmer and still holds world records to this day. I myself was also a competitive swimmer all through my growing-up years, and a synchronized swimmer in college, so this meant a lot to me. I was so proud to see the kids enjoying and demonstrating their skill.

Then it was Whitney's turn. Although he was still involved in intensive occupational and physical therapy, he was doing fairly well with swimming this summer. Maybe the water somehow eased coordination of his muscle movements. I was looking forward to seeing his demonstration.

I could feel my heart beat faster as I lined up with the other parents by the pool. We were to toss pennies into the water and the kids in Whitney's group were to jump in or do porpoise dives to retrieve them. We flung our coins and stood back. The water splashed over the sides as kids cannonballed in after them. After getting drenched, I opened my eyes to search the pool for Whitney. I couldn't spot him anywhere and panicked, fearful he was stuck underwater. Having been a lifeguard for many years in my youth, this was always on my mind. Then I saw a teacher crouching next to Whitney, who was seated on the cement and wouldn't budge. The teacher was trying to encourage him to jump in. As I approached them, Whitney lunged forward and pushed the teacher aside, bolting from the pool area. I ran after him, apologizing over my shoulder to the teacher.

By the time I caught up to Whitney, he had run across the street to our house and was in his room crying and rocking on his firetruck bed. I tried to get him to talk. "Whitney, you were scared by . . . ?" But he wouldn't respond to my leading questions. Finally, I soothed him by playing my guitar. Once he was calmer, I put down my guitar and smoothed the hair on his head. "How about we get William and Vanessa and go to the movies and have popcorn?" I am not sure if he understood me but he took my hand, so off we went.

As we sat in the dark theater munching on popcorn, I thought, *We aren't out of the woods yet. Too much commotion can still turn us backward.*

On one hand, I was feeling as if our intensive work with Whitney was paying off. On the other hand, incidents like this made me fear I was fooling myself—that we could only get so far before Whitney would retreat into his autistic-like meltdowns. Was it possible to draw Whitney any further into the verbal world? Was it possible to bring him completely into our world?

It was frustrating not to know if he understood what I was saying. Whitney was still not hearing properly or following directions readily. He didn't acknowledge that he understood me and there was no way of knowing what set him off. Was it the splashing and laughing—all of the noise? Was it being watched by all the parents? Was the demonstration too much of a change from the regular camp pattern he had adjusted to? The frustrating part was we couldn't anticipate what would happen—what would work out and what would be a disaster. Also, now that he was so much bigger than when he was two or three, these behaviors seemed much more atypical to outsiders. When he'd been younger, it was easier for others to see it as a temper tantrum. But these kinds of tantrums were more disturbing to see in an older child.

I longed to find more ways to communicate with Whitney—to be able to know that he understood what we were saying and have him communicate with us in return.

One night after watching an episode of *The Streets of San Francisco* in which a mime appeared, Vanessa came up with the idea of playing charades with Whitney.

"I think Whitney can act out things like that mime!" she told me.

I loved the idea. I searched the video store for movies where there was acting without words—the fight scene in *West Side Story*; the cowboys pretending to ride horses in the dance sequences in *Oklahoma*; the scenes on the Yellow Brick Road in *The Wizard of Oz*; or the Von Trapp kids climbing the mountain in *The Sound of Music*.

In the evening, I would play my guitar and sing while the kids Rollerbladed around, acting out the parts. William and Vanessa used exaggerated facial expressions but didn't speak. Whitney loved this game.

We developed a little "theater" at our house. There was a bank of windows where you could see yourself in the reflection at night. We would put on a Madonna CD. I would play the lead singer and William and Whitney the backup band. I would do dance routines that were simple and funny, and they would imitate me. Vanessa directed. I would do a series of hand motions, shoulder movements—sometimes we used hats and canes. Another one we could always get Whitney to take part in was our routine to the song "Me and My Cowboy," a song with a galloping beat about riding with a cowboy in the heat of the day. I would play my guitar and the kids would get on their horses (made from brooms and mops with big masking tape reins) and gallop up and down the stairs and around the house to the beat of the song, mopping their brows as if they were hot.

Not only was he participating, but there was an added bonus: We got such good exercise that it helped Whitney fall asleep. After dinner, exhausted from their blading and performing, the kids would go to bed and I would sing them sleepy songs or tell stories.

Later, we went to my parents' for my birthday dinner. "In first grade, you have to know how to tell your own story, Mom," said Vanessa. "Whitney can't tell a story with a beginning, middle, and end." She was right. Vanessa and William decided it was time for Whitney to go to the attic.

My mother's attic is an ideal spot for fantasy play. The attic has a round area in the middle, surrounded by little turrets. My mother was a harp and clarinet player, and her father was a music researcher, so in one turret are instruments of all kinds, including banjos, Chinese lutes, and the harp case, which we used as a pretend phone booth. As kids, my best friend and I played in the attic constantly, and my children followed suit.

Many of our relatives took part in theater through the generations, so there are costumes neatly stored in cedar chests, and hatboxes filled with fancy chapeaus and boas. My grandfather invented the song flute and manufactured it for the soldiers in World War II, so there were many prototypes from his experiments. Additionally, my father was a former Navy commander and fighter pilot squadron leader, so all of his old uniforms, parachutes, helmets, hats with scrambled egg insignias and log books were there. Will thought that being a corsair pilot was very cool.

"Let's go to the attic," said William. "We can show him how to make up his own plays instead of acting out plays with us from the movies."

I was a bit worried. My mother, "Grandma Dotty" as we call her, has the attic organized to a T, and Whitney could mix everything up in a heartbeat. Not only that, many of the instruments were antiques worth a great deal of money and were to be given as inheritance at some point. What if Whitney trashed the place? My parents said,

"Go ahead and have fun. You go too, Cheri. If you're there nothing will happen."

Right, I thought. Too much stimulation and Whitney could rip things to shreds.

Luckily, Whitney loved the attic too. He started pulling out costumes and trying them on—especially his grandfather's uniforms. The kids found a parachute and a box of pictures of their grandpa flying and teaching flying. Whitney was mesmerized by the military stuff.

It was a big nonverbal world—the kids put on one costume after another. My sister and I had been in so many plays and dance recitals as kids that there were tons of costume items to mix and match. Grandma Dotty let Vanessa, Will, and Whitney pack a suitcase of costumes to take home to continue the play.

"See, Mom, Whitney will learn a beginning, middle, and end, and he will also learn 'then and next,'" Vanessa insisted. "That's what they want you to do when you write in first grade, and it will help him understand his reading, too."

As the summer drew to an end, Vanessa, Will, and I thought that with all of our daily work, Whitney should be able to go to regular first grade. I hadn't let go of that goal for him. But the school district remained determined that Whitney was to "advance" to autism class—the class he had flunked out of in preschool.

Schools don't actually diagnose children; they determine appropriate school programming that will meet the child's educational needs. In order for the school to receive funding for the extra staffing needs, the child must meet the criteria set up by the funding source. It was when Whitney had done so poorly in the standardized testing after Chapman that he qualified for funding from Franklin County MRDD program. Thus, for the time he was with Mrs. Jones, his label was "multiply handicapped."

Now Whitney was moving on to Riverside and he had improved enough that he was being placed in the handicapped program supported solely by the Dublin schools without MRDD assistance—a step up, but still not the mainstreaming I wanted. "Autism" is a diagnosis that is made by observing the symptoms a child exhibits. According to the Autism Society of America (www.autism-society.org), those with autism may exhibit some of the following traits:

- Insistence on sameness; resistance to change
- Difficulty in expressing needs; uses gestures or pointing instead of words
- Repeating words or phrases in place of normal, responsive language
- Laughing, crying, showing distress for reasons not apparent to others
- Prefers to be alone; aloof manner
- Tantrums
- Difficulty in mixing with others
- May not want to cuddle or be cuddled
- Little or no eye contact
- Unresponsive to normal teaching methods
- Sustained odd play
- Spins objects
- Inappropriate attachments to objects
- Apparent oversensitivity or undersensitivity to pain
- No real fears of danger
- Noticeable physical overactivity or extreme underactivity
- Uneven gross/fine motor skills
- Not responsive to verbal cues; acts as if deaf although hearing tests in normal range.*

Whitney could still demonstrate all of these symptoms, so by definition he would meet the description of the syndrome "autism." I understood that he needed a label to qualify for special education and all of

*Reprinted with permission from the Autism Society of America.

the additional services that came with the label, such as OT, PT, and speech therapy. At this point in his school career, I had to accept this label for him in order to get him extra help. Still, the fact that I accepted the label to get him help didn't mean I accepted the prognosis that came with the label. For many autistic children, the prognosis is not for full recovery to normal capabilities. Every disease has a natural course, and the natural course of severe mental retardation or autism is not to end up free of all symptoms. I was still clinging to the hope that Whitney had some other disorder, something that we *could* help him with, and that he could overcome the autistic-like symptoms.

I also believed that labeling a child is a tricky thing. If the label makes the teacher believe that the child has limited potential and the child is nonverbal, not able to follow directions or speak, then it is very easy to think that teaching the child will be challenging at best, and potentially impossible. I didn't want Whitney to be considered unteachable because he was "autistic." What was the point of accepting the label to get him extra help if the help would come with a preconceived belief that he was unhelpable?

Although I still wanted more for him, I had come around to thinking it was good that the school officials thought Whitney had improved enough to advance from Mrs. Jones's "multiply handicapped" class (where he'd been completely isolated from all normal kids) to this class where the plan included mainstreaming him with other kids in the regular classroom.

I knew that it would be challenging for Whitney to go to yet another school and get used to new teachers, new routines, and new rules. Changing schools is difficult for any child. For a child with problems like Whitney's, it could be a huge setback. Making friends and adapting to new patterns was supremely difficult for Whitney. Every time he had to move and adapt to another group of classmates, teachers, and a new school, it was like starting all over.

When I drove up to Riverside on the first day of school, I was stunned to see Mr. Niemie, the principal, outside playing his guitar and singing to the kids as they arrived. A six-foot-tall former basketball coach, Mr. Niemie was handsome, strong, and physically fit. He looked more like a movie star than an elementary school principal. I jumped out of the car, grasping Whitney's little hand in mine. Whitney seemed surprised to see something so fun happening outside of a school, too. Whitney smiled at Mr. Niemie but continued to hold my hand. He was busy scanning the scene around the building: kids playing on the playground, parents talking to one another outside the building. In front of the school, a couple of boys were trading baseball cards. A young girl was showing off her new shoes that lit up with red sparkles every time she took a step, and was getting oohs and aahs from a couple of little friends. Whitney was smiling and looking from one scenario to another—he seemed quite interested. As we approached, Mr. Niemie started singing to us. Mr. Niemie knew Whitney was coming to the school because there had been plenty of behind-the-scenes planning meetings with the administration. Whitney's permanent folder had been on his desk, with pictures of Whitney included with each year's portfolio. He took off his guitar and threw Whitney up in the air and gave him a hug. "Great to see you, Whitney. You are going to love it here," he told him.

What a wonderful human being we have stumbled upon, I thought. I have always believed that the boss sets the "corporate culture," and I knew instantly I would move heaven and earth to stay around Mr. Niemie.

When Whitney and I arrived at the special education classroom, we lost some of our enthusiasm. The classroom was small, as it was for only about five children. A large section of the room was devoted to an area to practice toothbrushing and hand-washing. Otherwise it was fairly barren. Whitney started waving his hands and trying to leave. He did not want to stay there.

Ms. Meyer, the teacher, came up to us and greeted us.

She tried to get Whitney to put away his coat and sit down at the desk that had his name on it. But Whitney tried to run out of the room.

He seemed to want to go back outside where there had been so much to see.

While I tried to get him settled, I heard her tell another parent that the main focus of the class would be safety, rather than pushing the kids.

This felt like such a major step backward. "Can I help in the classroom?" I asked her, grasping for a way to make this situation better. Maybe I could get involved, the way I had with Mrs. Jones.

She told me to check at the office about the rules, since the program was new at Riverside. I left Whitney in his new classroom while I went off to see what I could do to change his situation.

When I asked Mr. Niemie's secretary, Alice, my question about helping in Whitney's classroom, she responded, "I am not sure about room moms for the handicapped, either. You will need to see Mr. Niemie. He will be with you in a moment," she assured me.

As I stood, waiting, a woman came in carrying a shoebox and holding a very spacey little boy's right hand while his left hand was flapping repeatedly. She set the box down on the counter and told Alice, "We've just been to a doctor in Akron and he was wonderful. He changed the kinds of meds our son was taking. We need to go over it with the school nurse." She lifted the top off of the shoebox and I saw a row of pill bottles stacked inside with notes about how they should be administered. Alice introduced us.

"I heard your son's going to be in my son's class," the mother said. "You should go to this doctor. I'm sure he could help your boy. We have seen such a change in him on these medications. We use this med for behavior, this stimulant for focusing and alertness, this for going to sleep easily, and this for emotional self-control—and these are vitamins," she explained as she held up the various bottles.

I thought it was ironic that Alcoholics Anonymous started in Akron, and here was a six-year-old who'd gone there to be put on a shoebox full of some highly controlled substances and who was being held up as an example of how to attain good behavior.

"He doesn't try to get into the kitchen cupboards anymore, he goes to sleep better, and he is not as disruptive or impulsive."

"What *does* he do?" I asked, but before she could answer, Mr. Niemie appeared and ushered me into his office. I was frantic about Whitney staying in class with such severely impaired kids, fearing Whitney would relapse to the old behaviors we had worked so hard to get rid of. I dove in: "Whitney can do a lot of things that are higher-level than the requirements for the autism class," I explained. "I want him to switch to regular first grade full-time."

"You have goals for your son, I like that." Mr. Niemie smiled and leaned back in his chair. He seemed much more relaxed than the other principals and school officials I'd encountered. He had a direct, commanding, and yet gentle way about him. I felt a glimmer of hope.

He leaned forward and pushed a legal pad toward me. He stabbed his pen at the top of the page. "You know, we have the triangle approach at our school, and the child is at the top."

He looked at me to see if I was with him. I forced a smile, not sure where he was going.

He took his pen and drew two more dots below the first one. "The *parent* and the *teacher* are on either side." He connected the dots to form a triangle and then jabbed his pen at the two dots at the base of the triangle: "You are our equal partner here."

I could tell he'd given this speech countless times, but I didn't care. I loved it.

"We love parental involvement. With parents helping, we can offer the kids so much more. For instance, we have a parent who knows sign language who's going to teach an after-school workshop, another who's volunteered to teach typing, one's doing science, another will do art. Let me show you around."

He jumped up and within minutes I was hurrying after him as he strode down the halls, bubbling with enthusiasm for the many ways parents were getting involved. I listened and agreed that it was a great approach.

At the end of his tour, he gave me a sign-up sheet with a list of options for parent volunteering and told me to turn it in when I'd thought it over.

"I will move in. I will do anything you need or want me to do," I assured him. I took the pen, checked off everything, and gave it back to him.

He glanced down at the sheet: secretary of the PTO, room mom for son's class, learning partners committee, testing procedures committee, fun fair committee, yard clean-up committee, publishing shop committee . . . He looked at me as if I was kidding.

"I am serious; I will do anything," I told him. "But what about Whitney and first grade?"

Aha. I could see him realize that even though I was acting agreeable, I was stubborn. "Let's start with this," he said firmly. "We can't just make changes like that. Whitney has an IEP and we are legally bound to do what is on it." Now he was all business.

This was an area I knew about. "I have written IEPs all over the country; the IEP can be changed at any time," I assured him.

He squared off again. "The IEP is not my area of expertise. But . . . I'll check with administration and get back to you."

I decided to leave it at that. As I turned to go, though, I made one more appeal. "No more testing, please. Whitney doesn't speak clearly; he can't take tests. He doesn't hear things correctly so he won't know what they are saying. But he can read, and that is what first grade is about—reading."

I knew that not being able to speak and follow directions certainly were big concerns for first-grade success—but my hope was that Whitney's reading skills might carry at least part of the day and could be used to supplement the other areas. I also knew, though, that what I was calling Whitney's "reading" was going to be a stretch for the school administrators and teachers. He wasn't reading books yet. He was able to select words on printed cards from visual sight memory and had a corpus of about two hundred words he could recognize when I said them. He could string some words together to make sentences. That was about all I had to show them. It was hard to convince people that he even had these skills, since he rarely responded to spoken words, or even spoke himself. He spoke sometimes, but in his telegraphic sentences, saying words here and there. Sometimes he just made noise—sounding like a machine gun, or babbling nonsensically.

But his ability to do these logo exercises, plus his visual problem-solving skills showed a lot of potential to me, and I had a plan for how to continue to build on these skills. Just as Annie Sullivan knew that once Helen understood that water was water from spelling into her hand, I knew that Whitney's current abilities were the beginnings of teaching him how to master a system of verbal processing for reading, writing, listening, and speaking. But I must admit, from a traditional school curriculum perspective, it didn't look like much. I was absolutely out on a limb, but I knew where I wanted to go with this if I could get the school to go along.

A few days later, after dropping Whitney off, I ran into Mr. Niemie and he took me aside. "I see you signed up to be Mrs. Moore's room mom."

I smiled, nodding my head.

"Whitney is in Ms. Meyer's class."

I pointed out that Ms. Meyer wasn't using parent volunteers and Whitney was supposed to be mainstreamed as much as he could handle. I said, "Remember we are working to get Whitney into regular first grade? I figure we'll have that worked out by Halloween, so it would be good to get acquainted with Mrs. Moore's class—it'll help me help him make the transition."

He looked like he wasn't sure whether to laugh at my audacity, or get annoyed. Taking a deep breath, he patiently explained that the administration would be happy to test Whitney to see if he could be mainstreamed for some of his schoolday, but once the testing began, they had ninety days to complete it. My mind started to multitask quickly, trying to formulate how to manage this situation as I heard him list the steps: meetings, tests, reports, more planning meetings. "Nothing can happen until after Christmas break at the earliest," he concluded.

By now I was getting more worked up, stomping down the hall, and he was quietly walking beside me. He stopped and turned to me.

"You know, you're not giving us enough credit here. You're ignoring that we have experience, that we know things about working with special needs children. You're just trying to get your own way, you're not giving us a chance to show what we can do."

"Whitney's going to MIT for college. First grade sets the foundation for schooling; he can't change in the middle of the school year, he will be lost!" I blurted out. The moment the words flew out of my mouth, I could see my mistake, but I couldn't help it.

Mr. Niemie took a deep breath. "I think there's a gap here."

I knew there was a huge gap. But I thought there was a better chance of filling the gap in first grade, where they are systematically working on adding elements to reading every day. Whitney would be off to a better start surrounded by a classroom of twenty visual role models than in the autism class where they were working on potty training and hygiene.

"I do too." I tried to hold my ground.

He saw I was off balance and he charged ahead, reminding me that I was the one who had approved and signed Whitney's current IEP back when Whitney started in the Chapman program at age four. The IEP was good for three years so there was no obligation to redo it until he was in second grade.

I explained that he had come so far that it made no sense to work from an IEP that was written when he was much worse off.

He tried another tack. "Maybe we can get some compromise."

"We're not going to get a compromise!" I pointed into the classroom where Whitney was now sitting in the corner. "In ten years, those kids will still be in the special education class. Whitney won't."

Mr. Niemie looked at me long and hard. "Since you are so firm about having us take another look at Whitney, I have talked to those at Central Office and they have agreed to revamp after only two years instead of three."

He thought I'd be thrilled, but I wasn't. *Oh no, there goes the triangle,* I thought. *It's a hexagon now.* I had pushed too hard. It was hard enough for me to hold onto my own conviction and argument for why a nonverbal child should be in regular first grade. I knew it would be hard to convince others. I thought I had a chance with Mr. Niemie. I knew this meant more testing. Whitney had improved, but he was still a far cry from being able to excel in standard testing. Past experience made me fear starting over with new testing and meetings with a group of new school personnel. I feared I'd lost my ally and I'd now have a whole team to convince. Maybe Mr. Niemie was right—but my intuition told me that Whitney could make it in the first grade and we should give it a try.

"I thought you would be pleased at what I accomplished."

I could see I was really trying his patience. "Look, you are clearly a one-in-a-million principal and human being—"

He stopped me abruptly. "I am just doing my job . . . nothing special, and my ego doesn't need flattery." I could hear the anger in his voice.

"This is not idle flattery," I argued. "I've never seen a school official roaming in and out of classes, playing guitar, telling jokes. You know every child's name, and the parents—parents are a second labor force here, working sometimes forty hours a week for free." I had quickly learned about Mr. Niemie and how much he'd done with his school. "I am beyond grateful to be at your school. But Whitney is a special case and needs to be handled carefully."

I explained how we had worked day and night for six years to bring Whitney out. "Last year, Whitney exhibited no hand-flapping or rocking by the end of the year. He did his seatwork at his desk and learned how to read independently." We were only a few days into the school year; now in the autistic class, he was already reverting to these old autistic behaviors at school and at home. He was rocking and isolating in his classroom. He was staying up all night, sitting and staring at things for long periods. He was retreating into his own world again. I pleaded with Mr. Niemie. "I am not sure how we will get him back if he relapses. I did eight years of research on relapse for the federal government, and relapse is like death for someone with a communication disability. We don't want to go there!"

He stared at me. My outburst shocked both of us. I reached into my bag and pulled out a portfolio of my professional work that I'd assembled. I took a deep breath and handed it to him—research papers, press clippings, and more. "I know a lot about how to correct brain disorders. Please trust me."

I could see he was struggling to make sense of my intense, manic blabbering. He was not expecting a mom of an autistic six-year-old to tell him about how many times she had been on CBS news or how many school programs she had set up all over the country.

In his calmest voice, he asked, "What do you think we should do?"

I appealed to his sense of logic. "The way you will be conducting testing could harm Whitney, not help him. He will appear to be retarded because he can't talk. Thinking and talking are two very different things."

He could see my fierce passion for both my son and my work. By this time, we were seated in his office.

"I know you have the children's best interest at heart. But I am fighting for my son. I won't give up. I will be back every day until we get this right. I am not a troublemaker. I try hard to avoid criticizing professionals. I don't like to focus on negatives or bad-mouth people. But I won't let you or your system harm Whitney. He has come too far to let a system crush him."

Mr. Niemie nodded and I could see his wheels turning. After a silence that seemed like hours, he said, "Tell me what you want and I will help you."

To my dismay, I burst into tears and started crying uncontrolably. Here I'd been going on about all of my professional credits and I had done the least professional thing I could do—cry! I tried to regain my composure. "There are federal guidelines for mainstreaming children like Whitney. All I want is for you to help me make the administration adhere to these."

He smiled with the relief of a coach who has just hit upon the winning play. "Then I am sure we will be fine." It turned out this district was so picky about following the laws that they'd just hired a secretary at their school for the sole purpose of law compliance. He could see a way to solve this problem.

We made an appointment to prepare for meeting with the administration.

As I left, I chastised myself again for crying in Mr. Niemie's office. Even though we were arguing, he was the first person I'd felt I could confide in freely about the problems we'd faced with Whitney and the schools. I told myself not to be embarrassed by the display of emotion and instead focused on preparing for our meeting.

I arrived at my meeting with Mr. Niemie with a big storage tub of videotapes, books, handouts, and our TV set with a built-in VCR. I showed Mr. Niemie a video first. Suzy was a former client who'd been referred to me by one of the pediatricians in my office building. The tape began with her mom explaining that she was a reading specialist and she had taught thousands of kids to read, but she couldn't reach Suzy. Now she was homeschooling her daughter because school made Suzy feel so sick she wouldn't get out of bed. Suzy was becoming a seven-year-old recluse and was potentially suicidal. "We are all a family of readers, but not Suzy," her mom explained. "She would sound out a word like s-o-a-p and then say 'horse.' It was like she forgot what the sounds were before she got to the point of saying the word." Then she explained that after six months of therapy, Suzy went from being unable to read *Hop on Pop* to reading chapter books. I asked her, "Did we work on reading?" She replied, "No, you worked on the auditory and visual memory systems that were the biology under reading. When those systems functioned properly, all the reading skills we had been teaching all along fell into place—"

"Turn that off," Mr. Niemie said kindly.

I looked up.

"I have someone in my own family with a problem just like that," he said. "I understand." I couldn't believe the providence. I don't know what made me decide to show Mr. Niemie a video to explain Whitney's problem. Looking back, maybe I'd sensed that this athlete, musician, coach, and principal with such a strong intuitive sense of people might be a visual thinker and would respond to the video more than to all my talking.

Of course that didn't stop me from explaining anyway. I told him that Suzy was a high visual. She could think fine, she just didn't understand the verbal coding needed for reading. Whitney was beyond that; he already had the verbal code to read many words. Neither Whitney nor Helen Keller could learn language by hearing. I was teaching language to Whitney through his eyes, like Helen Keller learned through her hands. Although Whitney couldn't talk, hear, or write, he did have a concept that words were part of a language code. He could recognize logos and words, so his receptive language was coming along nicely. I explained, "His expressive language is behind, but we learn receptive language first so I believe we can build this skill. The kids in the handicapped class do not have language. The kids in the first grade do. I want him around the language users. *See?*" I stopped for a breath.

"I really do see," he assured me.

I pulled out the Ohio Department of Education (ODE) handbook. The department had set up a system that was perfect for Whitney, and I explained it to Mr. Niemie. Teachers filled in a series of checklists: one for listening, one for reading, one for writing, one for speaking. Using these checklists, we could formulate a plan for how to accommodate what Whitney can't do. "He doesn't have to be labeled with anything. It won't cost any money. We just need to teach Mrs. Moore how to help him. I can teach her how to do this and help her every step of the way." My voice was rising with excitement.

I waited, anticipating his response. Slowly he reached for the handbook. "Give me the checklists and I will have Mrs. Moore, the speech therapist, the LD tutor, and the special ed teacher fill them out."

I shook Mr. Niemie's hand until I thought it would fall off. I was so happy to have him on my team.

Mr. Niemie quickly assembled the necessary school administrators to meet with us about Whitney. When I arrived for this meeting, the conference room was crowded with the group of administrators, Mr. Niemie presiding.

I decided to dive in. "I would like to help set up Whitney's reevaluation. I noted in the foreword to the ODE handbook that Dublin schools are represented on the steering committee that wrote the book. I love this book. Can we use this method?"

They agreed, saying they were very careful to follow the law here in the district.

"Great, so we will just follow what the book says then, and we can move Whitney into first grade tomorrow?"

"What?" two of the administrators asked simultaneously. "Why do you think that? We have to do testing."

I opened the book and pointed. "That is not what the book says—it says no testing is needed, just the checklists."

"No, you're misinterpreting. We need to do our testing. That is what we always do . . ."

I told them, "Whitney can't talk or hear correctly. That makes him really hard to test. Especially with the tests in the standard battery. It says in the ODE handbook that tests that are language-dependent are not appropriate for children like Whitney, and they will not reflect his intelligence correctly because he has language problems."

Now they were getting annoyed. "Look, we know how to adapt the tests so that we can work around language deficiency, and we can pick tests that don't have that much language dependence."

"Which tests? How can you do this without listening, reading, writing, and speaking?" Testing nonverbal people was exactly what I did in my practice, and I knew that designing and administering these tests was complex. I didn't trust that they knew how to do this. I seemed destined to butt heads with the administration.

Thankfully, Mr. Niemie took control. "Cheri, this is not going the way I wanted it to. You need to trust the system." He quieted me and turned to the administrative team. "Thank you so much for coming. I am sure Cheri will go along with whatever you think is best."

They looked at Mr. Niemie with sympathy—how did he deal with this overly aggressive know-it-all mom?

"We want you to be pleased, Dr. Florance. But schools are very different from the hospital and university systems that you are used to. If you let us do our jobs, I think you'll find that we will take excellent care of Whitney. Think of how much he has improved in the past two years."

He has done well in spite of the tests and because of my hard work along with his teachers, I thought. I walked to the car, put my head down on the steering wheel, and cried, feeling defeated again.

But Mr. Niemie had a plan. Within days, he sent a memo outlining his plan to let Whitney try out being in Mrs. Moore's regular first-grade class for a couple of hours a day. He would spend the morning in Mrs. Moore's and the afternoons in the special ed class. I was pleased Mr. Niemie was taking a step toward mainstreaming, but I knew this setup would be problematic. I warned Mr. Niemie that a complicated routine might be hard for Whitney to adapt to—he would be better off in Mrs. Moore's class all day. However, it was clear I'd better not push it.

I wouldn't learn until much later that the first day Whitney attended Mrs. Moore's class, he got lost coming back from recess. For two hours, they couldn't find him. Teachers and even Mr. Niemie were scouring the school and playground, looking for him. Finally, they found him under a bush, rocking. Mr. Niemie told me later that they didn't want to alarm me unnecessarily once he was located and safe. I suppose they had no desire to get me even more worked up. I was upset at hearing it later, though.

In hindsight, I see that they could have used this incident to argue that Whitney was in no state to attend regular first grade. But Mr. Niemie realized that Whitney's running away was an example of what I'd been warning him about. Whitney had no set routine to latch onto. And so Mr. Niemie came to Whitney's defense. He assured his teachers it was a minor setback, that Whitney had lost his pattern. Mr. Niemie decided that pattern was the key for Whitney, so he began to think about how Whitney could spend more time in Mrs. Moore's class but still get the help he needed.

Meanwhile, Whitney started seeing a speech therapist, and she was working with him aggressively on his articulation, specifically the way he said the "L" sound. While he clearly needed help in this area, school-based speech therapy for children Whitney's age focuses on articulation issues. Whitney's speech problems were much deeper than articulation.

When he started speech class, I'd received regular "Speech Happy Grams" that the therapist sent home to parents. They said things like: "Please practice this at home: *Little Lillie. Little Lillie likes to lick lime lollipops.*"

Because there are an estimated 140,000 messages sent from the brain to a host of body parts in order for the mouth to say "Little Lillie," I thought she was asking him to do something that was too hard for him. He wasn't able to say single words so you could understand them. Tongue twisters are hard for everyone. Trying to teach Whitney how to articulate an "L" sound as part of speech therapy was like trying to teach a beginning skater a triple toe loop. He didn't have basic speaking skills yet.

A little later, she sent a note home that said, "Whitney does appear to have good vocabulary skills and evidence of general knowledge during his free activities. He does appear to experience more difficulty responding to questions by giving unrelated jargon or saying 'don't know' . . . His effort needs improvement."

Then I got a call from Mr. Niemie: "Whitney is trying to get away from his speech therapist and crawled under the table and ripped her hose."

I knew this would be a huge setback for Whitney's case. The therapist, Mr. Niemie, and I met, and she indicated she thought Whitney would be better off back in the full-time special-ed program. I was so disappointed.

I was frustrated that she thought that Whitney's problems had anything to do with his effort. Couldn't she see that he had a language-processing problem? In addition, she told us that the ODE checklists were not appropriate for a child like Whitney. She wrote "not applicable" on the reading and writing checklists. To my mind, listening and speaking are the foundation for reading and writing, and if you are not thinking about how all of these functions interrelate, you cannot develop a treatment plan for rehabilitation of speech and language disability.

We'd come so far, and speech articulation was such a small piece of the overall picture. He was not fluent in his verbal thinking, and he was using his big-picture conceptual understanding of situations to manage his day. Breaking down the act of speaking into a focus on one sound could interfere with the fluency of thought-to-word training we were building.

Certainly Whitney was not up to par in all skills that the other children could demonstrate. But already he was doing better. He was sitting at his desk doing his reading and writing assignments. He was beginning to draw pictures to illustrate simple stories. He was learning how to leave with his tutor to "chill out" somewhere else when he was overwhelmed. He was in OT, PT, and adaptive physical education, and each of those professionals saw improvement. Whitney needed to learn a huge repertoire of skills that other children acquire intuitively. He couldn't control his motor speech system to say tongue twisters, but that was not an essential skill in the classroom. Listening occupies about 76 percent of a school day according to the ODE, and reading is a way to improve listening. These are both receptive language systems. I was interested in getting his receptive language system to work properly so speech and writing could develop on a firm foundation.

How could she be arguing that he needed to go back to full-time special-ed class? I'd thought a speech therapist would be my ally, but she was turning out to cause more trouble.

"I think Whitney should drop speech therapy," I said.

The next day, Mr. Niemie sat me down in his office. "Whitney's therapist is insulted that you do not want speech therapy when he needs it so desperately. He can't speak correctly and you are excluding speech therapy from his basket of services. In fact, we all find this hard to understand." He paused, took a deep breath and looked me in the eye. "She's says you've caused trouble and a lot of people don't like you. What have you done to upset her so?"

My face was hot with anger.

"You need to answer or we won't know what to do next."

"I wasn't aware that no one liked me—how would you answer if someone asked you that? I have had a wonderful working relationship with all of my children's teachers."

"I don't know, but this is no small concern. The superintendent called me and told me to stop associating with you because you were way off base. I could lose my job for supporting you."

I felt socked in the stomach. I took a deep breath and said, "Let's take Whitney out of speech therapy and go on with our plan. She is pushing all of these rumors." I knew I sounded defensive and accusatory. But I no longer cared. If people didn't like me, so be it. If I was known as an overbearing, overinvolved mother, fine. Now when I walked down the halls I imagined the whispers: "She's too proud." "The doctor can't stand it that she can't fix her own child." "She's in denial. She just wants him to be normal." Maybe I was being paranoid, but being told that I wasn't liked was upsetting. I felt alone again—what happened to the triangle? Was I doing something wrong? I thought of myself as a quiet, peaceful person. But I also knew that I was like a mother lion—I would attack if someone tried to harm my young. As long as Whitney got the education he was entitled to and the help he needed, I could ignore my concerns about what others thought of me.

At our next big meeting, the room was full of people: the OT, the PT, the adaptive phys ed teacher, the special ed secretary, Mrs. Moore, tutors, administrators, Whitney's speech therapist, Mr. Niemie, and others. The discomfort I'd felt imagining what people were saying about me as I walked the halls was nothing compared to the nakedness I felt sitting in that conference room. I was sure they were all here to explain what was wrong with Whitney—and with my attempts to help. I was so angry, all I wanted to do was make everyone see that I was trying to follow the rules as written. But Mr. Niemie had ordered me to stay quiet.

Mr. Niemie began, "Dr. Florance is like someone who is given a wonderful Christmas gift but wants to return it. Our district gave her a service her son needs and she is rejecting it."

I wanted to scream, to storm out of the room—I felt betrayed by Mr. Niemie's speech. Then as the meeting progressed, I realized that once again, he had a plan. He was somehow managing to move Whitney full-time to regular first grade before the testing was completed. It took great courage for Mr. Niemie to do this for Whitney, when everyone was telling him I was a troublemaker.

He told the administration to go ahead and do the necessary testing, but that in the meantime, he'd put Whitney in Mrs. Moore's class for most of the day. If he needed to go back to full special ed class after they finished their testing, he'd do that. In the meantime, this is what he wanted to do now.

People raised objections about how disruptive it would be if Whitney fell apart. What if he started to revert to old behaviors? What if he threw a tantrum? What if he started biting the other kids? What if he ran away? What if he started his head-banging and rocking? There was no way to predict if he would fall apart—his skills were too newly developed and he was too fragile with all of the change going on.

"When he falls apart, you can bring him to my office," Mr. Niemie told the schoolteachers. "No matter what I'm doing or who I'm meeting with, he can come in and crawl up on my lap," he insisted.

"You can't do that. What if you're not here? What if you are at a meeting out of the building?" they asked.

"Then he can talk to the guidance counselor, or Alice, or Peggy, the school nurse." He stood firm. "We will make a safe haven for him here in school."

We all signed a memo outlining this interim plan. I signed a form to waive Whitney's speech therapy, but the therapist would remain a vocal member of his team throughout his years at Riverside.

At the end of the meeting, I stayed behind. I knew Mr. Niemie had gone out on a limb and that I'd made things difficult. I stumbled for words to thank him.

He stopped me. "We have a lot of work to do to get him ready for MIT," he said.

On Whitney's seventh birthday, September 30, Mr. Niemie moved Whitney to Mrs. Moore's first grade class for most of the day.

In October, I went to parent/teacher night. I waited nervously for my ten-minute slot to see Whitney's papers and talk to Mrs. Moore.

While I was waiting, I reread for the umpteenth time the text of a book Whitney had written in his own, nearly illegible scribble:

THE STAR

Me and Ben. We play with Mark and Cody and Terry. They are our friends. We play at recess. We play a game of power rangers. You get a dinosaur. You get a suit. You have to stay with the group. Have fun.

When it was my turn to meet with Mrs. Moore, as soon as I sat down she burst into tears.

Oh no, I thought. *What bad news does she have?* "What's wrong?" I asked tersely, steeling myself.

"Whitney," she said, still crying, "has adjusted to our classroom." She tried to compose herself. "He can read kids' names on folders. We wrote that story together about Terry—his friend from last year—and put it in his writing folder. He had a sense of story . . . and I added the sentences to make it complete." Her eyes welled up again. *Uh-oh, here it comes,* I thought. *She's too upset to tell me.* "He needs work on his math. He counted up to twenty-eight . . . but had a lot of trouble and needed a lot of cueing. Sometimes he doesn't finish his morning work . . . but we can work with his tutor, Mrs. Cleveland, on that. The kids treat him as they do the others . . ."

She composed herself and looked at me and smiled. "This is a miracle. Whitney is a miracle. Thank you for allowing me to be part of this."

I reached out tentatively and took her hand. "It's going to work out, isn't it?" I asked. I was so desperate for another adult to share the journey, to tell me everything would be OK. I didn't know Mrs. Moore very well, and she'd been wary of me no doubt, after the trouble I'd raised to get Whitney into her class. But here she was, moved to tears about his progress. At that moment, I needed desperately for her to tell me it was going to be OK.

"Yes." She smiled. "I think it is."

During that school year, the special ed core team would meet periodically and review Whitney's case. They had reports from Mrs. Moore, Mrs. Cleveland, his learning disability tutor, and his speech, OT, PT, and adaptive physical ed specialists. The teachers would report whether Whitney was making progress and whether his skills were below age level. For instance, in November, the speech teacher reported that Whitney's behavior was inappropriate for his age, he was undisciplined, and he needed to improve his social and verbal skills. She suggested that I needed to attend positive parenting and Whitney needed to learn teacher respect. Mrs. Moore reported that he had some inappropriate behavior in the classroom also. He was making disruptive noises, and when he was having difficulty completing class work and she attempted to help him, he refused to look at her and said he had a headache. She reported that Whitney could dictate a story in sequence but could not write or reread the story. Whitney's locomotor skills and object control were average; his motor skills were below age level.

He may have been below age level in all skills, but I only saw the success he was having in learning language. He could dictate a story now.

By February of that school year, Whitney was actually starting to write words. His handwriting was still hard to read, but improving. Mrs. Moore wrote in his report:

Whitney regresses occasionally and blocks everyone out. Sometimes he won't go to art or gym and won't write in his journal. His desk is unorganized.

By March, the core group reported:

Whitney is reading aloud at low average for first grade. He struggles with writing and refuses to copy. He doesn't take risks. His social skills are immature.

Again, I only saw the amazing progress. Reading aloud and struggling with writing were huge successes to my mind. I disagreed about
him not taking risks. Risk-taking has always been one of Whitney's
enormous strengths. He has been taking giant risks since he was an
infant—as long as the risk depended on his visual thinking system.
When he was asked to call upon his unreliable and half-built verbal system, he often did not know what to do—which appeared to be limited
risk-taking in verbal land.

It would be May by the time the school district finished their evaluation of Whitney. In their report they wrote:

> Whitney's ability on a nonverbal measure recommended for stu-
> dents with language difficulties fell in the average range. Speech
> and language assessment results indicate a significant discrep-
> ancy in the area of oral expression. Although academic achieve-
> ment results were commensurate with his ability, [everything
> was in the 8 to 19 percentile low-functioning range according to
> composite scores] in the classroom, his functioning indicates his
> struggle with most language-related tasks. The team discussed
> Whitney's autistic-like behaviors in communication and interac-
> tion, which were evidenced in the classroom at the beginning of
> the year. As Whitney felt more comfortable and confident, these
> behaviors have decreased in intensity in an environment specifi-
> cally tailored to meet his difficulties with adjustments. . . .
>
> Whitney evidences language-related difficulties in the regular
> classroom in terms of oral expression, articulation difficulties,
> and some problems in receptive understanding.

With all of my training and expertise, and with their own observation of Whitney's dramatic progress as a result of the plan I had fought
so hard for, the team showed no interest in what I was doing or what I
had to say. They continued to follow the standard protocol they had
established for all children. The school speech therapist continued to

make pronouncements about Whitney through fourth grade, his last
year at Riverside. When I asked her why she thought Whitney had
improved so much, she said he had an "odd developmental profile."

They decided he could be mainstreamed at Riverside, and he was
now "upgraded" from "multihandicapped" to "learning disabled"
(LD). Of course, now that would be for second grade since, thanks to
Mr. Niemie, he had been mainstreamed for most of first grade while
the evaluation for placement was being undertaken.

II

Learning from

Maverick

Minds

During the summer between first and second grades, Whitney again improved dramatically. Everything was looking up. My practice was becoming more stable. Whitney attended summer camp and was enrolled in a one-week drama program called "Snow White and the 7 Sports." I'd thought that with his experience at playing charades and his enjoyment playing make-believe, he'd enjoy being in a kid's play. After all, he was playing "Power Rangers" now. I had done my master's thesis on the use of creative dramatics and music therapy to increase communication success and academic readiness in kindergarten-age children. I had written the plays and the musical scores for the research project, and divided the children into three groups for the experiment. Children in the drama and music groups made significant gains in articulation and language skills when compared to the children in the control group. This early work became the basis for my work with Head Start. Now, with this opportunity with the theater, I saw a way to mainstream Whitney into better communication and social interactions.

I remembered that when we'd gone to the Dublin Irish Festival, a woman named Candace Masur did mime and creative dramatics games, and she said Whitney should sign up for her summer camp. She had a bigger-than-life personality—a Shirley MacLaine–type dancer-gypsy with scarves flying, she pulled up for the first day of drama camp in her "theater mobile," with original music and scripts crammed in the trunk, and costumes and sets tucked away in compartments. Rather than make kids fit into the mold of her preconceived view of a play, she'd mold her plays to fit the talents of the kids.

When I introduced Whitney to her, I said nothing about his problems. Right away Candace realized she couldn't understand everything that Whitney said. Whitney was still not attempting to converse much, even though his vocabulary had improved, and what he did say was still hard to understand. This didn't faze her. She simply assigned him the role of Sneezy. She showed Whitney how to sneeze a number of different ways. He loved this, and inventing another "fifty sneezes" immediately became his new mission. Candace acted as if each new sneeze Whitney showed her was a gold doubloon. He could be facing upstage and his sneeze was still a masterpiece, as far as she was concerned. Whitney *was* putting himself body and soul into every *"Achoo!"*

On the big day of the show, Will, Vanessa, and I fidgeted nervously in the audience. I was afraid of a reenactment of last year's swim demonstration. I sat on the aisle, in case I needed to run after him again. All of my concern was for naught. Right on cue, with perfect blocking, Whitney followed Candace's direction to a T. Every sneeze was a unique episode, and the audience roared. In our minds, Whitney stole the show.

Afterward, the kids presented Candace with roses, and the cast gave us their autographs while we enjoyed punch and cookies. Candace approached me. "Can Whitney do this again next week? We're having a repeat camp in Delaware at the Arts Castle."

My mother had helped create the Arts Castle in Delaware, Ohio. My father helped to build it. Jack and Dotty Florance's grandson—

playing Sneezy in front of all of their artist friends? It could be the added pressure that would tip the scales. If I felt pressured for Whitney to do a good job to please my mother, Whitney might pick up on this without my realizing it. I have often seen this happen with parents and children in my practice. Vanessa and William are very sensitive and seem to know my mood even when I am trying to hide it. Whitney was not that in touch with other people at this time, but I still could never be sure what triggered his shut-downs and I didn't want to take any chances. Why not quit on a win?

But Candace persisted—she acted as if she had not noticed that Whitney was limited verbally. I found myself wondering why she and Whitney seemed to be able to relate to each other so well. Is acting visual? Maybe a play is a picture—a visual story—and the words are pasted on. I've heard Meryl Streep say that she reads a script once and sees it. Tom Cruise reads a script once and knows exactly where the movie goes wrong and how to fix it. Were Whitney and Candace two visual minds communicating in their first language?

So Whitney went to Delaware to be Sneezy. The first day, I drove him the thirty miles to camp and he did just fine. My parents lived down the street from the Arts Castle and offered to have Whitney stay with them for the rest of the week to reduce my commute. I was nervous about how they'd handle him; I didn't think they'd truly grasped the degree of Whitney's problems. They knew Whitney was in special education for severely handicapped, but no one on either side of the family tree had experienced raising a child in a program for the developmentally disabled and mentally retarded. They wanted to be good grandparents to all of the kids, but they hadn't ever spent any one-on-one time with Whitney. Moreover, Whitney had never stayed overnight by himself anywhere!

But he was doing so well, we decided to try it. I stayed the first night, and when I asked Whitney if he wanted to stay at Grandma and Grandpa's without me, he smiled. I gestured to him that he would stay here and I would leave. He seemed OK with it. I didn't know if he understood me or not, but we only lived about thirty minutes away, so I knew I could come back if there were problems.

That first night, I urged my parents to keep up the traditional rituals that the kids were used to at their home. For example, Grandma had "norcpop" parties (our word for popcorn) with a movie I had carefully selected for them. And Grandpa rose the next morning to make pancakes that looked like airplanes for Whitney's breakfast. They reported that Whitney was having the time of his life, and so the visit was extended for the rest of the week.

At the end of the week, we all went to the Delaware version of "Snow White and the 7 Sports" and again Whitney held court. "I told you so," Candace said proudly.

Meanwhile, I was reading in a lot of different areas, trying to understand and find solutions to Whitney's problems. Around this time, I turned to a new book by D. P. Cantwell and Lorian Baker, *Psychiatric and Developmental Disorders in Children with Communication Disorder*. I'd followed Dr. Cantwell's work for quite some time, but this book made me feel like I'd happened upon scripture. I read the book twice in one afternoon. Dr. Dennis Cantwell, a contributing author of the DSM (Diagnostic Statistical Manual of Mental Disorders—the manual used to diagnose psychiatric disease) and arguably one of the most influential professors of psychiatry in the world, was suggesting many, if not most, psychiatric disorders in children are due to, or coexist with, communication disability. Cantwell had studied six hundred children in a speech and hearing clinic following a sabbatical in London. His interest in this idea was triggered during his stay in England when he found himself constantly making mistakes because of language processing problems. He took a train from London and was trying to figure out how to change trains and get to his final destination. He asked several people for help, but because of their accents he couldn't understand them. He was from Los Angeles, and he had not anticipated that he would not be able to communicate in an English-speaking country.

He soon realized that as a direct result of misunderstandings in listening and speaking, he was developing what could be deemed the symptoms of the "psychiatric disorders" he treated. He became anxious and sad and appeared noncompliant, defiant, and oppositional. This brilliant and articulate professor said he felt the panic of getting lost without a way to verbally reason his way back to safety.

After studying children in speech and hearing clinics, Cantwell posited that a primary reason children have a poor sense of self-worth is their inability to say the right things at the right time. He also noted a particular problem area for addressing these issues: speech pathologists are minimally trained in mental health; mental health practitioners, psychologists, and psychiatrists do not understand communication disorders; and educators are not trained in any in-depth way in either profession. He said that until all three areas worked together, we would have problems taking good care of our children. Reading this book gave me the courage to trust that I really did understand Whitney: it was the communication disorder that was causing his "psychiatric" symptoms. Autism is thought to be a chronic and lifelong psychiatric disease with a poor prognosis for treatment if you set the goal as full recovery. But Whitney was getting better—perhaps because he was really suffering from a communication disorder. Maybe I *could* "fix" his autism—or more accurately, rehabilitate his communication disorder, which would in turn resolve his autistic symptoms.

Cantwell's book affirmed so much of what I'd been moving toward in my work—that communication disorders were misunderstood, misdiagnosed, and mistreated. By treating these disorders, a host of other problems could clear up. Almost any breakthrough or new idea I'd had in my work could be traced to the outrage I'd felt about how communication disorders were misunderstood and how this led to discrimination (at least) and pain and suffering (most frequently) and even suicidal tendencies (at worst). When I opened my Stutter-Free Speech

Center in 1978, I was proud to create a place where people with severe communication disorders could improve their speech. I also discovered that as their speech improved, many of their mental health problems improved. They got better jobs; they began dating and developed romances. Once they could communicate, their new abilities allowed them to share themselves with others.

When I opened the Center for Independent Living, I was driven to do so by my outrage over the elderly being institutionalized in nursing homes. In daily hospital rounds, I saw social workers make decisions that gave power of attorney over a patient's finances to her children—houses were sold, cars given to grandchildren, and dignity destroyed all because these elderly could not communicate. These indignities didn't happen because they were too sick to live on their own; they happened because of decreased or absent communication skills. The most common reason for referring the patient to the nursing home was the statement "we want to make sure the patient is safe"—just as the teachers wanted to keep Whitney "safe" in special ed. When people can't communicate appropriately, it appears to others that they will be unsafe. To address these problems, I invited a number of companies, including the Big Bear grocery store, the Huntington National Bank, *The Columbus Dispatch* newspaper and, indirectly, the NASA space program, to participate in building the Center for Independent Living. We created labs that simulated skills needed for independent living—shopping, banking, driving, cooking, and grooming. If patients could master these skills, they could stay out of nursing home institutions even if they couldn't speak. We could objectively measure skills they needed to be "safe" in their activities of daily living with or without communication skills. Probably most of us have some issue that causes us to feel outrage, issues that make us aware of incredible injustice. For me it was this form of discrimination against people who cannot communicate correctly.

I remembered reading *A Leg to Stand On* by Oliver Sacks, in which Dr. Sacks told of a wound to his leg that caused a sort of paralysis that concerned him. He wrote to the eminent neuropsychologist A. R. Luria in Moscow, who wrote back to him that this syndrome was common, though not commonly written about. When Sacks recovered and returned to doctoring, he did in fact see hundreds of patients with a similar syndrome. Sacks wrote, "The applications of my clinical findings to a large group of patients and the pondering of their implications and meaning led to a vision of what may be the neurological medicine of the future." I hoped that by contacting Dr. Cantwell I might discover whether, because he had such a diverse clinical practice, he had seen cases similar to Whitney's.

Would Dr. Cantwell be interested in the work I was doing with Whitney? Why not write him a letter and see? Feeling worthless and worn out, one voice said, "He won't answer his own mail. He is world-famous." But the other voice said, "What have you got to lose?" After all, Dr. Cantwell had followed hundreds of autistic people in longitudinal studies; maybe Whitney's case would be of interest.

Although Whitney had done well with his drama camp, I knew that for the new school year and second grade, it was going to be important for us to get a great teacher. To my delight, our new teacher, Mrs. Homon, was exactly what we needed—the ideal combination of discipline and kindness.

On the first day of school, Mrs. Homon invited me to teach a writing workshop for kids in the class. "We can make the most of your special talents and you can keep an eye on Whitney, too," she suggested. "That way I can see how you handle him, and we can work together to make this a great year for Whitney."

I began to check in with Mrs. Homon at the beginning of the school day on a regular basis. We worked to teach him how to advocate for himself even though his speech was still hard to understand. He'd learned some self-advocacy and self-evaluation skills the previous year: When he needed to chill out or was confused, Mrs. Moore took him to

Mr. Niemie or his LD tutor. He was learning to know when to do this by himself, before he started to fall apart. He was also beginning to understand which people he could go to for different kinds of help— his guidance counselor, his tutor, his principal, and the nurse all could augment his day in the classroom. It was working wonderfully; Whitney was catching up.

Mrs. Homon told the class that Whitney's mom would be teaching a writing lab for anyone who wanted to sign up. Whitney and three kids signed up the first week. I used stickers and awarded points to reinforce their good ideas and had them working for their awards. The next week, the whole class wanted to come. We divided them into five groups of four children each Wednesday morning, and it was a great way for me to get to know all the kids. I was helping them write stories about themselves, so I learned a lot about each kid's life.

Mrs. Homon would give me the assignment they were to work on and I would help them elaborate, give spelling models, and assist them in the writing process. They had their writing tablets and "books" they made in the publishing shop: paper stapled inside of folders or cardboard covered with wallpaper. The kids drew a picture in the top half of the page and wrote captions under the picture. Whitney wrote this story at the beginning of that year:

> *My name is Whitney. My teacher is Mrs. Homon. I am in second grade at Riverside school. I have to fun at school. I live at Ashford Court. My phone number is 555-0410. I have is fun home and at fun school. Those are the people in my family. I have a loving family. I am glad when I go to Leps and bounds. I am sad not go to Leps and Bounds. I weigh 66 pound and am 53 inches tall. My favorite school tings are publishing shop recess Mrs. Cleveland.*

This story followed an outline that Mrs. Homon had provided. Other times we worked on stories from the children's imagination. I would help them develop an idea and get them started. To get story ideas I would interview the kids about their families, pets, weekend activities, holiday times, or favorite TV shows, and then I would help them get from the idea to the paper.

Not only was the workshop a great way for me to get to know the kids in Whitney's class. When we got home at night and Vanessa and William told us about their day, I could tell about the kids in Whitney's class and he could fill in pieces and parts of the story without having to compose a complete story. Whitney felt like a full participant and I was learning more about how to cue his language processing to get his message across to the listener.

Another benefit was that as I got to know the kids and the parents better, we were able to invite kids over to play. Whitney was starting to have playmates. Life was beginning to seem more normal.

I decided to have a birthday party for Whitney at a new children's gym, which he loved: Leaps and Bounds, the place he had written about in his story. There were twelve-foot-tall ceilings and lots of tubes and plastic gym equipment to run through and play on. After stopping by the gym to finalize details for the party, I had to stop by the post office to pick up a certified letter.

I had a nagging concern that told me this letter was not going to be good news. In February of the previous year, I'd received a letter from two school psychologists asking me to explain why I gave tests to measure change more often than once every three years. They indicated that they thought that the scores could be changing due to repetition or chance, rather than any real improvement. They were also concerned that I did not use composite scores. I figured this inquiry was the result of my arguments to keep Whitney's visual and verbal test scores separate in his assessments. I assumed they were interested in learning about why I did this, so I'd written back a several-page explanation and invited them to my office to observe therapy sessions.

No one responded, so I figured my letter was sufficient. Then I received another letter from another school psychologist in another district specifically asking me why, in my practice, I thought visual processing had anything to do with language. Well, visual and auditory processing are the central neurological systems needed for language processing of listening, speaking, reading, and writing. So I wrote a long explanation about psycholinguistic processing and speech pathology treatment planning. Again I offered an invitation to visit my practice and discuss any questions. I got no answer.

Standing at the window of the post office that Friday afternoon, I felt my heart sink as I signed for a certified package from the American Speech, Language and Hearing Association (ASHA). I ran to the car and sat there quietly for a minute before ripping it open.

It was a letter informing me that a complaint had been filed against me by some school psychologists, and that the Ethical Practice Board of ASHA would be investigating the allegations. I had forty-five days to respond.

The words jumped out at me.

A complaint had been filed against me? Enclosed were more than twenty pages of criticism that was based on out-of-context clips from reports I had written and what I would learn are called *ad hominum* complaints—personal attacks. There was also a TV clip in which I was demonstrating how to identify and treat language delays in young children—the voice-over at the end of the segment identified me as a psychologist. The Board was investigating criticisms from this group of school psychologists, including accusing me of representing myself as a psychologist who provided mental-health services. The program was on speech and language development, not mental-health issues. It was meant to help patients identify normal and delayed communication skills. I had had no idea that the reporter had referred to me as a psychologist—the reporter added the voice-over after he'd left my office, and when they checked with him later, he said he knew I had a Ph.D. and didn't realize it was misleading to call me a psychologist.

The main problem, as I saw it, was that my accusers (school teacher–psychologists) were from another profession and were not aware of the depth of speech-language pathology. My licensure is in auditory and visual processing, treatment of disorders of reading, writing, listening, and speaking, and disorders of thinking and swallowing.

I had been working with the schools for twenty years before I had Whitney, and I had been the guest speaker for school psychologist conventions in the past. I suspected that the genesis of their problems came from my arguing about Whitney with the school administration, not about the attempts I'd made to work with the schools on my treatment plans for the school-aged children I treated. The school personnel saw a severely handicapped child and I saw a child learning how to enter the verbal world from a very different, visual thinking system.

But if I failed to respond adequately to the complaints, I could lose my license and lose the only source of income we had for our family. And Whitney's continued placement in a regular classroom could be in jeopardy. I had come far with Mr. Niemie by my side. But if I lost my credibility, it would endanger Whitney's progress. If I lost this fight, I could lose Whitney too.

I felt so sad at being misunderstood. I knew the names of some of the people who had signed the complaint, but I had never met any of them. I couldn't figure out why they would be so upset about my belief that Whitney and other children with high-visual thinking abilities could benefit from a new approach. It baffled me that they would jump to the conclusion that I was doing something inappropriate. What made me the saddest was that they would take the time to cause this investigation, but would not take the time to come to meet with me to discuss the issues face to face.

Even worse, they copied the complaint to two other boards: the Ohio state boards of speech pathology and of psychology. That meant I had three boards to answer to—even though I am not accountable to the psychology board, since I am not licensed by them.

The Ohio Board of Speech Pathology wrote to me and said they would agree with whatever the National Board said. The psychology board said they would do their own investigation even though in reality I am not under their jurisdiction. The ASHA assigned a group of experts to study my practice patterns. I had to create a defense for all of the allegations raised by the school psychologists. This would become a bigger job than writing my dissertation.

One good thing would come out of the complaints. In order to explain my work to the school personnel and others, I invited people to come to my office and observe therapy. I called some of my well-known and highly respected colleagues and paid them to fly in and give workshops. I asked the parents of my clients to bring their children's teachers and principals to the office to learn more about what I was doing. Through this process, I developed and strengthened some invaluable professional relationships and gained moral support for my work.

One of the experts I invited was Dr. Ron Goldman, a longtime friend and colleague who was the author of many of the tests I use. Some of his tests are used in nearly all schools and training programs across the country, so he is a very highly respected and well-known professional. He is one of the most knowledgeable people in the country on auditory processing and reading. Before my children were born, Dr. Goldman invited me to the University of Alabama to set up programs in his graduate training program. For the following ten years, when he was traveling on business, Dr. Goldman stopped over in Columbus to visit my clinic several times a year. He wanted to learn about our work and observe therapy sessions to take back any new ideas to the University of Alabama. He'd also invited me to the university several times to give workshops or set up programs, though I had not seen him since the kids were born. The last time we met I was working on creating the Center For Independent Living for stroke patients and *Stutter-Free Speech*.

I invited him to give a workshop for the families in my practice to counteract the criticisms of the school psychologists. I made the workshop a Valentine's celebration of the child who was working on building his brainpower. William, Vanessa, and Whitney were the ushers.

Dr. Goldman eloquently explained the relationship between hearing and reading. The families responded very positively to Dr. Goldman's talk, which helped ease any nagging doubts they might have had about the appropriateness of the treatment we were offering their children.

In addition to wanting Dr. Goldman to help counteract the criticism and help educate the community, I had another agenda: time with him to discuss Whitney's treatment plan. Dr. Goldman is one of the best thinkers I know regarding problems such as autism, hearing, processing, and reading. I wanted to pick his brain and get ideas about next steps. After the workshop, I had dinner with Dr. Goldman and talked to him for a long time about Whitney. "Maybe he never was really autistic? Maybe he was misdiagnosed," he suggested.

I explained that he met the criteria for autism, but that I thought the problem was really his hearing. "You taught me the basics of treating auditory processing and I am now using what you taught me to help Whitney."

He laughed. "I don't doubt your passion. I treated a lot of stutterers before I met you, but once I saw your program, I changed what I was doing to incorporate your techniques." He said what I was doing was very exciting and he thought there was a chance that it would work. But I could tell that he had significant doubts. "We have never thought that autism was a hearing problem, we have always believed it to be a psychiatric disease," he pointed out.

Dr. Goldman's workshop had been so helpful to the parents that I scheduled another event. I invited David Daley, chair of speech pathology and audiology at the University of Michigan, another national expert whom I'd worked with many times as a consultant. He is an excellent motivational speaker. We crafted workshops on learned helplessness and depression versus learned optimism and hope. He used the work of Martin Seligman of Stanford to create a spellbinding series of talks on self-regulation and self-management. (Dr. Seligman says that a person's explanatory style—or what you say about yourself and your goals—influence the way things pan out. He proposes that the treatment of a problem will only worsen if you spend your time tracking and discussing what is wrong.) Everyone loved Dr. Daly's work and his charisma. The program was a huge success. I learned a lot also and treasured my time with him.

When I asked Dr. Daly what he thought about Whitney, he said, "No one will agree with you that autism is a hearing problem. Your ideas about using the visual system to correct the auditory system are way out there." He urged me to keep my practice focused on what classic work I'd done within our field. "This program for Whitney is hard to buy," he admitted. "Even for me, your fan, I can't see the treatable hearing part of autism."

"I didn't say that," I clarified. "I don't have any idea about autism and hearing. But I do know that Whitney demonstrated all of the symptoms of autism for many years, and Whitney also had a hearing problem and the hearing problem was treatable. That treatment is how we got rid of the autism symptoms." Dr. Daly just shook his head and said, "When you are the mother, you lose your objectivity. That is why they say that doctors should never treat their own families. You know I have always loved your work and I will support your zest in helping Whitney. Keep me informed about what happens. I think you should start writing again and write this up."

Meanwhile, I had prepared a portfolio of my work and Whitney's case for Dr. Cantwell. I closed by asking him if he would be willing to consult with me on Whitney's case and also do consultations on patients in my practice. Nervously, I put the package in the mail. Maybe I was sending too much material. I was attempting to show the progression of my thinking about the natural course and treatability of information processing disorders and attention span—a subject of great interest to Dr. Cantwell—with the ultimate hope that it would lead us both to new understandings about Whitney.

I received a prompt reply from Dr. Cantwell stating he would love to come to spend some time with me. He indicated that he was very interested in what I was doing and would be most pleased to consult. So in correspondence back and forth between UCLA and Ohio, Dr. Cantwell and I planned an agenda for a three-day visit in which he would give a public address at the local Barnes & Noble bookstore, where I had also been giving a series of lectures, and see each of my patients on an individual basis.

When Dr. Cantwell gave his talk at Barnes & Noble, a large group of school administrators came. They fired questions at him in an attempt to prove publicly that what I was doing was wrong. But he told them point-blank that what I was doing made sense. He stated that his own work in the schools had been misunderstood, but never to the extent of having a complaint made to a licensing board. His experience was of having work ignored: he'd made a video tape series on Attention Deficit Disorder and spent time working with school administrators and specialists trying to get his program implemented. Instead, he said, it just collected dust.

Doctors Cantwell, Goldman, and Daly understood what I was talking about in ways no one else locally did. Dr. Cantwell was awarded the lifetime achievement award from the American Psychiatric Association for his many years of studying the human attention span and his diagnostic and treatment work with Attention Deficit Disorder. Differentiating psychiatric disease from communication disorder in diagnosis was Dr. Cantwell's passion. In particular, he was very interested in treating the brain's attention system and resolving psychiatric symptoms. At the time that Dr. Cantwell walked into my life, he was trying to figure out the issues facing Whitney as a scientist just as I was as a mother. Goldman and Daly had made major contributions to my big-picture thinking. Dr. Cantwell was here to help me plan for the short-term needs of working with Whitney and the schools.

It was a huge relief to find in Dr. Cantwell such a professional kindred spirit. While he had not been thinking about rebuilding the brain processing pathways through special training, he understood what I meant by my evaluation of Whitney's visual brain. He instead focused on medication and how learning to talk through a problem in psychotherapy can help with psychiatric disorders. Additionally, he was working diligently on how teachers could make accommodations in the classroom to help students who process differently. But he was not thinking about re-engineering how someone thinks, and this concept fascinated him.

By this time, I had collected families of visual people. I was searching to find guidance from other patients who were similar to Whitney, and so I was attempting to steer my practice toward patients with visual thinking abilities above the ninety-ninth percentile and verbal abilities below the one percentile. I had a radiologist, a professor of photography, a mansion landscaper, quite a few corporate CEOs and highly successful entrepreneurs and their children, as well as some medical students. The adult patients were changing how their brains worked so that they could access both the visual and the verbal pathway, depending on the task at hand.

These patients met with Dr. Cantwell and explained what they felt was happening to them. I set the agenda so Dr. Cantwell discussed all of this with them first, before meeting with Whitney, because physicians, attorneys, and community leaders are highly credible when they report their presenting symptoms and the effectiveness of their treatment. They could pave the way for Whitney. Having a radiologist explain that he thought only in pictures and had communication disabilities that had been successfully treated was a highly credible baseline for establishing Whitney's story.

I wanted to show Dr. Cantwell, step by step, that whatever Whitney's real diagnosis was initially, he was a high visual and he was learning to become a verbal, just like the other patients. Maybe Whitney was the extreme example of a new syndrome. Just as Oliver Sacks had said, we can study our patients from our practices, but what does that mean for the larger group? I hoped that Dr. Cantwell, with an international perspective on these issues and in his more wide-ranging experience, might offer us his expertise.

Finally, on the third day of the visit, Whitney walked into the conference room full of self-confidence and happy to meet Dr. Cantwell. He knew from all I had said that I considered this opportunity a great treat. Now in second grade, he was beginning to speak in a fragmented way, but we could understand him. He would gesture and use enough words that we could make out what he was trying to say most of the time, though only if we were in the room with him—on the phone I had no idea what he was saying.

I was concerned about how the conversation would go with Dr. Cantwell. But he was one of the greatest child interviewers of all time. He knew just how many words to use to help the child expound on a topic. He cued Whitney and wove the conversation around Whitney-centered topics. Right away, Dr. Cantwell started interviewing Whitney about Power Rangers, *Star Trek*, and Hulk Hogan.

After the interview, Dr. Cantwell told me he thought Whitney was quite remarkable: "What a delightful young man." He thought one of the key things I had done was teaching him to use his visual attention to cue his auditory attention. I agreed. I said I was beginning to understand the attentional systems of the brain in a new way based on Whitney's responses to my therapy and to his own natural development. I knew that Whitney could easily find places after having been there only once. He could put complex models together without looking at the instructions, and he had a natural aptitude for fixing things. These adult genius patients with communication disabilities were the same way: highly visual and great attention to detail, great visual figure ground perception with severe listening and auditory memory problems.

After Whitney's interview, I showed Dr. Cantwell my attention lab, where I had patients working on memory drills with distractions such as changing background music or the door opening and conversations spilling into the room. Dr. Cantwell said, "We have been accommodating auditory selective attention problems by asking for a distraction-free environment, a quiet space with extra time for tests. That is a standard and here you have them trying to work in noisy chaos." He wanted to know why I was doing exactly the opposite of the standard. I explained to him I was teaching the selective hearing system to tune in and tune out information or sound signals on purpose. Teaching people to work in quiet teaches the system not to activate. Dr. Cantwell smiled and said, "Amazing."

I asked if he would be willing to come back and consult with me on a regular basis. He told me that he was not in the best of health and had to limit his travel to only a few trips a year. "But if you can get me Notre Dame–OSU football tickets, we have a deal. In any case we can stay in touch. I want to follow your work closely. You are ten years ahead of me," he said, grinning. He came to see Whitney and me many times until his death a few years later.

While I was doing all of these workshops to help explain my practice, I was also preparing a written explanation and materials for the American Speech and Hearing Association. The ASHA reviewed what I sent to them and found no problems with anything I was doing. However, they were fascinated with my theories and my work with Whitney and the other visual people, so they developed their own list of questions, which I also answered. Clearing myself with ASHA would take one year. In the end, I was cleared of any wrongdoing. The head of the committee even called me to tell me how proud the committee was of my work.

After I was cleared by ASHA, I made an appointment to see the assistant superintendent in the school district where the complaint originated. He said he would have the accusers present so we could clear the air.

"OK, but first I would like fifteen minutes with you alone." He agreed.

On the day of the meeting, my three children and I walked into the school district building. I left them out in the waiting area while I went in alone to see the assistant superintendent. I began by showing him the report from the school psychologists saying that Whitney had a low IQ of 46 and should be in the multihandicapped class, and then I showed him Whitney's IQ score of 90 at the end of regular first grade. He nodded politely. I explained that Whitney is a perfect example of how a family, the child, outside professionals, and the school working together can help a child overcome the symptoms of his handicapping condition—yet Whitney was really never a 46 IQ or in the low intelligence range at all. Again, he nodded politely. I took out the storybooks Whitney had written. All decisions about Whitney's schooling, I explained, were based on his low score on an IQ test that was given to him verbally—Whitney could barely speak or hear. He continued to nod, not understanding where I was going.

I opened the door and called Whitney in. "He can speak and hear now. A great deal of progress happened in less than three years. He didn't have low intelligence, he had a treatable processing problem. And we are treating it."

Whitney crawled up beside the superintendent and read him one of his storybooks. The man smiled. I gave Whitney a hug and sent him back outside to play with his brother and sister.

Then I showed the superintendent the letter from the boards clearing me of any wrong practices and hailing my work. Then I handed him a copy of the original Worthington school letterhead report to ASHA.

"None of this turned out to be true and it caused me a lot of heartache, loss of my good name, loss of my reputation, and loss of my entire savings in legal fees. Is this the position of the school district, or just the school psychologists who used your letterhead?"

Before he could respond, the school psychologists began to arrive. I sat on one side of the table by myself, and the seven of them sat on the other side.

Finally, we began. The superintendent said, "We are here to bring closure to a disagreement. We all have our sides of the story. And we each have good points to make. Dr. Florance, I am sure we can come to some compromise, don't you think?"

"No," I said. "There is no compromise here. I am right and the school psychologists are wrong. I have presented the answers to their questions to three boards, and my answers were accepted by national experts. These psychologists were criticizing me for things that they don't know about."

One of them said, "You think communication problems cause people to be anxious and depressed."

I said, "Yes, I do, don't you?"

"No, you make it sound worse than it is. And that is not your job."

I took out the ODE handbook. "This handbook explains that school is a verbal game; those who follow the rules succeed and those who can't fail. Failing at school is a heartbreaker for a child, and comes with emotional side effects. Communication disorders can often be treated."

The superintendent asked, "Do you give the ODE handbook to all of your patients?"

"I sure do—that is the reason you have my reports. We follow the step-by-step procedures for coordinating outside services with the schools, and I have the parents follow each step to a T." I passed out a handbook for everyone.

One of the school psychologists argued, "We understand that stuttering is emotionally disturbing to patients and we think you are good at addressing that particular problem. But when you go off into language problems, you indicate that people feel just as bad about that as stuttering, and that is where we had to stop you."

"People do feel bad! . . ." I could feel myself getting riled, when the superintendent who had been browsing through the ODE handbook as well as the letters of apology from ASHA and the State Board of Speech Pathology indicating I'd done nothing wrong, interrupted.

"We all owe Dr. Florance an apology. From this minute forward, no one will say a word against her if you wish to remain employed by this school district. You don't have to endorse her. But you will never criticize her to anyone again if you want to work here." Then he looked at me and said, "I am sincerely sorry for what we have done to you."

I swallowed hard. Words were not enough, but they were better than nothing. The room was silent and tense as I rose and tried to walk out the door with as much pride as I could muster. As I opened the door to leave, I was greeted with the sight of Whitney and William making Legos, with Vanessa supervising.

I stepped out into the waiting area and closed the door behind me. I smiled as Whitney ran up and took my hand. *This is a hard fight,* I thought, *but definitely worth it.*

"Did I help you, Mom?" he asked.

"Absolutely, Whitney," I hugged him. "You are the smartest one of the bunch."

12

Talking

to God

For Whitney's third- and fourth-grade years, Mr. Niemie wanted to put him in a new experimental classroom he was establishing at his school. It would be a multiaged classroom combining both grades. The idea was that children could mix according to ability levels, rather than by age: If a third-grader was great at math, he could take math with fourth-graders; or if a fourth-grader was struggling with reading, she could be in a group with more third-graders. I was dubious of Whitney's ability to function in this situation. It would mean about fifty students in a combined classroom, with only two teachers. This wasn't the level of attention Whitney was used to—plus, there would be the extra children and stimulation to deal with. Mr. Niemie was confident it would work out.

"Just give him six weeks to try it," he convinced me. "We know transitions are hard for Whitney, but I think it will really be good for him in the long run."

The transition *was* hard. Whitney began reverting to a lot of his old isolating behaviors. He was disoriented and disorganized. He would answer questions in class with responses that didn't match the questions and seemed to come out of left field. His teachers were very concerned and were worried that he was in the wrong place. They couldn't imagine he could do third-grade work. He would often stare into space, doing nothing when the class was all doing their seatwork. At least it appeared to the teachers he was doing nothing; I imagined he was puzzling out some problem, triggered by what he thought he was being asked to do. He would not follow directions, instead doing something radically different from what had been asked of him. He would be hyperfocused on reading something about the Civil War, for example, and if the teacher told all the kids to get their math books out and turn to page 32, Whitney would continue reading about the Civil War and behave as if he didn't hear her. (In fact, I believed he did not hear her because he was visualizing what he was reading.)

Whitney would behave as though he couldn't move on to the next task until he finished comprehending the last one. The teacher at first took this to be noncompliance, but Whitney felt she was being illogical.

"If she wants me to learn about the Civil War, why does she interrupt me when I am halfway understanding something and tell me to do something else? I will forget what I have read and have to read it over again," reasoned Whitney.

He would also use words incorrectly. For example, one day he told the gym teacher he couldn't participate because of his "cows." The teacher said, "No excuses out on the gym floor. Time for jumping jacks." Whitney persisted that he couldn't because of his cows. That night, Whitney came home mad and said at the family meeting that the gym teacher made his cows sore. We finally figured out that he meant he had sore calves. When these things happened, Whitney would be flustered and withdraw. He would be horrified that he had done something wrong and yet not able to figure out how to prevent another illogical episode in the future.

He was also talking less and interacting with others less—both in the classroom and at home. We had to work harder to draw him out. I brought out my guitar and started playing at night for the kids again. I'd sit on the top of the stairs and play with William and Vanessa beside me. At first, Whitney stayed in his room, but eventually he ventured outside his door and slowly crept down the hallway until he was sitting with us again. Then, as if it was the magic amount of time he needed, right around the sixth week of school, he settled into the new routine of the new classroom quite well.

During the next two years, school went much more smoothly for Whitney. Mr. Niemie had let us set up a system where Whitney attended his OT and PT and worked with his LD tutor unobtrusively. He was adept at using his safe havens when he became confused or started to fall apart. In addition to Mr. Niemie, he had a great working relationship with his guidance counselor, the school nurse, the office staff, and several of the parents who volunteered in various helping roles at school. We had carefully built Riverside into a sanctuary where he had many cues to help him stay with the program. He wasn't singled out as a kid with problems. Instead, he got to be mainstreamed with the other students, and left quietly for the special extra help he needed. He still couldn't hold a pencil quite right, so his writing was hard to read. His speech was hard to understand. He muttered to himself a lot. But in terms of the "heart" he put into his interactions with others, he was doing great. Everyone knew he had a heart of gold, and he was truly accepted and beloved. He also started developing an insatiable appetite for knowledge about certain topics; once something piqued his interest, he would research these topics to the last detail.

He became completely fascinated, for example, by the Civil War and started reading everything he could find on this topic. He would go to the library and find every picture book, encyclopedia, or history book he could get his hands on. Even if the book was beyond his reading level, he would pore over it for hours. Mr. Niemie told me years later that he would go home and search for questions about the Civil War to try to stump Whitney, but he never could. Whitney became a walking encyclopedia on that subject and many more to come.

Meanwhile, as William and Vanessa completed lower-school life at Columbus Academy, I decided that now it would be great for all of the kids to be in the same school system. I had sent William and Vanessa to Columbus Academy to give them a part of life that was separate from Whitney. The idea of having the same schedule for school days and after school events, and the same vacation times like a normal family, struck me as a life-simplifying luxury. Even though Whitney was mainstreamed, his placement was still for three years of special ed. As long as we lived in Dublin school district, Whitney could stay at Riverside.

We moved to a new house in the woods that was within the Dublin district, really a dream house for all of us. For the first time, we'd have a big yard and property all around for the kids to play in. The house itself was like a work of art. Built into the side of a ravine on five and a half acres, it had a one-acre lot in the front, with a driveway that crossed a covered bridge and a bubbling stream before arriving at our funky front door. At first glance, the house looked like a barn made of cedar with just a little door and no windows; but inside, there were views of a waterfall and the woods from the large windows that practically covered the other three sides of the house. It was a fantasy house, and the kids loved having all of the outdoors to explore. In the woods out back, they could forge trails, make forts, and have campouts.

Once we settled into the new house, and William and Vanessa were adjusted to their new schools, I tried to take a breath and assess where I was. I was relieved that Whitney was able to function better in school now because, frankly, I felt like I had nothing left to give.

I realized it was time to make a change for myself the day I was getting ready to give a talk for the leaders of Dublin sponsored by the Rotary Club and couldn't find anything to wear that made me feel professional and in control of my life. It wasn't the lack of clothing in my closet that was troubling me, it was the person looking back at me from the mirror.

My weight had ballooned from all of the stress. Not only was I out of shape, but my bad eating habits had taken their toll on William and

Vanessa as well. We were all eating badly and not getting any exercise. Ironically, Whitney was unaffected by the rest of the household. Active and wiry, he ate if he was hungry and stopped when he wasn't. His emotions weren't governing his eating the way they did mine.

That day at the Rotary, one of the other guest speakers spoke about health and fitness. His name was "Todd the Body Man"—an energetic body builder who was a local celebrity for his "Body by Todd" segments on the morning news. He came bounding into the Rotary Club in tight neon pink-and-black-striped Lycra with a small tank top. A huge linebacker with a tiny waist, he looked like a Superman cartoon doll. I watched him give a rousing talk about staying fit to a bunch of conservative businessmen. Everyone loved him, including me. I clapped loudly, inspired by his encouragement to take charge of my life and well-being.

I went back to my office, still exhilarated by his talk. But when I looked in the mirror, I felt hopelessness and despair. *No*, I thought, *I'm not going to give in to this*. I picked up the phone, called Todd's body building club, and made an appointment.

When I got out of my car at his gym, I was pulling a luggage cart, wearing baggy pants, a big top, and green high-top Nike tennis shoes. Todd pulled up at the same time. As he jumped out of his white Porsche with his athletic bag over his shoulder and looked at me, I could see the dismay on his face. Todd trains professional athletes, Les Wexner, the CEO of Victoria's Secret and The Limited, movie stars and celebrities. I was not his typical client, to say the least.

He had me fill out a questionnaire. There were the typical questions about health and fitness, but some of the questions I found a bit odd— *How many books do you read per week? Why do you think you gained weight? What are your professional goals?* I checked off "more than ten per week" on the books, and said I wanted to be an athlete again as I had been in years past.

Todd looked over my questionnaire and asked again, "Why do you think you gained weight?"

It was hard for me to talk about my feelings. I'd spent years holding them inside. It was my job to help other people with their problems, and sometimes I felt like I took on the pain and suffering of those around me all day. Add to that the stress of trying to do what was best for Whitney and struggling to earn a living—and there was no chance to feel anything. I feared that if I were to let the feelings start, they'd drown me. So I stuffed them down mindlessly. I knew this was the root of my weight problem, it led to overeating and poor eating habits—and years of not making taking care of myself a priority.

Todd seemed like someone who could help. But I would have to let him in. I took a deep breath and poured out my story: how my hospital-based practice was closed because of hospital administrative difficulties and how my son was critically ill. I explained how Whitney's severe problems were so time-consuming, along with all of the other issues of working and raising kids, that I had lost my own sense of health. Worse than that, the problems fighting with the schools about Whitney had taken their toll on my sense of worth and I was feeling pretty bad and lonely inside. The story poured out, and so did the emotions. The goal of getting in shape was going to be hard.

But Todd clapped his hands together and said, "I think I understand. We can get this problem solved."

Todd liked to solve problems. He also liked a challenge. I was different from his usual cases—but I was also perhaps the biggest challenge he'd faced.

Todd started coming out to the house in the woods, where he helped me set up a home gym. After a short time of working with me on a nearly daily basis, I asked him if he could help train the kids as well. I knew they needed a healthier lifestyle, and I thought it would be good for the boys to have someone to teach them sports. I may have been great about teaching them about the arts, but they needed someone to socialize them in the ways I couldn't. Todd was perfect for the job. He got them excited about sports, pop music—and eventually even talked to William and Whitney about girls.

Within a year, our family became active runners, Rollerbladers, swimmers, tennis players, kickboxers; we tried our hand at racket ball, basketball, football, rock climbing, cycling—you name it, we started doing all the sports we could think of and Todd guided the process with humor and enthusiasm.

One day Todd pulled me aside after he'd been working with the boys. He'd coached William to the point where he made his middle school football team, and he was working to teach Whitney basic football skills. He told me Whitney was saying some strange things.

This didn't surprise me. People always thought Whitney said strange things. I waited for the latest.

"He says he's talking to God. And that he thinks he may be called by God to explain to people about what he's overcome."

This was stranger than usual, I had to admit. "He must have seen something on TV."

Todd looked doubtful.

"Well, I doubt he's really talking to God," I said, trying to make a joke.

Todd didn't laugh. Todd, it turned out, had urged Whitney to read the Bible, because in preparing him for football, he'd often tell him he needed to "feel God" inside of him. Whitney said he didn't know what this meant, so Todd told him that reading the Bible would help him develop a spiritual sense.

As usual, Whitney did what Todd suggested. But he didn't skim the Bible, he pored over an illustrated children's Bible carefully and started spouting to Todd his theories about what the stories meant. Todd was floored with Whitney's analysis. For instance, he questioned the story of Moses parting the Red Sea. "Maybe the sea opened because of natural occurrences, and that caused the pharaoh to drown," he suggested. "And the story of David and Goliath—they could have made that up so that people would believe in a hero at the time." Or Todd's favorite:

"I'm not going to mess with any woman," said Whitney. "They just get control of you. Look at Samson and Delilah."

Todd had to laugh. "He's not afraid to say the un-PC thing," he said admiringly. Todd thought maybe that was why Whitney was so perceptive about these stories. "He doesn't have that layer of guilt or fear or judgment—or whatever it is that we all have—he just cuts right to the truth of the matter."

Nonetheless, Todd was alarmed. "I've worked hard, read tons, and talked to so many people to understand things on this level. Whitney's just naturally coming to these deep understandings without all of the work most of us have to do. Whitney told me he was going to heaven, talking about these stories, and coming back."

Now I was concerned. "I'll ask him about it," I told Todd.

The next morning at breakfast I asked Whitney about what he'd been telling Todd.

"I told him that anyone who says that money isn't important is a dumb ass," he said.

"Whitney!" I chastised him.

"Look at Solomon, Joshua—all of them. God made them rich first. So then they could do the things they did."

I thought that was an interesting interpretation but I tried not to get sidetracked. "What's this about going to heaven and coming back?" I asked.

Whitney wiggled in his chair. "That's what it feels like to me, Mom," he said. Whitney said he could see all of the stories in a movie in his head. He could sit in a chair and watch the stories from the Bible just like he was there.

I thought I was teaching Whitney language and that fixing this communication problem was eliminating the psychiatric symptoms of autism. He wasn't isolating anymore; he was learning to socialize. But it was often one step forward, two steps back, and in the midst of correcting his problems it was hard to predict what would happen next. Whitney was not within normal limits in all of his skills yet. He still needed extra assistance at school. His writing and spelling was at the second-grade level even though he was in fourth grade.

He would still get confused with following directions. His personal leisure-time activities were building models and painting them, visually complex puzzles, engineering sculptures from twigs and leaves. His social skills were not normal, he had a hard time figuring out the right thing to say for the right situation. But those issues felt like things we could conquer. What was this? Seeing movies in his head?

It was like a daydream that was almost real to Whitney. Was this the visual mind being used for thinking through a problem?

"Tell me about the movies."

Whitney continued with a long discourse—not just about Bible stories, but also about ideas about religion from a host of sources. He had been watching the History Channel and learning about stories through the ages, as well as looking up references on the Internet.

I was very pleased that Whitney was examining moral issues and thinking about religious and spiritual implications. He was analyzing the Bible stories, making comparisons to today's society, to lessons in morality. His summary may have been blunt, but it was showing an analytical and critical thought process, and a thoughtful analysis of beliefs.

Whitney started using stories from history or the Bible or other great books to explain his life. We were reading the children's classics at night, like *Great Expectations* and *Oliver Twist* or *Moby-Dick*. I was reading them as bedtime stories and Whitney was using these stories and things he watched on TV to help him understand his life and how he fit in.

One day he announced that he thought he should use what he knew about how he got better to help other people get better.

"There are a lot of kids out there worse than me, Mom," he said.

I had never discussed Whitney's situation with my patients or anyone other than school officials and professionals. I felt I should give out information on a need-to-know basis. I thought Whitney's privacy should be protected because we weren't home free yet. So I was not sure

using Whitney's story to help others was a good idea. We had high
school ahead and Whitney still had some big improvements to make in
the next few years, or else high school would be very tough. He still
couldn't express himself normally, and his ability to follow directions
accurately was off the mark. He still depended on following set patterns, and I was sure that going to middle and high school—where he
would have to change classes and teachers—would be a big adjustment. So I didn't pursue this with him right away.

I thought there was something else going on with Whitney. It wasn't
just movies in his head. There was something to his idea that he was
"talking" to God. I tried to figure out what was going on. I thought
about how once Whitney started talking, he talked out loud to himself,
especially when he was upset or if he was trying to solve a problem. He
had conversations under his breath. He still does. The night before a
big football game, he will have conversations out loud in his room, in
the bathroom, walking around the back yard or in the woods across the
street. He carries on animated conversations with his teammates, his
coaches, his brother—but there is no one there. I do the same thing, but
I do it in my head. Whitney does it out loud.

Having an inner dialogue with oneself is called "subvocalizing." It is
something most people, but especially verbal people, do all of the time.
I have come to recognize from my practice that highly visual people do
not do this automatically. I often have to carefully teach them how to
have an inner dialogue.

When I tell a group of high visuals that I hear voices inside my head
when I'm working out a problem, they think I'm insane. "But you don't
think daydreaming is weird," I remind them. Now I understand that
highly visual people tend to see movies in their heads, rather than have
conversations. They recall a feeling or what a place looked like more
easily than a verbatim conversation. When I dream at night, I hear
people talking; visual people tend to see pictures. I know this now
about visual people, but back then Whitney was teaching me about
this, I was realizing just how different my brain and Whitney's brain

were. We were opposite in the way we thought: I was all words; he was all pictures.

When we are reading, we subvocalize into memory. We hear the words that we are reading, and that is how we understand them and remember a story. Think of when you read a book with a lot of words or names you don't understand, for instance. If you don't know the Russian names or how to say them, you may skip over them, which makes it hard to follow who the characters are. When language doesn't make sense, when we can't subvocalize the words, we can't understand what is happening and lose interest in the story.

I think Whitney's sense that he was talking to God was his first experience with the way we all talk to ourselves, or hear an inner voice that we have mental conversations with. It was the first time he'd had a dialogue with himself without having to say it out loud. Whitney never had an inner voice speaking back to him because he didn't have language. Now that an inner voice started talking back, maybe Whitney thought it was God.

Whitney got embarrassed when he sensed that "talking to God" wasn't something that everyone did. He quickly stopped reporting it and kept to himself whatever inner conversations he was having. This was one of the first examples I recall of him starting to adapt socially. He sensed something wasn't socially normal, so he adjusted his behavior. On the one hand, this was progress, and at the same time, it made me kind of sad. I realized how some of our social norms can prevent us from showing our unique sides. Wasn't it special that he felt he was talking to God?

Today Whitney insists that his "talking to God" must have come from something he had seen on television. Or maybe it was just dreams he'd had at night that he would talk about in the morning.

"I just wish we could all sit down and talk together," Whitney complained one day during our usual morning mayhem. We were all in the kitchen, bumping into each other as we grabbed what we wanted for breakfast. I was trying to ask the kids what they wanted for lunch while talking on the phone to my office. William and Vanessa weren't answering me because they were caught up in an argument about whether William had a crush on a certain girl in his class. (At this point, Whitney was in fourth grade, William was in sixth grade, and Vanessa was in seventh grade.) A CD was playing in the background. Whitney now liked and responded to structure at school, and our madcap household was getting on his nerves.

Because Whitney seldom expressed a need for this kind of contact, I felt I had to give his request the attention it deserved. I stopped what I was doing and said, "That's a great idea, let's start tonight. A family meeting right before dinner."

Whitney grinned.

That night before dinner, we all sat down at the table. Vanessa and William were grumbling a bit about the interruption to their homework but Whitney was eager to start off. He told us about his day and covered everything that had happened at school. We were amazed. Whitney had never made a point of sharing things with us so directly. If he told a story, it was usually spotty and it was up to us to figure out what he was talking about and why he was telling us. But here he was, taking the spotlight to tell us about how he'd played with the kids in his class.

William and Vanessa understood that this was important to Whitney and showed a big step in his emotional development, so they joined in with their own stories about their day. Thus our tradition of "family meetings" began. Before, I had taken the pressure off of Whitney by being in his classroom. I could then generate a conversation based on knowing his fellow students and what was going on during the day. In fact, I did this with all three kids—I'd guide the conversation and allow them to fill in the blanks. This usually constituted our "evening bonding." Now it appeared that Whitney wanted to have a say in the agenda.

I was thrilled. After a long day at work, to come home to a discussion generated by all three kids was a great pleasure. And they all seemed to enjoy the conversation. But most thrilling was the chance to sit back and observe how Whitney was turning into an extrovert. I was thrilled to see this visual child not only use his new verbal systems but maximize them. He was turning out to be a great communicator. His potential for thinking and sharing himself was astonishing to me—this thoughtful, compassionate mind had been buried under so much disability.

So about once a week, we would have family discussions. Over the years, they have evolved to include serious topics like capital punishment, abortion—any issues they were pondering. To this day Whitney blames himself for getting the idea. Now he pretends, "I can't stand having to sit through the long discussions you like to have with the kids!" He accuses me of wanting to talk over every family decision at length—from where to go on vacation, to where they should apply to college. "Why did I ever come up with family meetings?" he wails. "I hate listening. You blab too much, Mom, why can't you just get to the point?" We both laugh at the truth in this: he thinks in bullet points and I have to ramble around in circles to decide what I am thinking about.

Of course, in spite of his complaints that having to listen too much is draining and ambiguous, if we dare to leave him out of a family meeting he becomes furious and very insulted.

Whitney's request for family meetings was exciting to me as a mother—and as a scientist. It fit in with what Dr. Cantwell and I had been discussing regarding my clinical work—a link between communication disorders and certain psychiatric symptoms. To me, the family meetings were Whitney's way of taking charge of his own "treatment." He needed to connect and bond with us, he needed to practice social skills, storytelling, sharing, and asking questions. It was also an indication that fixing his language problems was improving his other symptoms related to emotional and social development.

He was not only less isolated and in his own world, he was actually drawing himself further into our world.

About this time, a book entitled *Driven To Distraction* (Pantheon Books) was published by Edward M. Hallowell and John Ratey, two psychiatrists at Harvard. I was trying to figure out if ADD was a mild form of what Whitney had. One of my patients was related to Dr. Ratey and arranged for me to meet him. Dr. Ratey was very interested in ADD and autism.

Ratey's belief was that ADD was a permanent psychiatric condition. In fact, he believes he suffers from ADD. He said his staff had given him as a holiday present a T-shirt that had a big black hole on it. The black hole was to signify that any patient record or chart or piece of paper they gave to him was quickly lost in the "black hole." They had learned that they could only give him copies of things, because he would misplace everything so that no one could find it.

I told him that sounded a lot like Whitney. I showed Dr. Ratey around my office, which had portals showing the entrance to each training lab. There were labs for listening, reading, writing, and speaking. On the portals, the purpose of the lab was identified in bullet points. On the writing lab, one of the points was sequencing. Dr. Ratey noted, "Sequencing is the opposite of ADD. That is what ADDers can't do. We jump ahead." He said he could only talk for a couple of hours and he then would have to go running to get his attention span back. He said exercise was a good way to focus.

He told me, "The treatability of these disorders, the way you are describing re-engineering a brain, is not the way we think about all of this in psychiatry. We think of chemical imbalances and how to use medication to put the brain back in homeostasis. Once the medication is working, then we use accommodations or work-arounds to adjust the environment."

When Dr. Ratey met Whitney, he wasn't sure what diagnosis would fit Whitney at this point. He was not showing symptoms that would profit from medication. He was not depressed and his visual attention span was superior. An ADD diagnosis isn't consistent with sensory impairment and Whitney had hearing problems. And ADD existed across all modalities, whereas Whitney had high visuals and low verbals. Still, Whitney did have many of the symptoms that ADDers have. In fact, there is a passage in *Driven to Distraction* that very eloquently describes how I see Whitney's relationship to language:

I think people come to words much as lovers get together. They stumble on to each other at the oddest of times in the strangest of places. They will meet in an empty Laundromat on a rainy Sunday afternoon or they will catch each other's eyes across a ballroom dance floor in the middle of a wedding waltz. They will meet without appointment and strike up a relationship without an agenda. There may be a long courtship or a whirlwind romance. There may be protracted avoidance. Even what looks like phobia. There may be instant avidity, what amounts to love at first sight. Some carry on a kind of epistolary relationship with words, expressing their feelings through the formal prose of elegant notes, while others jump at words and bark them out at the world in the immediate poetry of certain street corner vendors. Some slap their words up on posters on telephone poles, while others keep them in reserve, like a pistol concealed in a pocketbook. Some read haltingly, like the nervous lover, hat in hand, while others seem born to orate. We all woo language differently, and language grants us her favors in different ways. Sometimes the relationship takes off, although it is rare there is a ride without bumps. While utterly beautiful, endlessly varied, and thoroughly transfixing, language can also be frustrating, confusing, exasperating, and unforgiving. . . . Language is not an inert tool that you take down from the shelf like a hammer. Rather, it is a living companion, whose company you keep for most of your waking life. For many people, language is a best friend they take for granted. For some others though, language never comes easily. The company of words is always an effort to keep. These people—and I count myself among them as one who

*is dyslexic and has ADD—never know quite what to expect
from words. Our relationship with words is rooted in unpre-
dictability. One moment we are Abraham Lincoln composing a
Gettysburg Address, and the next moment we are as clumsy with
words as a boy on his first date.*

I brought my discussions with Dr. Ratey to Dr. Cantwell. I was
grappling with how to treat people with processing problems like
Whitney's, for both the emotional and the linguistic problems. By this
time, I had collected over a hundred high visual/low verbal patients,
and I was beginning to limit my practice only to patients who were
genius visual thinkers with communication disorders. Many of them
had been misdiagnosed with ADD, so I wanted Dr. Cantwell to help me
design a protocol to distinguish communication disorders from psychiatric disorders like autism and ADD.

Dr. Cantwell urged me to form a relationship with Elizabeth Weller,
an expert on childhood depression. At the time, she was the chief of
child psychiatry at OSU, and we'd met with her during his previous
visit. If the National Institute of Mental Health couldn't figure out a
case, they referred the patient to her. Dr. Cantwell said she was a world-
class thinker and arguably one of the best child psychiatrists ever. Dr.
Cantwell thought I would learn that the patients who walked through
Dr. Weller's door were very different from those who walked through
my door. There was a distinction he wanted me to grasp between
people whose communication problems caused psychiatric symptoms,
and people who suffered primarily from psychiatric disorders. He saw
these as distinct populations and thought it was crucial that practitioners be able to recognize the differences for proper diagnosis and treatment. Additionally, he hoped I would learn how to think like a
psychiatrist, which would give me a better understanding of psy-
chopathology and mental illness. During Whitney's fourth and fifth
grade years, I began interacting with Dr. Weller, whom I found to be
brilliant. The more I learned, however, the more questions I had. We

decided that I needed to have a "senior fellowship" where I trained right beside the psychiatry fellows, working up patients as if I were going to become a psychiatrist.

Dr. Weller asked the psychiatry department to give me a faculty appointment as an adjunct so I could teach in exchange for the training she was giving me. We decided that I would spend one morning a week shadowing her on her clinical rounds. I would provide communication disability evaluations for the patients to demonstrate these services to the medical student residents and fellows; in exchange, she would teach me how to think like a psychiatrist.

I would drive to Dr. Weller's house early in the morning and pick her up so we could talk on the drive over together. Then we saw patients together for two hours and then we did a multidisciplinary team meeting for three hours.

The first patient we evaluated was a three-year-old who had been locked in a closet all of his life. He was totally sensory-deprived. Many of the children Dr. Weller saw had suffered significant physical and mental abuse. Many were children of schizophrenic parents; others had parents who were severe substance abusers. This was a population unlike any I had seen before. When I got in my car to drive home from the OSU neuropsychiatric hospital, I often felt ill from what I'd observed. I found I wanted to get back to my clinic and my kids as fast as I could.

Still, I was learning a great deal. Dr. Weller is one of the best teachers I have ever had, and the population she attracted was fascinating, so I continued the fellowship for two years. I saw many very severe situations. Dr. Weller ran a school in the hospital so the children admitted for inpatient psychiatric treatment at the hospital could go to school while the health team worked out a plan for each one. My admiration for what she does is limitless, but I soon realized Dr. Cantwell was right—my patients had communication disorders and hers had psychiatric disease. The two populations are very different—except for the fact that my patients did have a lot of psychiatric symptoms.

One evening, doctors Cantwell, Weller, and myself were together and I was quizzing them on how to distinguish between the psychiatric symptoms and communication problems and how to decide what to treat first.

"How do I know what to treat when?" I asked them both. I still had concerns about how to stabilize Whitney's gains so we could prevent a relapse. I had seen the movie *Awakenings* recently with Vanessa. In the movie, Oliver Sacks, played by Robin Williams, discovers an effective treatment for Robert De Niro, his patient. However, Robert De Niro was only better for a while and then relapsed. I wanted to create a foundation for Whitney's brain development where he would continue to improve and not revert backward at some later date. I also was very aware that many of Whitney's skills in thinking and reasoning were very advanced now. If I had the opportunity to engineer Whitney's brain to work the way I thought was best, then I wanted to take this as far as I could. Why settle for normal range if we could develop genius verbal skills to complement his genius visual skills? So I exhausted these wonderful doctors by begging them to teach me every minute I was with them.

"Break off the most treatable part and treat the hell out of it," Cantwell said. "The most treatable will be the communication issues. So treat them as aggressively as you can. Push the patient to learn to listen, speak, read, and write better. Once they are better, see what happens to their emotional symptoms. I think you will see that these emotions are tied very closely to their communication failure. When communication is better, the psychiatric symptoms will resolve."

"What about Whitney?" I asked. "Do you think his emotional risk factors are going away . . . could he relapse?"

Dr. Cantwell and Dr. Weller looked at each other. They didn't know. None of us did. "We have never seen someone with autism change in the ways Whitney has," they said.

Dr. Cantwell thought Whitney was a single-subject research project. William and Vanessa and I had been his primary treatment providers.

There was no one to talk to professionally about Whitney except for us, and we were his family. "You could be on to something very big," he said. He urged me to establish a research and training lab where psychiatrists, educators, and speech pathologists could train and practice together. We were still discussing this possibility several years later, when Whitney was in sixth grade, when I got a call from the surgery resident at UCLA saying that moments earlier Dr. Cantwell had passed away on the operating table. He'd been sick for a while and I knew this day was coming, but I felt a greater sense of loss than I had imagined. The battle with school psychologists and people who thought my work made no sense had continued throughout the years. Having Dr. Cantwell believe I was ahead of my time had made me feel sane, grounded, and like I was right to keep pursuing what I was doing. His loss would leave a big hole. And yet I still find I can hear his voice, talking to me at my mental board meetings. He encourages me when I face naysayers and urges me to keep on with my work.

The summer after Whitney's fourth grade, I took the kids to Florida for vacation. I brought along *The Miracle Worker* and every biography I could find about Helen Keller, and while we sat on the beach, I read aloud to them about Helen Keller's life. I wanted them to understand the miracle we had accomplished with Whitney. We had taught him language, broken through to him the way Annie Sullivan had broken through to Helen. I thought it would help them understand how special their roles had been and help them understand their brother better.

I carefully paced how to introduce the Helen Keller books into the vacation. It was the first really successful vacation as a family unit we had ever had. No running after Whitney, no panic-filled hours because Whitney had wandered off or gotten lost.

We spent most of our days at a cabana at the beach. I let them swim and make fabulous sand castles until they were exhausted.

Then, toward the end of the day, we would order special frozen drinks and snacks: virgin piña coladas and daiquiris that came adorned with umbrellas, fruits, and plastic swords. Then I began reading. Our first book was called *Helen and Dr. Bell,* in which Helen and Dr. Alexander Graham Bell wrote alternating chapters. Every day for a week I would read long sections from these books. It became my favorite part of the day.

Everyone loved the story of Helen Keller—and since Annie Sullivan was Helen's teacher much as I am the teacher of my patients, there were a lot of parallels. It was the first time I had attempted to explain Whitney's disabilities and give them a name—hearing impaired—that made sense to Whitney, Vanessa, William and me. He was overcoming a hearing impairment and that impairment was caused by his high visuals.

Watching the kids play and tease and argue with each other all day, and having Whitney be able to sit still with his brother and sister and listen to me read out loud, I was very happy to be sharing the wonder of Helen's story with my own miracle workers.

13

Band-Aids

The screams and grunts and groans were ear splitting: William and Whitney were dying. It had been at least fifteen minutes since they'd shot each other. I was about to order them to die when William yelled, "Put on a Band-Aid!" and they popped back to perfect health, and started running around chasing each other, beginning the war game all over again.

There were times when the roughhousing between the boys made me second-guess my decision to get them involved in sports. Wouldn't it be quieter if they were watching a movie? But those thoughts were fleeting. I knew that they were having a blast. Not only was the physical activity healthy for them—but the aggression they got out in these games was an important stress reducer, something they needed, especially these days.

Fifth grade was another rough start for Whitney—it was for all of us.

After four great years at Riverside, at the end of Whitney's fourth grade school year, I learned that Mr. Niemie was moving to a newly built school called Bailey, and most of his staff was going with him. At first I was thrilled. Bailey was right near our house in the woods. The drive to Riverside was twenty minutes. Finally, Whitney would get to go to school with the neighborhood kids, making his social life so much easier to schedule and develop. Outside his specially crafted environment, Whitney was still at a loss with social nuance, so building new friendships was difficult for him.

Much to my dismay, Mr. Niemie told me that our house wasn't in the Bailey school district. Apparently the cut-off was just one house away.

I wrote to the administration to appeal. I had school experts and doctors write letters explaining that after all we had been through, this much change was too much for Whitney and could cause a relapse— not to mention ruin the options for letting him adapt to a new set of school changes in stages and adding social skill training.

The IEP we created for Whitney at Riverside for grades one through four had expired, so we had the choice of writing a new IEP and staying at Riverside with a new cast of administrative support, or moving to a new school. I explained that Whitney already would be facing a big change moving to fifth grade because he would have a new teacher for the first time in two years. He'd been in the experimental multiage class that Mr. Niemie had recommended for third and fourth grades, and so he had the same teachers for those two years. The Riverside support staff that had served as Whitney's social touchstones (the secretary, the guidance counselor, and the nurse) were leaving with Mr. Niemie, so every one in those roles would be new.

If we went to Bailey, Whitney could adapt to a new environment and new kids and teachers but without the complete change of his crucial support system. I thought that would be like a halfway house for preparing him to move on to middle school in sixth grade, where a thousand kids change classes, and the teachers each see 250 kids in a day.

By this time, however, many of the things I had been saying about

Whitney's development and education were proving to be right. Those administrators in the Dublin schools who had been fighting with me over the years did not seem to be pleased to be proven wrong. When it came time for the administration to assist me in this process, even with Mr. Niemie and others asking for assistance, the administration did not budge.

I got Mr. Niemie to write a letter about how important it was to let Whitney go to Bailey, explaining how disruptive it would be for him. We explained how he didn't operate well without understanding routines, and that taking away his supports could cause him to crash. We all felt it was important for him to go to school with the people who knew him.

They held firm to the cut-off. I was desperate. In my attempts to force a solution, I found out that my father had a friend who had control over house numbers on a street. We were on a country road, so there was room to change our number. My father appealed to his friend and we had our address changed by a digit. This didn't work. Again, I was denied. We weren't going to get to Bailey. Whitney had to go to Deer Run, the school that we were zoned for. Under different circumstances, I would have been thrilled. Deer Run was fifteen minutes away and was considered the elite of the Dublin schools, serving the highest-income families in the Muirfield area, a group of homes centered around beautiful mansions and a pro golf course build by Jack Nicklaus. I had a chip on my shoulder about this school—not only was I convinced it wasn't in Whitney's best interest to switch to this school, but I thought it would be full of wealthy students and we wouldn't fit in.

I couldn't understand why they wouldn't let Whitney go to Bailey. Maybe Mr. Niemie needed a rest from me. Maybe the superintendent was mad at me over the school psychologist problems. Maybe I was being paranoid and rules were rules. I'd lost perspective on how to understand people's thinking when it came to Whitney. To me the best solution for him was always clear. But time and time again, my solution didn't match the system's.

All summer I tried to get us into Bailey. One day in the midst of a harangue about how illogical this was, Mr. Niemie stopped me and said simply, "Why don't you go visit Deer Run? The principal is very nice. I think you'd like him."

The school year was about to start and I could see I didn't seem to have a lot of options. So at Mr. Niemie's suggestion I went over to talk to the principal. Of course the principal was nice. He understood my concerns and tried to assuage them right away. "We'll work this out," he said, calming me. "Here's a list of the teachers we have for the fifth grade. I'm sure we can find a suitable match for Whitney."

I glanced at the list, on the off chance I would recognize any of the names. One name jumped out at me.

"Mrs. Lud!" I cried.

He looked at the list. "Mrs. Ludwizac? You know her?"

"She was Whitney's teacher when he was four," I said in amazement. "She's wonderful! She's knows Whitney."

"Well, she's here today, let's go see her." Off we went.

The school year was about to begin so teachers were in and out of the building, setting up their classrooms. We walked into the room and there was Mrs. Lud in her golf outfit, decorating her bulletin boards before an afternoon on the course.

When she turned to greet us, all I could imagine was Mrs. Lud in a big clown outfit on Halloween, entertaining the children with her enthusiasm for the holiday. We hugged and she was amazed to hear that Whitney was doing well enough to be in a regular fifth grade class—after all, she hadn't seen him since he was four. I explained my concerns about his ability to adjust to new routines. "Why don't you bring Whitney by and he can help me set up the room?"

When I told Whitney the good news, he said he had no memory of

Mrs. Lud. At first I thought he just needed to have his memory jarred so I drove him and William and Vanessa back to Chapman Elementary, the school he'd attended with Mrs. Lud, and had the kids play on the playground. He had fun, but didn't recall having played on this playground before. We walked inside and went to his old classroom, but he still had no memory of ever having been there.

How odd! Whitney had no memories until he was able to use language. I wondered if he would remember Mrs. Lud when he saw her. He remembered Mrs. Jones, his teacher from the following year, but by then he was reading. When we walked into her classroom at Deer Run, he did not recognize Mrs. Lud at all.

That first day I brought him to visit, I stayed with Whitney and Mrs. Lud for a while, helping organize the room, the three of us working together as Whitney became more comfortable. Mrs. Lud gave me a wink that indicated it was OK for me to leave and come back later. I left them with Mrs. Lud telling stories about all of the things the class would be doing as she and Whitney unpacked boxes and set up bulletin boards. Whitney was able to get a sense of what to expect by helping her create their new classroom.

As I drove to work, I was nervous about how the rest of their day would go. Many times I had left Whitney someplace with high hopes and within a half hour the phone was ringing for me to come pick him up. Would Mrs. Lud be comfortable having him in class with her? Would she see as much improvement as I had? All the difficulties and fights I faced trying to get the best services for Whitney made me feel like I was crazy sometimes and that maybe the rest of the world didn't think Whitney was doing as well as I did.

I went to work, and though my mind was on my patients, my heart was on the clock. Three hours had passed and no call. I had promised to pick Whitney up for lunch. I called the school.

"We're having a great time," Mrs. Lud told me. "Why don't you let him stay for lunch? I brought extra." Mrs. Lud was actually enjoying having Whitney around and thought it was a good idea for him to be

there with her to get used to the room. "Also, kids and moms are dropping by and I have a chance to introduce Whitney to them," she said.
"We are taping names on all the desks and making folders and putting
up all the bulletin boards. We also have to unpack all the workbooks
and put names on them and put them in each desk."

Before I hung up she said, "He is Miracle Boy. I cannot believe that
this is our Whitney!"

Though he took to Mrs. Lud again right away, Whitney was very
bothered that he didn't remember this earlier time in his life. It had
never occurred to me that Whitney's memory might have been impacted, but now that we quizzed him, he seemed to have no memory of
anything prior to Mrs. Jones's class, and even that was sketchy. I was
pondering how people made long-term memories without language.
Now that I have treated 435 highly visual people, I know a lot more
about how they store memories. I have a dentist patient who reports
that he sees the inside of each of his patients' mouths in his mind when
he looks down his schedule at the start of the day. Many of my medical
student patients also say they remember things nearly exclusively in
pictures. While I hear the conversations when I think back on a holiday
or a special event, I don't see a picture. One of my high school patients
once said, "How sad for you—when you think about last Christmas,
you don't get to replay the movie of the day in your mind." I said I
enjoyed hearing the conversations if I think back about a family time or
prior appointment. I can pull patient interactions from my memory
and they all come back to me in conversations that I hear in my head.
While the visual patients might see pages of a textbook on a slide in the
mental screen, they don't hear the words.

I think Whitney's senses were so disintegrated that he was not able
to retrieve long-term memories even from his visual filing system. We
knew he was using a short-term memory loop to solve problems, but
apparently these thoughts did not make it to a long-term storage facility in those early years.

Now he asked us for stories about his early years to fill in the gaps.

I soon realized it was probably a blessing that he had no memory of life before kindergarten, because hearing stories of his misbehavior upset him. When I would tell a story for him and there was something in the story that he did wrong, he would cringe. He would say, "Stop talking, Mom. I don't want to hear about it." If Vanessa and William started to laugh about some of the funny things he did, he would run to his bed and go to sleep. He would talk to himself trying to sort it out. He would go for long walks pondering things over and over, saying, "I just need time by myself to think." He would usually conclude that he "just wanted to move ahead with his life and not go back." I was all for that. Reliving our experiences in order to write this book has been very painful for both of us, even though we know the positive ending.

On the last weekend before school started, we had picnics on the school playground, and every night at dinner we'd talk about Deer Run being his new school and how we all loved it because his brother and sister would be in the middle school next door.

Still, the adjustment to the new school did not go smoothly. I knew he was struggling because he couldn't find his patterns, and school felt like chaos. Normally, Whitney is an early riser on a school day. He loves to get ready for school and have me fix him breakfast. This is the best time to talk to him. After school, he is often tired after a long day in verbal land. Now, I would have to drag him out of bed, and rather than scurrying to get ready, he would be muttering to himself in the bathroom. After school, he would go for long walks in the woods, talking to himself. He was withdrawing from us, losing his appetite and overall *joie de vivre*. At school he was not listening accurately and he was having trouble following classroom directions. He was getting most answers wrong on his homework papers. He was not following classroom routines. When it was time to go watch Will play football at the stadium behind Whitney's school, he said he was too tired and wanted to go home and take a nap. The established routines at Riverside were very important, helping Whitney to organize his day and fulfill expectations. He had arrived at the point where he took great pride in his work and had a thirst for knowledge. Starting at Deer Run was too much change, too fast for Whitney. There weren't regular people to go to for help yet. His new tutor was treating him like a special ed student. He was reverting to old behaviors.

I knew we had to get the pattern re-established as quickly as possible. I explained to Mrs. Lud and the principal that the first six weeks of the school year were always hard for Whitney. Until the routine got set in his head, life was chaos—and the amount of change this year was extra stressful. "He tries so hard to please. He doesn't get everything from verbal reasoning. Until he gets his visual cue system set up so he can watch and understand, he can't please, so it upsets him." I begged them to be patient.

Mrs. Lud and the principal were very concerned. Whitney's work was extremely below par, and his handwriting quite infantile. The ideas he wanted to express in his writing were at grade level, but not the act of using the pencil to write legibly and the ability to get the words down on paper, all there and spelled correctly. Thus his output often looked very immature. He was unable to figure out what he didn't understand so he could ask for help. What they were seeing was a fifth-grader capable of doing written work at a second-grade level, if that. They didn't know what to do with him. Just as much of first grade is devoted to learning to read, a major goal of fifth grade is learning to work independently, manage your time, and express yourself in writing. These are all skills that prepare students for the note-taking required in middle and high school.

In the midst of this difficult transition, I got a call from Mrs. Lud and the principal asking me to come to the school right away. "We have an emergency. Can you come over?"

"What's happened?"

"Nothing's happened. Yet. But we're very worried about Whitney."

I raced over to the school. Mrs. Lud and the principal sat me down and handed me a notebook. It was Whitney's journal. I read the page they had opened to. Whitney's scrawl was still barely legible; once I made out the words, it was even harder to read:

I have no friends at this school. I don't know anyone at recess. I am sad. Please let me go back to everyone I know at Riverside. I miss Mr. Niemie and Adam and Danny and the other kids. I miss seeing all my teachers. I want to die. I hate my life.

Even with wonderful Mrs. Lud, the change to Deer Run was too much for Whitney. For one moment I felt a wave of sadness for him, he sounded so lost. Then, my protective instincts sprang into action. I was not afraid. I knew exactly what to do. I turned to the principal and Mrs. Lud. "We can't wait for him to grasp the order of things. We need to set up support systems in this school like we had at Riverside immediately. I will be here every day until we have the systems set up."

I could see confusion and doubt in their faces at my declaration. "This is not a difficult problem. We need to re-establish routines and help Whitney to develop relationships."

"Don't you think we should get a psychiatrist involved?" the principal asked.

I was still corresponding with Dr. Cantwell and consulting with Dr. Weller, so I knew that I had the best psychiatric backup one could ask for. I also knew that the best way to help Whitney was to re-establish his sense of routine and comfort. Once that safety zone was in place, his depression would go away. To those who hadn't been intimately involved in Whitney's life, however, this cry for help in his journal was a big red flag. The idea that providing a sense of routine would be sufficient no doubt sounded like a mother's denial.

It would have sounded very pompous of me to tell them that I believed I was inventing a new disease model to describe Whitney—that he had a disease only I understood because I was discovering it. And at times, when he took these backward steps, I very much doubted myself.

I was frightened also. Maybe Whitney was relapsing in a permanent way. But Dr. Cantwell had said to break off the most treatable part and treat the hell out of it. That was the best thing I knew to do.

I explained to Mrs. Lud and the principal that I was working with the psychiatry department at OSU and if Whitney did not change rapidly we would involve them—but for now we would focus on the most treatable issue and treat it aggressively. And the most treatable part of Whitney's problem was communication, relationship-building, time management, following directions, and making visual patterns out of a verbal world. We could work on these issues very quickly.

Mrs. Lud was willing to let me come back to the classroom and help set up Whitney with a study buddy, recess partner, and lunch partner. Whitney, Mrs. Lud, and I worked out the plan together. In fact, Mrs. Lud made this a plan for all of the kids so it didn't seem like Whitney was being "baby-sat." Everyone had buddies now and Mrs. Lud, being such a high-energy exciting teacher, made the new plan seem very cool to the kids. They stayed with their buddies for a few weeks and then they changed and got new buddies.

The buddy plan not only built a wonderful esprit de corps in the class, it turned out to be an excellent system for Whitney. Whitney was very friendly with these new "buddies." He was eager to learn how to make friends with them and how to share in their games. He would come home and tell us about his new partners and what he did during the day. Mrs. Lud worked wonders at camouflaging Whitney's differences so that he wasn't teased or treated as "different."

His oral language was similar to someone from a foreign country who was learning English. He would leave words or word endings out. He often used the wrong verb tenses and still mispronounced words. His inflection was off—like a foreigner who is trying but is not fluent with getting ideas from thought to word. Recently Whitney and I were in France, and when we finished our lunch, I said "Billet s'il vous plaît" which means "Train ticket, please." I meant to say "l'addition," which means check. The waiter looked at me, perplexed that I was asking him

to get me a train ticket! I had picked the word in French that corre-
sponded to the word "bill" in my mind. Whitney was making similar
kinds of mistakes.

Mrs. Lud worked each situation so that Whitney's special requirements
were as inconspicuous as possible, and she helped the other children
learn to enjoy Whitney and he them. She had a way of making all of the
children feel affirmed and celebrated. She was so adept at doing this
that any of these differences were accepted, whether it was because
you were from a foreign country (and because there was a Honda
plant nearby, there were a lot of foreign students in his class) or had
disabilities.

These artificial systems helped Whitney build relationships and
start to see patterns. This, along with working out with Todd in the
evenings at home, created patterns that calmed Whitney down and
grounded him. Sure enough, within two weeks we had things going
smoothly and Whitney was back on track.

In fact, Whitney started to flourish that year. As writing skills
seemed to improve daily. They were still far behind his peers', but they
were improving. His reading skills were good and he was able to read
along with the class without major difficulties. He began to discover
things he was good at—his visual strengths—and for the first time get
positive reinforcement for these talents from people other than at home
or at my office.

His first triumph was an art contest at school. The kids were supposed to make a self-designed piece of art that symbolized a fable or
fairy tale. Whitney chose the house of twigs from *The Three Little Pigs*.

Deer Run was in a wealthy school district so the school projects
were often quite impressive because the students had access to lots of
great supplies and got very involved in competing to create the most
inventive arts and crafts. Whitney liked to do things on his own,
though, so he seldom asked for help. In fact, I don't think I even knew

there was a contest underway. Inspired by our house in the woods, Whitney decided to build a log cabin for his project. He spent hours outside, searching for the best, identically shaped twigs. He designed his house and hand-glued the twigs to form a perfect miniature log cabin. When we saw the finished project, even I was amazed. I knew he had superior visual skills, but this precise replica was very impressive for a fifth grader to make completely on his own. The school agreed. He won "Best of Show" in the art contest—which we discovered only when I went to his classroom for parent night. Among all the projects displayed in the classroom, there I found Whitney's with a big blue construction-paper ribbon on it.

Driving home from the school that night, Whitney said, "You know why I won, Mom?"

"Tell me."

"Because I made my project out of my imagination. I only used twigs and rope from around the house. I didn't get any help from grown-ups and I did not go to a store and spend a lot of money making it, either."

I was impressed with his perceptiveness about what was special about his project. "I think you are exactly right and I am very proud of you Whitney."

He grinned. "And making it was a lot of fun, too!"

His next achievement shouldn't have surprised me after his triumphant stage debut as Sneezy. The school announced the traditional DARE (Drug Abuse Resistance Education) contest for all fifth graders in Dublin. A required part of the school curriculum, the DARE contest is sponsored by the Dublin police. Fifth graders were the seniors of elementary school, and the DARE contest was like a rite of passage to middle school.

One afternoon I found Whitney in my closet, with clothes and hats strewn around. He was creating costumes and writing a one-man play about why kids shouldn't take drugs. He practiced day and night, working hard on developing his characters with different voices and personalities. I thought he was fantastic—a miniature Lily Tomlin or Robin Williams. He practiced making faces in the mirror and talking in hilarious cartoonlike accents. He also presented his act to all of us— bounding in with revisions by the hour.

The night of the big contest, we all went to a special evening party held in the school cafeteria. The police gave awards and each child was "shirted" by the police with a DARE T-shirt. These DARE shirts were big at the swimming pool in the summer because only kids who had "graduated" from elementary school had them, and that meant that they were much more grown-up than the younger kids. In addition to the T-shirts, the police singled out the top ten award winners and gave them a certificate. Whitney came in third. None of us could believe it— here he was being judged by the police, who had no idea of his history or his developmental problems. We were all thrilled for him.

For months afterward, it was hard to get Whitney out of his DARE T-shirt, even to wash it. He was very proud of this sign that he was graduating from elementary school—and on to young adulthood.

After over a year of working with Todd—almost daily for me and several times a week for the kids—we were all in tip-top shape. I had lost a lot of weight. I looked better and felt better. I'd even become adept at kickboxing. Todd was proud of what he'd achieved with my training, and he asked me to take part in a kickboxing demonstration at the Rotary Club—I was going to be an example of a great turnaround. What a victory!

The night before the demonstration, I went out to dinner with a friend. After our dinner, we stepped outside into an ice storm that had started during the meal. The sidewalk was slick, I was wearing high heels, and I slipped and fell, twisting my ankle. When I tried to get up by grabbing my friend's arm, I slipped again and pulled him down on my leg, breaking it so badly that I had to have surgery.

When I got home from the hospital the next day, with my leg in an external fixation device, we had a family meeting. I told the kids I was going to need them to help me because it was going to be hard for me to get around for a while.

My broken leg was painful and made everything more difficult. But it didn't stop our lives. I barely missed any work. At first, I used a wheelchair to get around, but I soon abandoned it because I got too frustrated trying to maneuver it and was always banging into things. Instead, I used crutches. I got myself to the car, drove to the office, made my way to my desk, and would not budge for the rest of the day.

The kids rose to the occasion. Vanessa had to take over the mom role at home. She helped me get dressed in the mornings. She had to take on most of the meal preparation duties in the kitchen—even if I was telling her what to do. The kids came to the office after school on the days they had no other activities and helped out there as well.

Our house was messier—and no doubt we all looked a lot more disheveled during this time, but we persevered. Even Whitney found a unique way to help.

We had a fireplace in our house in the woods, and occasionally bats flew down the chimney into the house. The first time it happened, we all screamed, especially Vanessa and I. The kids ran around the house—I wanted to run but couldn't move. The thought of a bat getting in my hair or flying into me terrified me. I felt so helpless.

Only Whitney seemed nonplussed by the bats. We were trying to hide from them, but Whitney got a tennis racket and calmly talked to the bats—telling them not to be afraid, that he was going to help them get outside. It was like he had a sixth, animal sense, the same kind of radar the bats had. Somehow he could find them and, with the head of his racket, scooch each bat out of the door and outside.

Here was my autistic child taking charge. He calmly found a solution to what could have been a fiasco.

After six months, the doctor removed the external fixation device from my leg and put on a cast. Then he told me the results from the X ray: the bone hadn't grown back at all. "The bone is sitting in the right spot, but it's not connected. You can't put any weight at all on your leg."

My father was with me at this appointment and I told him, "I'm not going back to that doctor."

"You can't *not* go back."

"Why? They say it won't get better, why do I have to go back to hear bad news?"

My father just smiled, knowing I was stubborn. "You have to go back."

I started doing physical therapy with Todd again, against medical advice. I did return to the doctor again, as my father predicted. But the next time I went back, the news was better. All in all, it took about a year, but finally the bones started to knit. Today, that leg is slightly longer than the other one. Sometimes, depending on what shoes I'm wearing, or the weather, it can still be painful to walk.

During that year, there were many times when I was confined to my bed, working on my laptop, and I could hear the kids living their lives around me—playing, arguing, doing their homework, fixing snacks. For someone like me who was always doing a million things, being limited in this way was torture.

I was glad we were living in the house in the woods because it provided lots of diversions, especially for the boys. Vanessa was in her early teen years and preferred to play with her girlfriends—exploring makeup and clothes, printing pictures of Leo DiCaprio and Brad Pitt off the computer to make posters for their rooms. But Whitney and William would play all kinds of games in the forest—we had five acres of trees with streams and an acre field in front of the house. They had a go-cart that they could drive around in together. They had campouts and sleepovers with a group of kids who lived down the street that were often over to play. When I could hear William and Whitney playing their shoot-'em-up games, I identified with their long drawn-out death scenes—I felt like I was in one myself. Then one of them would shout, "Put on a Band-Aid!" and they popped back up,

When I heard that, I thought, *Well, they learned that lesson somewhere:* the need to go on—to dust yourself off, slap on a Band-Aid, and keep on going. I sensed that I was reaching a turning point with the kids—a time in our lives where I was leaning on them, and finding strength in their resilience.

Thinking back to the beginning of fifth grade and how hard that transition was for Whitney made me realize that this broken leg was an even bigger change in everyone's life. And here's where the cloud had a silver lining. The children were strong—all three of them. Because we bonded together to help Whitney, they knew how to bond together to help me. All of them had the ego strength to not be scared when their mother was hurt and unable to do the things she always had. They rose to the occasion and took over many of the roles I had been playing, even Whitney. I couldn't believe what a change this was from the child who wanted to die because of too much change only months before.

14

From
Special Ed
to Maverick

I had high hopes for Whitney's sixth grade year at Grizelle, his new middle school. I knew and respected Grizelle's principal; Whitney's school nurse from Riverside, whose office had been one of his safe havens, worked there as well. And, for the first time ever, he was in the same school as William.

I had two remaining concerns. First, this was the first time Whitney would have to change rooms for each class. I thought once he got the routine down, switching would be fine, but the stakes felt higher at a school where the kids were older. Kids always tease each other, but adolescence brings on a certain mean spirit and viciousness, and I was worried for Whitney. He was developing into a boy who was terribly sensitive, but who also said whatever popped into his head, uncensored. I feared this could get him into trouble.

The second biggest challenge for Whitney was that he was required to attend a special ed homeroom. At Grizelle, there were a thousand kids in the middle school, and only two kids in special education besides Whitney. Since first grade, I'd fought for him to attend a regular class and slip away for his special education services: OT, PT, and LD tutoring. Now with special ed homeroom, he was visibly singled out again.

The ways in which our society in general, but our education system especially, tends to segregate and label people with communication disorders is a huge stumbling block to helping the very people who need it. It is an issue I have fought throughout Whitney's life—as well as in my practice. I am convinced that a major cause of childhood "behavioral" problems—acting out in school, depression, truancy—is the result of children who have trouble learning being made to feel "dumb." If not handled well, special ed classes can do this by separating children with learning difficulties so that other kids see them as different. As Dr. Hallowell said in *Driven to Distraction,* when he went to school there was one learning disability—stupidity—and one treatment—"try harder." For many children, this is still true today.

Even in schools where there aren't separate special ed classes, the children are often required to traipse out to a special van or building for special ed classes or tutoring. I'd fought hard to make these services for Whitney fit into his day seamlessly. Now with a special ed homeroom of only three people, and several special ed classes, he was visibly set apart as being different and he felt that this made him seem "less than" the other kids.

I visited Grizelle's principal to see if Whitney had to be in special ed homeroom. He was not at grade level in all of his work. His writing was of serious concern. He was unable to get his thoughts, which were now very complex and multilayered, into words on the paper. His handwriting was poor, but even more of a struggle was his ability to express himself—to encode words from his brain to his mouth or pen.

Whitney still needed tutoring and accommodations. The principal felt Whitney had to stay under an IEP so that he could qualify for this extra help. That meant he had to go to the special ed homeroom for the first period. I agreed that Whitney still needed the extra help, but explained that it was the homeroom that set him apart, and that was a major issue for him. The principal held firm that the special services cost the district money and many people who would like to have them didn't qualify. So for Whitney to qualify, we had to follow the rules. However, he suggested that we meet with the teachers and Dublin administration to see what we could work out.

In the meantime, I found out that some of the kids had started teasing him. This really was the first time Whitney had been teased. His behaviors had always called attention, but up until now the faculty at his schools made an effort for all of the children to be given respect at school. Mr. Niemie had been a stickler about people treating each other with respect, so teasing was not tolerated in his school. Along with the guidance counselor, the nurse, and his secretarial staff, Mr. Niemie worked hard to create a safe school environment for all of the kids. The previous year, Mrs. Lud had also fostered an atmosphere of acceptance of all children, and good manners was a requirement in her room. I understand the limitations of enforcing these standards—Mr. Niemie's school had a couple hundred students and Grizelle had more than one thousand sixth-, seventh-, and eighth-graders, so the situation was quite different.

Teasing was a new and upsetting experience for Whitney. One boy began heckling Whitney in the hallways and after school, calling him "Whitney Houston" (after the singer), saying, "Whitney is a girl's name." "Whitney Houston's a retard," he yelled. Will defended his brother against the primary troublemaker and they got into a school-yard tussle. While the fight wasn't much, the boy then stole all of Will's books.

Once again, I found myself in a meeting with school administrators. "Boys will be boys," they said. They had so many students; name-calling didn't rank as a severe enough for them to intervene.

"We can handle it, Mom," the boys chastised me. They were getting too old to want it known that their mother was fighting any battles for them. I didn't know what else to do. Whitney still needed protecting, as far as I was concerned. Whitney came up with a solution: He decided to start going by his real first name, which is John (he's John Whitney, named after my father), thinking that maybe this would solve the problem. But the name-calling continued.

We'd spent his entire life working to build up his strengths and not treat him differently. As a result, Whitney seldom felt different. When he did, or when he noticed that people were laughing at something he'd said or done, it really got to him.

I knew things were getting worse, not better, when he started coming downstairs in the morning for school looking unkempt.

"Comb you hair, honey. Tuck in your shirt." Hearing myself give these admonishments made me realize that no matter how much Whitney insisted everything was fine and he could handle it, the situation at school was getting to him. Todd made a big point of getting the kids to take pride in their appearance, teaching us all that how we presented ourselves reflected our self-esteem. I could see Whitney's self-esteem was taking a beating from the name-calling.

Then one afternoon that fall, I came across a letter while trying to clean up the clutter of Whitney's room. (Sometimes I thought that the disorder of his room must match the disorder of his thoughts at times—piles of things, obscuring any chance of ever finding what you needed.) I no longer have the letter, unfortunately, but it went something like this:

Dear Congressman:
I want to be taken out of special ed. I am not the one who needs it. There are kids in my class that need it more. I want to have a meeting to discuss this. I think Mark should have therapy with my mom. I think you should tell his mom that my mom can fix him. I think Jane needs to have special reading help and Billy needs help in math. They are not doing the work right. They are confused and upset. Kids should not feel that they are dumb at school. That is wrong.

The letter made me smile. At the same time, it left my heart aching for Whitney. On the one hand, I was impressed at his initiative and all that it represented. They were learning about the U.S. government in school and Whitney must be doing well enough in this class (which was one of his mainstreamed classes) to understand that if you wanted something changed, you should write your congressman. He went straight to the top to find an answer; I was surprised he hadn't written directly to the President. On the other hand, it revealed how hard it was for him to be segregated in special education classes and made me realize how desperately he wanted to fit in. The letter must have been Whitney's latest idea for how to stop the name-calling: if he could get out of special ed, they couldn't single him out. I confronted Whitney about the letter I'd found. "I think it's a great idea," I told him. "But maybe you should tell your message to the people that can help right away. Going through Congress might take a long time."

He agreed, and we decided he should try talking to his principal personally. I called the principal again, and asked if Whitney and I could both come meet with him, explaining that Whitney felt so strongly he shouldn't be in special ed that he was planning to write his congressman.

The principal said it was unusual for students to present their own case, but he agreed that Whitney could attend the meeting he had set up to discuss it.

I hung up the phone and thought, *I hope this is a good idea*. Whitney was to talk in front of twelve or fourteen teachers and specialists about why he wanted out of special ed. That night we had a family meeting. I told Whitney the outcome of our request and explained that he now had a chance to explain his point of view to his teachers. William warned Whitney that he should be careful. "You don't want to make the teachers mad at you. We had better practice what you are going to say." And so we did. We play-acted mock meetings for the rest of the week until Whitney seemed well prepared and eager to represent himself.

The next week he and I arrived an hour before school started and walked into a conference room to face his teachers. I didn't know many of these people and I felt intimidated and scared for Whitney.

Luckily, he was feeling very self-confident that day. The principal asked him what he wanted to say and Whitney very simply made his case. He told them that he was getting As in science, history, and art—the classes where he was mainstreamed. He was sure he could succeed in regular English and math (the classes where he was in special ed), given the chance. He also pointed it out that it made no sense to him why, if he was mainstreamed for history, he couldn't be mainstreamed for English.

Whitney finished his appeal and sat down. The teachers were clearly impressed with his initiative; but it was also clear they didn't think he was ready to leave special ed. His handwriting was poor and he made lots of spelling errors, and it was still difficult to follow what he was talking about at times. His speech still had a quality that sounded like a deaf person talking—he was somewhat nasal and monotone, and the inflections weren't always in the usual places.

"You need the special ed services," they tried to convince him. "You are actually lucky—we don't give them to many people."

"Everyone is making fun of me," Whitney appealed. "I can do the work and I want a chance to show you."

I could see the teachers still weren't convinced. They spoke quietly with each other, and became agitated over the fact that they felt it was inappropriate to argue with a student about their professional assessments of his education plan. I was becoming anxious that the meeting was going to backfire when the principal jumped in with a suggestion.

"What I hear you teachers saying is that Whitney could change from special ed math to honors math and stay in special ed English and special ed homeroom."

I looked around the room. That is not at all what the teachers were saying. Special education math to honors math was a huge jump. But apparently this was the only math class that would work with his schedule. For a moment I wondered if the principal was trying keep things status quo by offering a solution that we would reject. *They will never buy this and neither will Whitney,* I thought.

He continued, "This will work because Mrs. R is a great math teacher." (I knew this was true because Will had her.) Mrs. R, who was there, smiled. "And he can get special help in language arts where he still needs work. How does that sound to you, Whitney?"

I could see Whitney was excited. "I know I can do the math. I love math. But the homeroom is what everyone teases me about," he insisted, holding his ground. Whitney's smile was hard to resist. His energy and enthusiasm were infectious. By now, he was just turning twelve years of age, with a shock of dark brown hair that hung over his brown eyes. He had freckles on his nose, clear skin and rosy cheeks. It was hard to believe he wasn't a perfectly normal adolescent. If he laughed or told a joke, others couldn't help but laugh—whether or not they thought it was funny.

Everyone smiled at his tenaciousness.

"If you don't go to special ed homeroom, you won't get the help you need for your writing," the principal said. "We will make a special plan for your writing and meet again, OK, Whitney?"

"OK," he agreed. He rose to leave and I nodded that I'd meet him outside. "Thanks for helping me, everyone!" Whitney beamed.

The teachers were beaming too.

Once Whitney was out of the room, the school psychologist turned to the principal. "If you take him out of the special ed homeroom, he will no longer be able to get our services, so I think I should write up a plan for improving his writing and see what you think." She turned to me. "You can send us any input you want as his mother, Dr. Florance," she said half-heartedly—my reputation had clearly preceded me to this school.

After the meeting adjourned, Whitney and I went to celebrate at the Morgan House, an old log cabin gift shop and restaurant that served homemade comfort food.

I was impressed. Whitney had been a more effective advocate for himself in one meeting than I'd been in my years of fighting on his behalf. I enjoyed witnessing Whitney's emerging strong sense of self and his improving ability to access his verbal brain to express himself.

He wasn't out of special ed, but he'd maneuvered himself into the honor's math class and opened a door to possibly getting out of special ed if his writing improved. I couldn't believe this compromise. I'd sat in that room and knew that none of his teachers had recommended to the principal that Whitney be moved to honors math, or that his language arts program or IEP be revisited. But somehow Whitney had won the principal over, and he in turn had won the teachers over. It was as though all the principal had to do was suggest that his plan was *their* idea—and they believed it was.

After our celebration, I went home and wrote an IEP for a writing program for Whitney. The school incorporated my ideas and promised to implement them as long as he stayed in the homeroom.

I think things went so much more smoothly with the school this time for many reasons. Whitney speaking on his own behalf was one. Also, Whitney *was* better and more capable than he'd been in the past when I'd been fighting for him to be mainstreamed. Mrs. Lud had also written an excellent report. She met with the teachers before the school year started to explain her experience teaching Whitney in fifth grade—what worked and what didn't, and what help she thought he needed, so they were very familiar with his case. Also, by now I was more familiar with navigating the school special education system and the administration was getting used to me too.

Whitney did excellent work in his math class. But despite his success in getting this changed, he was still being teased. The kids continued to call him "retard" and William continued to defend him.

At this time both of my boys were studying karate with a champion teacher, who advised them on how he thought they should handle the situation: ignore the name-calling until the last day of school, and then on the last day after the bell rang, take the ringleader of the name-calling "to the mat." I told them this wasn't an acceptable plan. I don't believe in using physical aggression to solve a problem. I listened to the boys expand on their revenge fantasy, wondering how in the world I was going to talk them out of it. (Fortunately by the end of that school year, William and Whit ignored the kid so long that they were no longer interested in fighting him.)

Nevertheless, throughout sixth grade Whitney was fighting a reputation of a "dumb retard" at the school. He started telling me he wanted to change schools to get away from the teasing and the special education homeroom. I urged him to hang in there and ignore the name-calling; I tried to tell him how strong he was being to take the high road. But it continued to bother him. Whitney firmly believed that as long as he was required to go to the special ed homeroom, everyone would think of him as a "retard." And I was thinking about how hard it would be if he was one of three kids in high school in special ed when dating and sports are so central.

Victor Frankl, a neurologist and psychiatrist who survived the concentration camps during World War II, believed that people have a specific ego strength. Some people have a resilience that helps them forge through adversity, while others don't. As a camp prisoner and doctor, he noted that some people who were not very sick were unable to withstand the emotional pain of the experience and died, while others who were very sick were able to survive and also help others.

Whitney, I was starting to see, was being well served in his recovery by having a very strong sense of self. He was not only pulling himself through a brain disorder, but I was starting to see that he also had the inner strength to give of himself to others. Whitney had helped me through my broken leg period. He was contributing as a fully functioning family member, helping with daily chores and spearheading our family meetings. Fighting to get out of special ed, to not be segregated and teased, I saw he was developing a sense of justice and morality. His ability to help Mark is a case in point.

Around this time, I got a call about a tenth grader named Mark who was taking LSD and had run away. I'd first met Mark some time earlier through his relative, an executive CEO, who was a patient of mine. At that time, Mark was seeing a psychologist for taking drugs and school failure. I had explained to his parents that I worked on communication problems not drug addiction, but that often one can lead to the other. Ultimately, they had decided to stick with the psychologist rather than work with me because they were not convinced that his problem had to do with a communication disorder.

I have never advertised myself; I have built my practice on satisfied customers referring other patients. The parents who come to me are usually experiencing what are considered behavioral problems with their children. Until they see the results of my approach, it is hard to understand or believe that an auditory processing disorder could be the reason for school failure or behavioral problems. The irony is that treating many of these children as if they could just "snap out of it"— pay more attention, apply themselves, try harder—often creates more stress on the child, leads to a greater sense of failure, and exacerbates the behavioral problem. If you can treat the root of the communication disorder, once the child learns how to learn, the behavioral issues often disappear. Most of the children I see are smart kids, trapped and frustrated by an inability to excel because they don't have the language skills necessary to succeed in a traditional learning environment. Whitney was an extreme example, and he'd taught me to see how addressing the communication problem first worked with other patients whose visual and auditory processing systems were more balanced.

When Mark ran away to become a roadie for rock bands, his mother called me in despair. "Please help—we don't know where Mark is, but we have his email address. Maybe you can get in touch that way."

I thought it was a long shot, but I reached out to him via email. To my surprise, he replied. I got him to chat with me over the Internet, but barely. I was trying to figure out how to engage him when I got the idea that telling him about Whitney might help.

I asked Whitney if I could share his story with Mark. At first he said no. "I don't even know Mark," he objected.

"I know," I explained, "but I think it could help him to hear what you went through and how well you're doing now."

He must have remembered his "talking to God" sense of responsibility because when I put it like that, he agreed instantly.

Whitney sat beside me and together we typed away on the keyboard, telling Mark about all the challenges we had overcome. Mark was drawn to the stories of how we had to fight the schoolteachers and administrators to get accommodations and a good educational plan for Whitney. He related to the idea of being misunderstood.

Mark was full of rage toward the establishment.

An unusually gifted artist, he attended a small community Catholic school where everyone was supposed to look alike—same haircut, same clothes. Mark told us that his art teacher, whom he liked and who taught his favorite class, felt his hair was too long and was on him to cut it. He acquiesced, and then she complained it was the wrong haircut. The faculty became so involved in whether or not he had the proper conformist hair style that he felt picked on and singled out, without any respect for his own personal choices as a seventeen-year-old. He was getting hassled even in art class, the only subject in which he was thriving.

Whitney felt a huge sense of injustice over the situation. As Mark was typing these stories about his school, it was almost hard for us to believe that a haircut could cause so much trouble.

In his other classes, Mark explained, everyone was telling him to "try harder." His teachers had humiliated him in front of his fellow students time and time again. He was tutored after school for years. He was kicked off the football team for poor grades. He did not know how to please authorities any more.

As Mark began to describe his symptoms, I suspected that he might have a communication problem. I was beginning to think that it was not that he did not want to follow their verbal reasoning—he *could* not do it. Mark's mother had shown me examples of his artwork from preschool. He had been accepted at the prestigious nationally recognized College of Art and Design as a youngster and taken art classes there throughout his youth. His artwork definitely signified a highly visual thinker.

Through our exchange, Mark softened and wanted to hear more about Whitney's experience. Whitney began, now in his own words, to tell Mark about his feelings about being in special ed and how kids made fun of him.

By now it was way past Whitney's bedtime. Although none of us wanted to stop this very powerful Internet chat, I had to draw it to a close. Mark agreed to come in to see me for an appointment at my office and we signed off. That night was special to all of us. It felt like a real turning point for Mark and Whitney both. It was the first, and one of the few, times that Whitney has been able to talk so openly and effectively about his disability; he felt proud that Mark recognized himself in his story. Mark says that Whitney's story inspired him and made him feel that he was not alone—if Whitney could overcome adversity, then so could he. Today, Mark is a successful senior in college majoring in computer graphics for Hollywood movies.

I think helping Mark made Whitney feel proud—that he had something unique to give. He was developing into a very generous, empathetic human being—quite a change from the disconnected child who did not seem to know we were people.

This experience seemed to spark something in him—a real desire to help others who might be facing the same problems he'd faced. He seemed to be understanding the feelings of others, something that is classically very difficult for autistic people. This was more evidence that his disease was not autism, but something else.

One day Whitney came home very upset. Most of the world wouldn't be able to tell if Whitney was troubled. He always seemed laid back, as though everything just rolled off of his shoulders, and he seldom cried. I'd come to notice the signs of distress—a blank look, distracted, pacing and talking to himself. On this day, he came home looking very dazed, like he was in shock. I asked him what was wrong.

"They called me 'retard' in class today so I told them I used to be deaf and have autism but now I'm O.K." He thought that since he'd been able to help Mark, maybe by telling these kids about his story, they'd understand him too.

"I told them you fixed my brain, Mom," he said. "And they laughed. They said, 'You can't fix deafness, you idiot. You are nuts.'" He was astonished. "They don't believe me, Mom! They said I was an idiot. I am an idiot! I hate myself!"

I saw red. Here was Whitney, being open and honest, and getting punished for it. How dare these kids be so hurtful!

"I'll ask the teacher if I can come teach a lesson on how the brain works, and we can explain it to them together."

I was trying to figure out if we could stay in that school or would we need to move. I thought the best way to assess the situation was to go into the classroom and be the teacher myself and see how I perceived the children's reactions to Whitney.

The teacher agreed, so I came in and asked all of the students to write on an index card a question about the brain they wanted answered.

I read through the index cards: "How does memory work?" "How do we dream?" "Is the brain like a computer?" I kept the questions for later. Then I started talking about Whitney.

"When Whitney was younger, he couldn't speak or hear," I said. I explained that I could scream in his ear and he could not hear me. I told them I thought his brain would go into overdrive to the degree that it heard too much—exterior sounds like the fire drill and even the blood going through his veins, his heart beating, would be way too loud for Whitney. I explained that it was this system overload that caused him to bang his head in frustration and made him shut down at times.

Then I played a tape of Madonna singing "I Am Going Bananas," by her character from the Dick Tracy movie. In this song, there is a lot of complex orchestration and Madonna sings with a Spanish accent, switching from English to Spanish to Yiddish to Latin. It is a very hard song to understand and the kids couldn't figure out what she was saying. I decoded it for them and had them write down the words as I dictated. Then I played the tape again, and this time they could hear the words much better.

I used this exercise to illustrate how the brain can filter what you hear. In this case, they needed to understand language, and also be able to focus their attention to understand what they were hearing. The kids were fascinated by learning about their ears. They took hearing for granted and had not considered that you could train your ears to work in a different way or that your "ear's zoom lens" could be taught to attend to small aspects of sounds. I was showing them, in elementary terms, how what Whitney was saying was true: We had trained his ears to work a different way so he could hear better. They were simulating what we had done to help Whitney improve.

The most effective part of the class was when I had Whitney teach the class how visual memory works. Whitney had them draw some pictures on their papers: a flower that was droopy, Colonel Sanders writing in a journal, a harbor with barber poles, some creatures in a classroom being taught by a teacher. Then Whitney told the kids to write "lazy daisy" under the flower, "Colonel's journals," "barber harbor" under the pier, and "creature teacher" from a puzzle we had from *GAMES* magazine. In all, we gave them ten drawings to copy and name. After studying them for a few minutes, the kids had to put away the drawings and try to remember the names and write them down. Whitney then asked the kids in turn who remembered by seeing the picture in their mind, and who heard the words. We explained how some of us think more in pictures, and some think more in words, and how Whitney was so strong in thinking in pictures that he was not able to hear until I taught him how to filter and focus on sounds. It was a rudimentary explanation, but it helped because we gave them examples of how these concepts worked in their own brains. We showed them pictures of me at the governor's mansion, with Oprah and Gary Collins on TV, on the cover of *USA Today,* and in newspaper and magazine stories for my prior work. The kids thought this was very cool.

Whitney passed out candy treats to each student as a reward for brain training. When the bell rang at the end of class, they clapped and I could see Whitney felt happy about the class and the response we got.

I had other concerns, however. Here I was in the middle of the day coming into the school to correct a situation that Mrs. Lud or Mr. Niemie would have never let happen. The teacher didn't stay to hear the class presentation. When the bell rang, I went to find her and tell her how it went. She told me she was worried about her large number of students and how it was hard to get to know each one individually. I watched all the kids pushing through the halls to get to their lockers and then to the buses. *This is not the right school for Whitney,* I thought. It was not just the special ed homeroom—it was too big and impersonal. I only had two years left to get him ready for high school. On his current course, I knew we were not looking at a shot at a good high school experience, nor were we anywhere close to him being a college-bound student.

I thought there might be a better high school solution for all of my kids. The next school year, Whitney would be going into seventh grade,

William into ninth, and Vanessa into tenth grade. Vanessa was attending ninth grade at Dublin's public high school but she didn't like how big it was. I wanted all of my kids to have the best education possible.

There was an excellent private high school in our area, Bishop Watterson High School. From my years of helping students who attended, I knew it had an excellent reputation for academics and it was very family-oriented.

My interest in Watterson intensified when I started working with an eighth-grade boy named Alex. His family wanted him to attend Watterson, but the administrators from his current school felt his skills were too deficient to succeed there. They felt he wasn't ready and it would be a disaster if he attended; he would be better served by going to public school, where he would have better access to special education. When I tested him, he had high visuals and low auditory processing scores. His parents were desperate to have him attend Watterson, and we worked intensely over a four-month period to see if we could bring his language skills up.

Alex brought his verbal scores up from below the first percentile to the fiftieth, eighty-fourth, and seventy-fifth in various areas. When we showed Watterson's principal, Ms. Hutson, Alex's reevaluation results, she agreed to let him give Watterson a try. The true triumph came with his first report card—he earned a 3.5 GPA.

I'd been so impressed with Ms. Hutson's belief in a solution that was outside the box and with the leadership she had shown in many situations over the years, that I decided her school was where my kids should go—hopefully even Whitney. In spite of my determined pronouncements that Whitney was going to MIT, I was still worried that a school like Watterson and college were unreachable goals for Whitney. I thought if I was able to figure out how to help Whitney in the way I'd helped Alex, maybe it could work. Granted Whitney was a more extreme case, but the issues were similar. Both of these boys had high visual and low verbal scores on their testing. Whitney was more impaired, but he was processing information more fluently through his verbal pathways day by day.

William and Vanessa knew of Watterson from other kids who went there and were excited about the idea of attending this school. Watterson had a great sports program that appealed to both of them—but especially William. He was eager to go to a school highly ranked for his favorite sports: wrestling and football. And I liked that the school had a great college placement record. Most of all the parents were very involved in this school, and that was what I wanted very much.

That year, Vanessa and William did very well on the entrance exams and were accepted.

The solution for what to do for Whitney's next two years, so that he would get the attention he needed to be able to get into Watterson, came from Marion Hutson, who introduced me to Sally Lindsay, a former English teacher who was now the principal of a small private school near Watterson called Clintonville Academy. I realized that Clintonville would be a great place to prepare Whitney for Watterson. In fact, it was one of Watterson's feeder schools.

In the spring of his sixth grade year, Whitney had to take a series of tests to get into this private school. The faculty was proud of the fact that many if not most of the children were scoring about two or more years above grade level on standardized testing. Whitney did a good job with his reading and math entrance tests, but his writing fluency and his handwriting were significantly behind. Nevertheless, the teachers who tested him stated that they found Whitney to be totally engaging and intellectually curious. Mrs. Lindsay felt we would be very happy there, specifically because the student–teacher ratio was 10 to 1, which would give Whitney a lot of individual attention. The school also had a superb LD tutor and a great English teacher who, working together, would set improving Whitney's writing skills as a primary target goal.

By the end of Whitney's sixth grade year at Grizelle, I had as patients six college students referred to me by various sources. They were all failing colleges located in different parts of the country. They had all

tested as high visual, low auditory processing cases. These college
kids were desperate and depressed from so much failure. I realized I
could learn a lot about this phenomenon and the best ways to treat
it from these older patients because they were better able to explain
their experiences than my child patients. I was excited to work with
them since I saw a real similarity between their problems and Whitney's. The connection might have been obscure to others because
these students hadn't struggled with handicaps throughout their lives;
in fact, they'd all done very well in high school. Their parents thought
their problems were that they were partying or not working hard.
But the imbalance of the verbal and visual scores indicated to me
that their problems were much more similar to Whitney's than they
appeared to be.

I had an idea for creating a summer school plan to help these students improve their skills enough so that they could be readmitted to
their respective colleges. I knew my plan would mean getting these college kids very involved in our lives over the summer, so I started laying
out my new ideas to Vanessa, William, and Whitney. I wanted to enroll
the college students in a summer course at OSU—and I thought we
should take the class with them to teach them how to think and process
information in the verbal world. They could help me figure out what
skills the college students needed and what was causing them to flunk
out. I thought Whitney in particular would be good at this, because his
problems in the classroom were likely similar to these students': difficulty following spoken instructions and lectures; difficulty communicating and taking in information; difficulty with reading recall,
memory for test-taking, and participating correctly in class.

My ulterior motive for involving my kids was to see if Whitney could
find a way to harness his visual skills for classroom lecture learning—
or if he needed to learn other skills, and if so, what. I thought working
with the college kids would help William and Vanessa get ready for
college and figure out what kind of things they would need to learn
ahead of time, too.

"Cool," Whitney said. He had already met several of these college kids and he had hit it off with them—and vice versa. They seemed to have an instant understanding of one another, as if they were recognizing kindred spirits. I'd noticed that they all seemed to speak in a kind of shorthand that I couldn't always follow. They would speak in partial sentences that, to them, were clear as a bell. They understood each other, and Whitney understood these conversations too. I needed more words to follow what they were talking about. They were also all attracted to what things looked like, and talked a lot about their experiences in terms of visual memory.

Vanessa liked the college kids so she was enthusiastic too. William, who was looking forward to a summer of football training with Todd, wasn't interested in sitting in a classroom though. I thought this was fair enough and assured him he could stick to his summer football plans.

With everyone on board for this plan, I researched what might be the most verbal class on campus at OSU during summer school and chose Philosophy 101 taught by Dr. Diana Raffman. I suspected this class would really challenge the students' visual/verbal abilities.

I hypothesized that unharnessed associational thinking had caused the college students to flunk out of school. I had observed that visual people have a superior ability to think in associations. In fact, those with very high visuals make associations so quickly that they often leave the rest of us in the dust. It is a great skill to have; but it can also cause problems if a person doesn't know how to harness it.

An example of this occurred recently in a group I run called Communication Partners. Here, patients practice with nonpatients such as parents, teachers, friends, or observers. Whitney was sitting in with the other young people as a practice partner.

"Tell me about one of the scariest things that ever happened to you," I asked them.

Brett, the older brother of one of my patients who was visiting to learn about his sister's disorder, said, "I shot a BB gun into the TV set by accident."

"For a couple of weeks, our car door would always fly off when we were driving until we got another car," Whitney said.

"I am going to marry a doctor," said Sheila, smiling.

"What?" Whitney asked. "Why is that scary?"

"He is handsome and I have on a beautiful white dress with pearls all over it . . ."

Brett interrupted, "What are you talking about, Sheila?"

She looked as if she'd been shaken out of a dream. "Huh?" she said. Her feelings were hurt. "The wedding. I am walking down the aisle to see my husband."

Tracing back her train of thought, we discovered that Sheila had heard the part of Brett's story about the BB gun and then she saw herself go to the emergency room, meet a handsome doctor, and now she was getting married—and we were being invited into the movie in her mind.

Whitney laughed with recognition. "I do that all the time!"

Sheila was engaging in associational thinking. Most people have balanced visual and auditory processing and therefore do some visual thinking. They switch back and forth between associational and sequential thinking, depending on what's more appropriate for the problem they are solving. The shift happens subconsciously. I happen to have high auditory processing (meaning I'm a verbal thinker) and very low visual processing skills. I don't tend to think in associations; instead, I think in sequences. Many of the high visual patients I see think primarily in associations rather than sequences. They are two different systems, and when someone uses one more than the other to an extreme, it can make that person feel out of whack with the rest of the world. I believe that many forms of miscommunication and misunderstanding arise when people of different styles interact without realizing the other person is actually thinking—processing information—in a completely different way.

To figure out how to help these students learn to harness their visual/associational thinking and build their verbal/sequencing thinking, I thought about how to explain what their "problem" or "syndrome" was. Since they were in the ninety-ninth percentile in one system and zero in the other, I coined the name "Maverick Minds" to describe their syndrome. I told them they had an asset-liability. "Your asset—your visual brain—may actually be the reason your verbal brain is underdeveloped. Your visual brain's overly high performance may be overpowering the auditory pathway, preventing information from being processed and thus hindering development of your verbal brain. You are not in the middle of the bell curve, you are outliers—you are what I have decided to call Mavericks, Maverick Minds. You may have a handicap but it is because you have genius gifts in another area."

This was the beginning of a more formal approach, and a name, for the kind of practice I was developing: one that helps high visuals, Mavericks, build up their lagging auditory system.

The experiment with this class was to see if I could teach the Mavericks to harness their associational thinking—and see if this improved their ability to function in school, in turn alleviating their depression. The goal was to teach these college-age kids how to think verbally in an intensely verbal class that required very dense and difficult listening, speaking, reading, and writing skills. Could they turn off their picture thinking and operate in a verbal land as verbal thinkers?

Most of the visual mavericks could not imagine turning off their picture thinking. They thought that an impossibility.

"But I never see the picture in my head. I hear a voice," I tried to explain. "Besides, we don't want to get rid of the visual pathway for thinking. We at first want to harness it so that we can use it to teach the verbal system to activate. We will use the visual thinking pathway to cue up the verbal system. Then once we have the verbal pathway working with visual support, we will then turn the visuals off so that the verbal pathway will work on its own."

They seemed skeptical, but agreed to try.

As I drove to OSU that first summer Monday morning, one of my mental voices said, "You are crazy. What do you think you are doing?

You have these students' hopes up that they can learn to be verbal in a college class. On top of that, you are convinced this will help Whitney!"

I realized I was taking a huge risk. I'd be working with a very discerning group of patients and parents. The college kids were really a complex bunch. Many of the parents were wealthy, powerful, and nationally influential.

The huge lecture hall had seating for seven hundred, but the class had only sixty people in it. Tiny five-foot-tall, ninety-pound Dr. Raffman stood at the front of the auditorium speaking a mile a minute. A Yale graduate, she kept joking about people from Columbus. She often lost her train of thought and asked, "Now, what was I talking about?"

I could feel the college students drowning. I continued to take volumes of notes. Whitney was trying to imitate me, as was Vanessa. The Maverick college kids sat there doing nothing, looking like they were in pain and lost.

After class, I introduced myself to Dr. Raffman. The students were signed up for credit and grades, but I was sitting in without permission and so were Vanessa and Whitney.

I explained briefly what I was doing and we made a date to discuss my project further the next day.

The students, the kids, and I went to lunch to discuss the class. As we sat down, I said, "Only Whitney and Vanessa took notes today. Why didn't any of you?"

"We can't."

"Why not?" There was not one word on their papers.

Ginger said, "I don't see how you can listen, understand what she is saying, and write at the same time. I am still trying to figure out what she is talking about and you have pages of writing."

Whitney said, "If you start writing, you will understand better."

I said, "Whitney is right."

Jed objected. "We can't do this. Why don't you just have us highlight someone else's notes afterwards?" He had big expressive eyes, and was very artistic. You just didn't want to disappoint him, and this had probably made it easy for him to get through high school, but now he was in deep trouble. He was estranged from his family after a ton of terrible screw-ups, and he felt this was his only hope.

"No. We are not going to review later; we are going to learn it the first time it is said. This is what you need to learn," I said firmly. They continued to argue. I finally said, "I got As in college and you got Fs. Let's do it my way and see what happens."

The next day at lunch I explained to Dr. Raffman my theory of high visual and low verbal skills and how it was based on what I thought was Whitney's extreme case of this. I explained that I suspected that Whitney's autistic symptoms had actually been a problem with his auditory processing system. She had studied linguistics and autism as a philosopher and was interested in this theory, so she welcomed our participation in her class.

I asked her what study guides she used.

"None. I don't organize my lectures, I build them from discussion with the students, building from their thoughts until they understand the concepts. That is the way you make a philosopher. They need to learn the thinking system of logical analysis and verbal reasoning. I pride myself on the fact that this course is arguably the most difficult thinking class at Ohio State University!"

As I listened to her talk about her teaching approach, I felt the anxiety churning in my stomach. I knew this would be challenging for anyone—for the Mavericks it could be nearly impossible to try to find order in a sea of words. *What had I gotten us into?*

One blessing was that Dr. Raffman moved the class to a smaller room because she hated that lack of intimacy of so few people in a huge auditorium. The new room was a room I had actually taught in years before. We all were more comfortable in the more intimate setting.

I told the Mavericks they were to imitate my note-taking—they sat beside me and Vanessa so they could see how we took notes, and we compared our notes after class. I made up a note-taking method, based on work of B. F. Skinner, where the students learned how to make test questions while they were listening. When they finished a two-and-a-half-hour lecture, they had turned the teacher's declarative sentences into interrogatives. By taking notes in this way, the students went from being passive to active listeners.

So if the teacher said that we were going to cover three central themes in the class, they might write on their paper:

3 THEMES

1. art vs.   pornography
2. the mind   brain and soul
3. when is abortion   moral

Then, folding the paper in half later, they could test themselves by filling in the missing part. This technique of making listening and note-taking very interactive not only helped the students learn the material the first time, it helped sustain attention as the "zoom lens" for working memory and for creating word files.

I organized the experience so that we worked on listening during week one; listening plus speaking week two; listening, speaking, and writing week three; and listening, speaking, writing, and finally reading week four.

Week one passed while we worked on listening and note-taking. The second week Dr. Raffman called on Jed.

I met Jed after working with his sister. He had flunked out of a university in Georgia in the spring at the conclusion of his freshman year. He was a very artistic kid who had always been told to "try harder" and had great grades until his senior year, when he'd started rebelling: he'd stolen his friend's car radio as a prank and the friend's father had pressed charges. He'd gotten so mad at his parents for riding him that he moved into a family friend's house and did not attend his high school graduation.

In class, Dr. Raffman asked Jed to explain the meaning of ambiguity. Jed said, "It is the difference between the mind and the soul." This wasn't the answer. She asked the question again, and again Jed answered exactly as he had before. She asked again, and again he repeated his answer. Then Whitney piped up with the correct answer, that ambiguity meant that a word could mean two or more things. Dr. Raffman said, "Good job, Whitney, that is right."

A girl sitting behind me said, "Hey, that kid is answering and he is going to make us all look bad." I smiled—here was Whitney thinking along with the college students.

At the break Jed looked upset. "Why did Dr. Raffman turn mean?" he asked.

"What are you talking about?" I asked.

"I kept answering her and she just kept asking the same question like she hadn't heard me."

The other Mavericks agreed that she seemed mean, asking him the question over and over. I explained that what he'd answered had nothing to do with her question, so that was why she continued to ask the question. Jed somehow made an association from her lecture that led him to think about the mind and the soul. He thought he was answering her question. The fact that she just kept asking it was mean.

He was amazed. He said he always got frustrated when he thought the teachers were insulting the students. Now he was starting to grasp that maybe it wasn't meanness, but a communication mishap. This was an example of the associational thinking I'd suspected was a big cause of their problem. The Mavericks mishear things and then, convinced they are answering correctly, don't understand why people react in ways they perceive as unfair.

As the course continued, I had the parents go to class with us to see what we were doing. The Mavericks went to office hours every day with the teaching assistant and once a week with Dr. Raffman. They wrote weekly philosophy papers and turned them in ahead of time to the T.A. for critique; then they rewrote their papers as recommended before turning them in for grading. They wrote test questions prior to weekly tests and reviewed the questions in office hours before the real tests.

At the same time, we were doing therapy to build a verbal architecture in their brains. They had therapy for four hours each day, plus their study groups and meetings with the professor. Whitney and Vanessa helped with their therapy. I spent the evenings after they left figuring out what they were missing and building exercises to strengthen the problems areas. Each one had different issues he or she needed to address. It was an all-consuming experiment and much more complicated than I expected. As a result of all the training, they became able to turn off their visual brains for these lectures and use the verbal pathway exclusively for learning. They got the highest grades in the class. That class changed their lives. They went from believing that Dr. Raffman was a mean, disorganized teacher to the best teacher they'd ever had. Now they had the tools to succeed in college. Everyone learned how to think and engage in verbal reasoning—including Whitney and Vanessa.

Meanwhile, while we'd been in summer school, William had been playing football with Todd and going to football and wrestling camps. He'd begun to resent the Mavericks being around so much and taking so much time.

"We need our own lives back!" he complained. "This is too much. They are eating out of our refrigerator and making a mess in our house. I hate the Mavericks. *We're* your kids, not them."

"They're teaching us how to fix Whitney's brain," I explained.

"Please be patient. There's still a lot of progress he needs to make before ninth grade."

While this course had revealed that Whitney had the thinking capacity for college, he still didn't have a lot of the language skills that would be required to communicate his thoughts adequately. As a visual thinker, he could participate and thrive in a difficult class at OSU—but his speaking and writing were still severely off the mark.

When the philosophy class ended in July, we started working on his writing and speaking skills; it was time to get ready for Clintonville Academy. There would be no special ed classes there; but there would also be no more safety net.

It was times like this, when we were about to leap off another cliff, that I had moments of panic and self-doubt, wondering if I wanted too much, too soon for Whitney. Whitney wanted to be out of special ed, but I knew that a lot of that was because he had internalized my constant refusal to allow him to be treated differently. This summer he'd vaulted from special ed to Maverick.

I hoped there'd be no crash landing.

15

Never-Never

Land

We had another big project going on that summer before Whitney started seventh grade at Clintonville. With Whitney at Clintonville and Vanessa and William at nearby Watterson, I'd decided it would be best to move closer to both schools to make the commute easier and so the kids would live near their classmates. Vanessa began looking on the Internet for houses for sale in the area. William scanned the newspaper, clipping out ads and highlighting others. But Whitney announced that he wanted nothing to do with the decision. "You pick the house and I'll just live there."

"Why are you saying that, Whitney?" I asked.

"Because I have no feelings, Mom. I don't care."

"What do you mean?" I asked, wondering why he would say such a thing.

"I don't feel things like other people, like sadness, happiness, anger. I just don't feel," he insisted.

"You mean like Mr. Spock on *Star Trek?*" I queried.

"Yeah," he answered seriously.

I decided to challenge him. "That's not true. If I died, wouldn't you be sad?"

"No," Whitney said matter-of-factly. "I would just need to get my stuff done and someone else would take care of me instead of you."

He was being so honest about what he was saying that I knew he wasn't intending to hurt my feelings. But that didn't stop me from feeling crushed. I love my children more than life itself—and here my youngest was telling me that whether I existed or not was irrelevant. A part of me felt, *Hey, wait a minute, after sacrificing for you, you feel no gratitude and I mean nothing to you?*

But the scientist in me was perplexed and curious because I had seen Whitney experience a range of emotions. He got angry and frustrated. And he could be incredibly empathetic and sensitive to what was happening with other people. To hear him say he didn't feel anything struck me as not quite right. Was he unable to register his feelings? Did he feel them in the moment and then not remember them? What was it like for him?

I had read that the well-known autistic doctor Temple Grandin said that people thought from her reactions to her surroundings that she didn't have feelings because her emotional reaction to events seldom matched others'—her response was not "typical." I'd observed a similar phenomenon in many of my patients. Sometimes they had strong reactions to situations or comments that would not strike the average person as noteworthy. Then again, there were times when, like Whitney, they were totally oblivious to others' emotions. For example, they often commented on not understanding why audiences got scared or cried in certain parts of a movie.

One of them said, "I went to see *Titanic* the movie and my friend was crying at parts that I didn't think were sad, and then the parts I thought were sad she didn't."

The other Mavericks had similar stories of having different reactions to films from verbal family members or friends. I hypothesized that the Mavericks tended to pick up on visual cues for their emotional

reactions while verbal people reacted to words. The visual and auditory systems are sensory systems. People who are operating above the
ninety-ninth percentile in one of the sensory thinking pathways may
feel things much more intensely than others but react to things that
other people find ordinary.

Maybe the Mavericks'—and Whitney's—lack of feelings was really
a problem with the regulation of feelings: they over- or underreacted in
various situations. Seeing an obvious disparity between his own feeling
states and those he was observing in others made Whitney think he had
no feelings. Perhaps it wasn't that he had no feelings—he just had the
"wrong" ones at the wrong time. I decided to watch Whitney closely in
emotional situations while I pondered this further.

Meanwhile, after a long search (involving everyone in the family and
primarily my father, the engineer in the family), we found a home that
was laid out beautifully and located conveniently to not only a nature
preserve but a very quaint old-world shopping area as well. We all loved
it—even Whitney. There was only one problem. Because the house
needed major renovations, we weren't able to move in until the end of
September. The timing wasn't great—I'd really wanted to be settled
before the school year started.

Just before Whitney was to start at Clintonville Academy, I took him
with me on a consulting trip to Vermont. I was going to see Patrick, a
young boy who was struggling with school and also having some social
problems because of his weak auditory processing.

Whitney spoke to a small group, consisting of some of the school
faculty, as well as to Patrick and his father about his experience and
how he'd overcome so many of his disabilities. The school faculty was
interested, but it was Patrick and his father who really identified with
Whitney's story. Once again, there was an uncanny sense of recognition and bonding that occurred between Whitney and these visual
thinkers.

Patrick's father was a cardiologist, and I was starting to realize that many doctors were visual thinkers. The visual brain is an excellent thinking system that doesn't require words. The visual thinking pathway is in many ways a far superior thinking engine than the verbal one—but only for thinking. We still need to be able to communicate what we are thinking. I was seeing more medical students in my practice—students who had always done well in school, but who began to struggle when they got to a point in their studies where they had to communicate with patients or quote reading material, rather than work with their hands or solve problems at home during homework, when they had time to plan the verbal component carefully.

We made a special arrangement to work further with Patrick, and in fact, Whitney would prove helpful in creating some long-distance therapy, using email, our teleconferencing center, and Internet chats. His teachers agreed that Patrick could go to the tutoring center twice a week and do therapy on the phone with Mavericks, Whitney, and me in Ohio.

I decided to stop in New York City on the way home from Vermont as a treat for Whitney. I wanted to extend this special one-on-one time together, and I thought Whitney would love all that New York City had to offer. As Whitney and I sat at a small table at the famed Algonquin Hotel, we were riveted to a cabaret singer performing "Never-Never Land." Whitney recognized the song from hearing our video recording of Mary Martin as Peter Pan, and I felt it was providence that it was the first number of the evening. I felt as if I was in Never-Never Land with Whitney that day. The very fact that he could hear the song was wonder enough, but the past few days we'd spent together had shown me a new side of Whitney—a boy who was growing into a man in spite of the odds against him.

I'd never been on a trip with Whitney alone before and I was amazed at how much fun we were having. Trips with Whitney up until then had always been hectic family events—and usually we'd been chasing after him or worried about losing him. I knew he was no longer at the stage where he'd run off on his own, but I'd had no idea if he'd be moody or talkative, withdrawn or interested in doing things. When we arrived in New York, we discovered that the airline lost our luggage. The airline gave us a clothes voucher and we decided to spend it all on Whitney. At the Gap, the sales people made a big fuss over him, outfitting him from head to toe. Whitney told them of our plans to go to Ellis Island, the Algonquin, Broadway shows, the top of the Marriott Marquis, and about the other sights in New York City he wanted to see. To hear Whitney talk with such animation about doing so many things was astounding. Here he was, unfazed by the lost luggage (certainly a major upset of routine), enjoying the connection to these strangers, and forecasting the wonderful weekend he was to have. I enjoyed seeing how social he was, and how interested he was in carrying on adult conversations. Maybe it was time to stop thinking of him as the little kid we were always worrying about.

At Ellis Island, Whitney was a fountain of information, due to his intense hunger to learn anything and everything about history. We walked slowly through the exhibits, Whitney studying every minute detail. He didn't want to miss one artifact or skip reading one sign. He was explaining everything to me and elaborating on all that he was absorbing. He was enjoying every minute.

I was never more impressed with his gigantic thirst for knowledge. Here was a child who could not remember the first seven years of his life now hell-bent on learning everything he possibly could. It was as if he was trying to catch up.

Whitney was the perfect travel companion for hyperactive me. We rode tour buses around the city to take in all the sights. We ate at the Plaza and roamed through FAO Schwarz looking for presents for Vanessa and William. We spent a long time down at the harbor and wandered along Wall Street. We discovered Sam's, a café on 45th Street near all the shows, where show people, wannabes, and actors spontaneously get up and sing at the piano bar. It was so much fun to hear the tunes we had listened to over and over for all those years driving around in the car, trying to get Whitney to sing along, now being sung by actors right in front of us.

Whitney was up for anything and everything. He really loved the city that never sleeps and neither of us wanted to miss a minute. A few years ago I couldn't have imagined that he could be such an enthusiastic and wonderful travel companion. I didn't want the trip to end.

"America, America, God shed his grace on thee . . ." More than a hundred kids age five to fourteen strained to hit the right notes as the teachers pulled the song along, and I felt a lump in my throat. It was early morning and I was standing at the back of the cafeteria at Clintonville listening to Whitney and his new schoolmates wrap up their morning assembly. It was a Clintonville tradition to start the day with an assembly in the cafeteria. The principal, Mrs. Lindsay, would make announcements and celebrate birthdays, and the meeting would end with a good-morning song. I loved to walk Whitney into the building and stay through the opening ceremonies.

Clintonville was a huge step. It was yet another new school for Whitney—but the biggest change was that he was no longer in any special ed classes at all. Clintonville didn't have special ed, but I'd felt that the small size would provide the extra attention he needed. I'd finally gotten what I wanted for him, and now I found myself tossing and turning at night over whether he could do it. Had I done the right thing, getting him so mainstreamed? Clintonville prided itself on having students that test on average a year or two above grade level. It was a tiny private school. Whitney would be in a class of twelve seventh-graders. I thought that with this much attention, he would be able to really focus on his writing and improve it enough to qualify for admission to Watterson. I was hoping that with the principal and the individual attention such a school offered, we could correct Whitney's learning problems completely before ninth grade.

Right from the beginning, Whitney was having trouble keeping track of his assignments. At Grizelle, the entire school used the same system for giving assignments and they had a homework hot line. Although changing classes had been difficult for him, this system had at least provided a consistent pattern for Whitney to learn.

At Clintonville, each teacher had her own system for giving assignments, and Whitney was lost. Whitney thinks in the big picture and not in sequential details. He had papers and note cards everywhere. He was getting in trouble for not doing his homework assignments, though he had only misplaced it.

"Whitney, we go through this at the beginning of every school year. Mrs. Lindsay told me I can work with Mrs. Springer, the tutor, and see what we can come up with to help you. Don't worry."

Whitney was quiet for a moment, then he looked at me and said, "Mom, I am too old for you to come into the school and work with my teachers. Please let me work this out myself."

I was about to argue but the look on his face stopped me. Granted, he was at the age when kids typically begin to be embarrassed by their parents. A seventh grader didn't want to be seen with his parents at the movies or in public, let alone have his mother in school helping him with his schoolwork. But this was something more than adolescent embarrassment. He seemed determined. Maybe his wanting to handle this problem on his own was a step in the right direction.

I offered a compromise. "I'll bring you and Mrs. Springer lunch every Friday and check on your work. If there is no problem, I'll stop coming. But if there continue to be problems, I will come until they are fixed. OK?"

He grudgingly agreed.

When I came the first Friday, Whitney and Mrs. Springer were working together smoothly on writing a paper about *Animal Farm,* an assigned book he had read for English class.

Whitney smiled and insisted that my services were no longer needed. Mrs. Springer agreed they could work it out themselves. I smiled inwardly thinking, *Wouldn't this be wonderful?*

On the other hand, suddenly my school involvement came to an abrupt halt. It was an odd adjustment for me. It was what I'd worked toward, but at the same time it was very hard to trust and let go of watching what was going on with Whitney in school. As I walked to the car that day, I glimpsed my mom job coming to an end. I had a premonition of the kids all going off to college and suddenly being on my own. I realized my life built around the kids would have to change. It was an odd and painful state: Whitney was at the point where I was no longer needed to hover around at his school, a sign of success but which also left me feeling a sense of loss.

Commuting from our new home in Worthington to my office in Dublin, combined with dropping the kids off at school and picking them up, was turning into a hassle. The traffic between Worthington and Dublin was terrible, and commuting time was very unpredictable, varying from thirty minutes to two hours due to road construction.

Also, I wanted to be closer to their schools so I could attend school events without taking a half-day off from work. As a result, I began to consider moving my practice to our new home. I thought of our new basement, which was now just a gravel floor. I'd always had very creative office spaces—finding ways to make the space visually interesting, conducive to doing mentally challenging work, while also creating an inviting, supportive atmosphere that allowed people to feel safe and comfortable and willing to take risks. It would be a challenge to turn the basement into such a space. I wasn't sure how professional a home office would seem to my patients. But what I really wanted to do was subspecialize in the Maverick patients. Having my office in my home would help us financially as I moved to seeing this subtype of patient only.

I was anxious to increase my work with the Mavericks so I could continue to fine-tune and refine Whitney's progress. I was now interested in how to help him grow into an emotionally and psychologically mature adult. And I was convinced that working with other Mavericks would help show me the way.

I had six more months on the lease for the Dublin office and had scouted out a new office nearby in Worthington, but the idea of working out of our home was becoming more and more appealing. When I broached the possibility with the kids at dinner one night, William protested loudly. "No, no, no!" he objected. "I don't want your clinic in our basement—I want a home. Please, Mom, don't do this."

Although it would be more cost-efficient, I thought I would appeal to William with a benefit for him. "I'll have more time to run over to school to see your sports and other activities," I pointed out.

"I don't want to come home from school and have patients in my house," he insisted.

Whitney and Vanessa didn't mind and tried to convince William along with me. "We go to her office all the time anyway—what's the difference?" Vanessa said.

William ran upstairs and punched a big hole in the dry wall by the bathroom. "Can't we have any privacy?" he shouted. "No patients in the house!"

My punishment for such behavior is what the kids call my classic "write me a note" line. I find that the best way to discipline my children is to have them write down their version of the story before we discuss it. This gives them a chance to get their message out uninterrupted, and also forces them to think through their actions and realize at least some of their responsibility for the consequences. It also helps for me to read their point of view without getting into a verbal argument about who did or said what. I seldom punish my kids with traditional things like taking away privileges. To me, the point of punishment is to decrease the chance of the behavior occurring again, and I've found it effective to confront it in this way.

William's response to this incident made me see that he needed a boundary between himself and my work. I'd thought it was fun to have the Mavericks around. There was a part of me that felt that now that the kids were almost grown, this might be the next stage of my career—a way to return to my prior life as a research scientist and study the Maverick brain. But I began to see that William felt like they were overrunning our lives.

He knew I was planning another summer college class for the struggling college students, as well as high school seniors who wanted a head start on going to college. To him, that meant a lot of Mavericks in the house during summer vacation. I proposed that I see patients in a basement office during the day while he was at school, and then for after-school appointments, I would see them in Dublin for the next six months. "If we don't like it, I will get another office when the lease runs out," I promised.

William finally agreed. I decided I would only see patients Whitney's age or older, with very rare exceptions. Younger kids would have to be genius visual Mavericks for me to take them, and parents would have to be in therapy with them.

In the end, we've found having the office in the basement to be a huge advantage. We made it separate enough that it didn't feel like they were in our home, and because it cut down on commuting time, I was actually home more, and more available to my kids than before. William came to appreciate this.

I couldn't stop thinking about how Whitney's emotions were tied into his language and communication issues. When I thought back, I noted that it wasn't until Whitney gained language that he began to demonstrate emotions. And it was only recently that he was beginning to show a range of emotions.

I thought about this in terms of other patients who'd had more severe sensory impairment. I'd always known that when auditory problems improved, people were able to identify more of their emotions. I'd assumed this was because they improved their ability to identify and communicate about those emotions. But maybe it was more than that.

Maybe we were creating a sensory integration with the brain-building work we were doing. And now that Whitney's auditory and visual processing systems were becoming more integrated, he might have more access to understanding his emotions.

Todd's assistant, Melinda, was an interesting example of this. She was severely hearing impaired; she had sensory neural hearing loss in both ears from birth. She needed to wear two hearing aids to hear anything, but she hated them and went about most of her life not hearing much of anything. When Todd started working with me, he'd suggested that Melinda and I barter—she'd train Vanessa in exchange for some sessions with me. So we began working on her auditory processing each week.

Melinda thought her hearing problem was just a matter of physical volume—she just had trouble hearing. On audiometric testing without her hearing aids, I could crank the audiometer up to 90 decibels and she heard nothing. I didn't think I could teach her to hear, but I figured I could teach her to process language better, including listening, reading, writing, and speaking.

I told her that there are two pathways for information to get to the brain: via the eyes or the ears. One of her biggest concerns was her inability to remember what she read. (She had gotten so frustrated with this, she told me, that she'd taken all of her books from expensive seminars she had attended and thrown them in the Dumpster one day.)

When I tested her auditory processing, even correcting for her hearing problem, she was well below the first percentile on all the auditory processing tests. I began by playing just a sentence or two and stopping the tape recorder. I would say, "What was just said?"

She couldn't repeat it. I'd ask, "Did you hear it?"

"Yes, but I don't know what it was."

"I couldn't do it at *all*," Melinda recalls. "Even if I thought I was following the story, I couldn't repeat a word of it."

This is a common experience for patients with auditory processing problems, and it is incredibly frustrating. They think I am tricking them, or giving them extra hard tests on purpose.

But Melinda was disciplined and worked hard in our sessions and on her own. For two years, we worked on her auditory processing. She trained her brain to be able to hear. After therapy, with her hearing aids in she was better able to talk on her cell phone, she could take messages off voice mail, and functioned better as a hearing person. When we started, her visual thinking skills tested at genius levels while her auditory scores were well below the first percentile. After one year, upon retesting, her auditory scores ranged from the seventy-fifth to ninety-sixth percentiles, significantly above the average of fiftieth percentile.

In Whitney's and Melinda's cases, I believe there were organic problems with the ear-to-brain connection, which caused processing problems, which in turn caused the behavioral and communication problems (to varying degrees—severe autism symptoms in Whitney's case, communication problems and emotional disconnect in Melinda's). By building an effective verbal pathway for thinking and processing verbal ideas, we were learning that, just as Dr. Cantwell predicted, the emotional, behavioral, and communication problems were resolving.

I was struck by the emotion issue in Melinda's case. When we first started therapy, Melinda was a very angry person. As she says, "I felt only two emotions: pissed or happy on a 90 to 10 ratio. I didn't know sadness, I didn't know how to identify frustration . . . all I felt was pissed."

About six months into therapy, she started crying during a session. She came to me and said, "I don't know what's happening. I feel scared. I feel sad . . ."

As she was able to hear better, she was able to understand her feelings better. This was similar to the way Whitney's connectedness to the world and his emotionality improved as his language and communication skills improved. Perhaps Melinda's improved verbal abilities allowed all of her senses to integrate and therefore she was able to regulate and modulate thoughts and feelings concomitantly. Or maybe she was succeeding as a communicator, and that allowed her to develop more effective coping and defense mechanisms to manage the roller coaster of feelings that Mavericks experience. Maybe her increased ability to express her feelings to others permitted her to give her feelings a home, and thus she could understand them better. All of these ideas seemed plausible to me. Regardless, I saw a definite parallel between Melinda and Whitney in terms of how they increasingly experienced and expressed feelings.

Whitney was thriving at Clintonville. His teachers told me he was very vocal with all of his classmates about how he'd been in special ed up until this year. I was touched that he was proud of his progress and eager to explain how hard he'd worked to get better, rather than hide it or feel stigmatized by the disabilities he'd overcome. I had concerns, though. It was great when he shared his story with people who knew and understood him, but I feared his openness would make him vulnerable to naysayers or people who neither knew him nor had seen his progress.

I watched for repercussions, but his enthusiasm and his intent to help others seemed to be helping him socially; it also gave him a sense of drive and purpose.

When Marion Hutson asked me to give a fall workshop for the Watterson teachers to explain my work, I did not want to include Whitney for a variety of reasons. Remembering what had happened to him in sixth grade, I thought his story was better left out. Instead, I asked the Maverick high school and college students, and some of their CEO parents, to help with practice labs so the teachers could rotate through the labs and have hands-on experience. The Mavericks agreed to participate but only if Whitney would be the first speaker. They reasoned that no one would believe that they were just not trying hard enough unless Whitney spoke first and explained how he had overcome his problems. Whitney's successes were their inspiration, they pleaded. Whitney wanted to do it, so I asked Mrs. Lindsay, his principal, to open the workshop with him. I had about twenty of my patients sitting in the front two rows to provide Whitney with support for his opening remarks. Whitney matter-of-factly laid out his history: "I was diagnosed with autism and I had a serious hearing problem. I did not start talking until I was in first grade, and now I go to Clintonville Academy."

Mrs. Lindsay explained how Whitney was now a superior thinker with very insightful and complex thoughts, but his verbal skills for test taking were not as developed as they needed to be. She continued to describe how we developed a plan to make his school day support his visual thinking while we worked on improving his language skills. The teachers seemed to find Whitney's story incredible. Mrs. Lindsay quoted from Whitney's records about how severe his problems had been in school and how throughout this difficulty, he'd had very strong visual skills. She made an impassioned case for how learning about Whitney's story might well help at-risk students at Watterson.

Next was Ginger, and I stood by the podium with her. I knew she was nervous but I watched proudly as she spoke with poise, explaining that although she was a cheerleader, won poetry contests, and her days and evenings had been packed with academic and extracurricular activities, she had learned nothing in high school. She realized this when she got to OSU—facing the demands of college without her very supporting and nurturing home had overwhelmed her. The amount of reading and listening to lectures had increased dramatically and she'd begun to fall behind. Her old strategies of asking teachers to allow her to do extra credit and studying materials over and over again were not working. She was afraid of flunking out, when she learned about my therapy from another student who was a patient of mine.

At that moment, there was a rustling in the audience, and Ginger and I noticed that all of the Mavericks seated in the front turned and looked behind them. When they turned back, they looked upset.

After Ginger finished, Dr. Raffman jumped up and spoke about the philosophy class everyone had taken. I could tell she was trying to take command as she explained how far the Mavericks had come in her class. I was dying to know what had happened in the audience, but I had to play emcee until it was time for a break.

The minute we broke, one of the high school kids ran up to me and said, "We need to go in the library and talk." While walking to the library, she told me that right in the middle of Ginger's speech, one of the teachers had said, "Bull. This workshop is a bunch of bull."

I was stunned. When I walked into the library, the Maverick students were sitting there looking downcast. They wanted to go home. No one wanted to continue. "Why should we tell our stories when people are going to accuse us of lying?" I didn't know what to do.

I understood how they felt, but I didn't want them to leave. I knew that if they left now, they would feel like our workshop had been a failure, and I was worried how that would impact their treatment.

I knew I had to stay, and I wanted their support. "You can leave if you want to, but that leaves me here by myself," I told them.

Whitney and Mrs. Lindsay were supposed to go back to Clintonville but Whitney insisted on staying. "If anyone thinks what I said or the others said is bull, then I am going to stay and let them say it to my face," he insisted. I looked at him, his face red with emotion, and I realized he was wrong about not having feelings—at least he felt anger.

I suspected it would be better for Whitney to leave. I didn't want to expose him to more criticism, and I didn't want him to blurt out anything that would disrupt the afternoon. But if I was asking the others to stay, I realized I had to let Whitney stay as well. When we resumed, I had the teachers write down three things they liked about the workshop. Except for one teacher who didn't write anything, they all found the workshop very exciting. In the main, however, they did not really understand what it would be like to be a visual Maverick. Only two or three of the teachers thought in pictures, and they suggested that they were not very smart themselves. Good verbal students are easy to see as smart. The idea of being a genius picture-thinker was a hard concept to grasp.

Although the rest of the day went smoothly and the majority of the teachers enjoyed the workshop, I could tell that the Mavericks were still impacted by the teacher's response.

Maybe the concept of Maverick Minds was just too complex or unusual for people to understand. While I was building a unique architecture for each very complicated Maverick, underneath I was following a firm protocol for all of them. At this point, my work with the Mavericks had to be customized. What worked well for some didn't work for others. For instance, I couldn't simply say, "All students with listening comprehension and auditory processing problems should sit in the front row," because for many of the Mavericks, this made the problems they were having worse. They felt they were center stage and everyone was staring at them; sometimes the second row worked better. For some students, taping a class was helpful; for others, getting a classmate's notes was more effective. Accommodations were different for each person and required a trial-and-error period of testing and determining which approach increased learning efficiency. I had to try different methods for each client until I found what worked best for that person, but in any case I needed to modify the environment to enhance their ability to learn until the patient could work without the accommodation or use a strategy that would be helpful to any student. The teachers, however, wanted specific techniques of what to do, a simple formula for how to help a struggling student. Although we covered a host of possible strategies, and provided everyone with a handbook on accommodations, explaining the diagnosis and treatment of the Mavericks was harder than I thought.

Soon after this workshop, I decided to take Whitney and his buddy to Shocktoberfest—a spooky series of haunted houses and rock bands set up to raise money for charity.

I also invited Dr. John Stang to join us. I had met him through a patient of mine—a failing med student who was able to get back into med school and graduate as a result of our work together. He had been interested in my work, and we had met a couple of times to discuss the medical students I'd helped, and had become friends socially.

I wanted to make this a fun day and not talk about work, but I soon found myself venting about what had happened at the workshop.

Dr. Stang insisted that I start writing about Whitney and the Mavericks so that other professionals could benefit from my work. I told him it was very hard to explain all of this and that I wasn't sure how to go about writing it up. He suggested I start teaching seminars with him at the medical school.

"You can teach the medical students about the Mavericks, and from these discussions you can learn how to build a more understandable explanation. The medical students are all learning how to be diagnosticians, and you can start to create a foundation for your research. Plus, maybe Whitney wasn't autistic," he said. "Maybe you are identifying a new disease model—a new syndrome. Can you identify what it was that allowed you to achieve your success with Whitney?"

After fourteen years, this was the first time someone was really showing this type of rigorous scientific inquiry about how Whitney's brain was actually re-engineered. I felt hope reigniting. Dr. Stang was very respected on a national level. Many physicians see him as the doctor's doctor and diagnostician par excellence.

After Shocktoberfest, we decided to take the kids for a snack.

Later, while waiting for our food, Dr. Stang said, "I wonder where the food is?"

I said, "Maybe they had to go milk a cow to make the shakes?"

Whitney looked at me with an unusual expression. "I don't think so. I think they get the milk from the grocery store."

Dr. Stang looked at me and smiled. "He speaks English like a second language, doesn't he?"

It was true, there were nuances of language that Whitney still didn't grasp. Whitney had learned verbal language second; visual language was his first language. He didn't always get irony, jokes, idioms—the subtleties of language that are hard to learn in a language that's not your native tongue.

Dr. Stang's support encouraged me to pursue defining the Maverick syndrome more formally. Following the guidelines set up by ASHA and the Americans with Disabilities Act, I began developing a protocol for evaluating each part of the visual and verbal processing pathways. I worked to chart the natural course of Whitney's disease and to create a battery of tests that would specifically diagnose a Maverick and create a baseline for therapy.

I knew that the work would still be viewed as controversial. My battery was very different from that used for learning disabilities. Even though all of the tests I was using were commonly used and highly respected, I was pulling parts of different tests to create a battery that was more predictive and more customized to explain the organicity of Maverick symptoms. Thus, the battery itself—and as a result, its inter-pretation and treatment planning—was unfamiliar, but as I worked on this at the medical school, it became easier and easier to explain.

Meanwhile, the more I thought about it, the more I was convinced that Whitney's comment about not having any feelings stemmed from the fact that he felt some things differently. Because his reactions were not the norm, it seemed to him—and sometimes to others—that he didn't feel. I thought it would be good for him to understand how unusual it was to have overcome all he had.

For the school science fair that spring, I urged Whitney to do his project on autism. Vanessa and William and I came up with a test that would measure visual and auditory processing on a laptop, and we taught Whitney how to give the test. Whitney brought my laptop into his science class and gave the test to everyone. At home, we made graphs of his work and created a posterboard presentation.

When it was time for judging, Whitney gave a speech about autism. His primary judge was his science teacher's daughter, who was herself a science teacher in another school. After the kids had given their presentations and we were waiting for the results of the judging, Whitney's science teacher beckoned me into the back room.

"My daughter is in the bathroom crying," she said.

"What's wrong?" I asked.

"Nothing's wrong, she is so touched by Whitney's project!" I thought her eyes looked moist as well. "It really is remarkable—your autistic child is now teaching us about his own disability."

I turned and looked back at Whitney, who was grinning happily. He won the ribbon for his class and would go on to win state honors. At that moment, he was just reveling in a good presentation. Look at all that emotion on his face! I thought back to the presentation at Watterson, when he'd been so matter-of-fact. This time he had put his heart and soul into the project. He was connecting to his feelings and proud of what he'd accomplished. He felt a need to express it to others.

I told Whitney he did have feelings. "You have very deep feelings. They just may be triggered by different circumstances than some of the people around you."

16

Football

and Girls

In the two years that Whitney attended Clintonville Academy, he worked hard at school to get his reading and writing skills up to high school levels. Now that I wasn't working with him at school anymore, most of our efforts with Whitney focused on helping him connect to his feelings—and in particular, learn the complex nuances of social skills. To be accepted in high school, he had to be accepted by his peers. And high school kids could be vicious about anyone who appeared to be slightly different.

Whitney's charm was his openness, his passion for the things he loved, and his honesty. Unfortunately, these qualities, unharnessed, could come off as being slightly off-kilter. Vanessa and I especially had always tried to point out to Whitney that he shouldn't say certain things to people—even if they were true. But teaching this kind of social nuance proved difficult.

Todd and Melinda got a real kick out of this quality of Whitney's. As a high visual with a life-long hearing problem, Melinda really related to Whitney. "I spent my life watching people from the outside, feeling like an alien. I didn't understand why people cried over certain things. It was so foreign to me," she said. Watching Whitney interact with others often made her laugh with recognition. One of her favorite stories happened while she was driving the kids home one afternoon and overheard a discussion among Whitney, Vanessa, and a friend of Vanessa's who had a huge crush on one of the high school's star football players. Vanessa's friend was obsessed with the player and talked about dating him.

"Why would he date you? You're overweight," Whitney said.

Vanessa, mortified, elbowed Whitney. He'd gotten an elbow enough to know that he must have said something wrong, and he shut up.

When they dropped off her friend, Vanessa turned to Whitney and chastised him. "You can't say that to people! You hurt her feelings."

Whitney didn't understand. "But he's not going to date her."

"Whitney, people should learn to become friends because of the qualities that make that person unique. You can't judge a book by its cover," Vanessa said.

The last thing in the world Whitney ever wanted to do was upset someone. But he didn't understand what caused upset. Working on this kind of emotional intelligence was a next step for us. Todd had a nice way of explaining things that respected Whitney's ability to see the truth. "You can't be afraid of the truth, because you're right," Todd told him. "But only certain people can handle certain things, so you have to be aware of who you're talking to."

The time that Whitney spent with Todd proved immeasurably helpful in building his social skills. I wouldn't have predicted that football, in particular, would play such an important role in teaching social nuance, but it turned out to be an incredibly valuable source of socialization lessons during his teenage years.

Todd met Whitney when he was nine or ten, and said it was hard to imagine him being the little kid we talked about—the one who'd caught his arm in the car door and not responded, or didn't talk for so many years. Now, in his middle school years, he was more talkative than William. It was also hard for Todd to imagine Whitney being such a wild kid, because he had become the one of us four who most followed directions. "I never have to harp on Whitney to follow my regimen— he follows every exercise and eats right with devotion," Todd would say. "Vanessa and William and you on the other hand . . ."

During many of my training sessions with Todd, we would discuss my theories and therapies for the visual and verbal mind. Because Todd now trained some of my clients, he was interested in understanding what I was working to improve. The more he understood the difference between visual and verbal thinkers, the more he started to identify examples from the rest of his clientele that he suspected were highly visual. For instance, he thought Whitney reminded him of many of the CEO businessmen he trained. "They are direct and abrupt. They see the solution and don't get caught up in the emotions of solving a problem or worrying about taking care of everyone else's feelings."

Todd gave me an example. "The other day we were at the studio and I'd just finished working Whitney out. I stopped to say hi to a woman client who was on the Life Cycle. Whitney said, 'You're going so slow! You're not gonna lose any weight like that! You're barely moving your feet!'"

I paled at the story, but couldn't help but laugh. "That's his version of small talk," I said.

"I know. And she *was* going too slow. But I would have said, 'How many rpms are you doing? Let's get this up to eighty.' But Whitney's bluntness reminds me of the CEOs I train."

I thought about this in terms of the adult Mavericks I'd been working with. Many of them were accused of being gruff, cold, and unfeeling. I'd assumed it was because as visual, big-picture thinkers, they grew impatient with those whose thinking process felt too slow or meandering. Whitney wasn't impatient with others, because he had had to go through his own frustrations learning language. But he did jump straight to the point in a way that could feel out of context or even blunt to others. Maybe this was what was really going on with the

Mavericks, too. Maybe they were just jumping ahead and assuming everyone could follow them.

Some researchers have said that if you look at thinking in terms of a ratio, a visual thinker can think at the rate of 2000 while the verbal thinker is thinking at the rate of 6. This estimate is made to illustrate the point that visual thinking can occur much faster than verbal thinking. I said to Todd, "Just look around this gym at all of the photos and equipment. If I were to write the description of all of this, it would take a very long time to capture. That old adage that a picture is worth a thousand words is true."

Another day, Todd told me he'd had an epiphany about Whitney's visual thinking, versus verbal thinking. He and Whitney were playing one-on-one football during a training session, and Todd was trying to get Whitney to run routes and catch the ball. Todd said he would explain how to run the route and then throw the ball to Whitney.

"He wasn't doing it at all. It was like he was purposely doing the exact opposite of what I told him. Now I know that he's not a kid who tries to be difficult. He always follows the routine to a T. So I couldn't figure out what was going on. Then I remembered about him being visual, so I decided to show him what I meant. I ran the route and said, 'Now you do it.' And he got it right away."

Todd was excited to have figured this out. He began applying the concept of visual versus verbal thinkers in training his clients. Not everyone is one extreme or the other, but many people do have a subtle preference. After a few sessions, he began to be able to assess whether someone was more visual or verbal. If a person was visual, then he would demonstrate new skills, whereas if someone was more verbal, he'd explain it. I, for instance, did better with verbal explanations. It just didn't help me to "see" something the way it helped Whitney.

Todd thought he could use football to help Whitney learn to socialize and enjoy being part of a team athletic effort. Todd, a former military airborne ranger, fully believed that when you work on a team, you learn a lot about leadership and building a unit to accomplish something together. Further, Todd believed that Whitney's emotional development would mature through this experience. "He needs to learn to connect his emotions to the game," Todd explained. "Logic is crucial for football, and he's got that. But he needs to really care, to feel the emotion, to get charged up to play."

He decided to get Whitney ready to play on the Falcons, an inner-city football league, in the summer between eighth and ninth grades. Todd noticed that when their workout routine changed abruptly or he put Whitney in a new situation, Whitney would shut down and seem paralyzed. For instance, when Todd tried to get a bunch of kids together to play a game, Whitney, who was fast if running alone or doing sprints, wouldn't always run fast on the football field. "I need to get him motivated or he'll get creamed out on the field. He won't make it," Todd said.

I assumed that the problem was one of focus. With all the distractions of practicing with other kids, he would lose focus and lose his physical edge.

"Whitney has a lot of physical grace. Watch him run. He is gorgeous," Todd said. "He has a lot of natural physical talent."

Was this the same kid who'd had ten years of physical and occupational therapy and adaptive physical education in elementary school because he was too impaired to attend gym class with the other kids?

To work Whitney's mind/body connection, one Saturday Todd took Whitney out to a football field. "You have to connect to your emotions to play football," Todd explained. "You have to run fast, you have to put energy behind every tackle. You have to get excited."

Whitney nodded in agreement, but when Todd put him through a route, he still wasn't pushing. Todd was getting frustrated. Then he got an idea.

"Watch this," he ordered Whitney.

Todd jogged out onto the field, and turned to Whitney and called out at the top of his lungs, "Picture this: There are eighteen seconds left in the game. You're on the forty-two-yard line. We're in a huddle . . ."

Todd crouched down. "It's gonna be a fly pattern to Whitney on two. OK? Ready, break!" Todd snapped into position. "Whitney draws back. The crowd is screaming!!! The stands are filled, everyone is look- ing at you!" Todd ran his route and made his play, jumping up and down, playing the parts of the athlete and the crowd all in one.

Barely winded, Todd jogged over to the sidelines to Whitney, who was grinning. "Your turn," he said, snapping Whitney the ball.

If there was one thing Whitney loved, it was playing make-believe.

Whitney ran out onto the field and reenacted Todd's play. "That really helps," Whitney told him.

From that point on, whenever we'd see Whitney practicing, we could hear him narrating the scene under his breath, motivating him- self with his own inner movies of the game.

There was another area that I was glad to have Todd around for—girls. The boys were starting to notice the opposite sex. I was the last person they wanted to turn to for advice, and Vanessa was a little too close in age for her brothers to really confide in her regarding their crushes. When the boys started talking about girls to Todd, he gave them advice on how to approach them. Whitney had no qualms about walking right up to a girl and talking to her or asking her to do something. If she said no, he'd just try someone else. William, on the other hand, was very shy. At school dances, Whitney is often the one out on the dance floor all night because he keeps asking girls to dance.

"I think this one girl likes me," Whitney told Todd.

"How do you know?"

"She looks at me, and I heard her talking to her friends," Whitney said matter-of-factly. He wasn't bragging. It was just a fact. He was insightful and picked up on these kinds of cues—he just didn't know how to use the information subtly.

"So why don't you ask her to a football game?" Todd suggested.

The next day Whitney came to work out and told Todd, "Oh, man, she is so stupid. We're in class and she sits off to the side behind me. So I turned around and asked her, 'Why do you keep staring at me?'"

"Why did you say that?"

"'Cuz she was staring at me."

"Whitney, she was looking at you because she likes you."

"I know. So why didn't she just say it, then?"

"I don't know. That would be embarrassing for her. It's just the way it works—" Todd suddenly realized he didn't know how to explain.

Whitney concluded, "These women just play games. I think that's why women control the world. They control men with these games. I'm through with girls. I'm just going to play football."

At the end of eighth grade, Whitney had his eye on a cute red-haired girl in his class. Now that he'd discovered that the blunt approach wasn't so effective, he wasn't sure what to replace it with. He hated being laughed at, he wanted to fit in. But when he realized his first instinct was "wrong," he didn't know what to do instead, so it left him adrift and frustrated for a while. He asked all of my high school and college patients week by week how to approach her. Everyone gave him different ideas: put a rose on her desk; send her a note; invite her to the movies. Normally he wouldn't have been afraid to do any of these things, but he really liked her and he was thinking about her as a potential girlfriend, which made this seem like more of a risk to him. To me this seemed like a normal adolescent feeling of how to go about approaching a special person of the opposite sex.

Finally, came the end-of-the-year dance. Whitney was very excited about going. He took special care getting dressed and combing his hair, asking Vanessa's advice for what to wear. Vanessa carefully selected the outfit and talked nonstop about how he should behave. He was determined to talk to the red-haired girl tonight.

Vanessa and I waited excitedly at home until it was time to pick him up, guessing at how things went as we drove to pick him up.

As we pulled up to the school, Whitney was standing off by himself.

"Uh-oh," Vanessa sighed.

We pulled up and Whitney got in the car and slammed the door. He was white as a sheet.

"So?" I smiled expectantly.

Vanessa shot me a you-should-know-better look.

Whitney burst out, "She slapped me! In front of everyone. I don't know what her problem is."

"What did you do?" Vanessa asked.

"Nothing! I called her a skank and a ho—you know, like she's phat!"

I did not know what a "skank" or a "ho" was. Vanessa said, "Oh no, Whitney, why would you say that to her? That is awful! That is not like phat. That is calling her a whore. That is bad!"

Whitney had wanted the red-haired girl to think he could use cool talk. He'd heard these words on TV and assumed the names were compliments. He didn't understand irony. The news that these words were bad hit him hard. He looked out the window aghast.

Adolescence was painful enough without this added burden of not knowing how to decode the verbal parrying that surrounds teenagers. I looked over to see how he was taking the news of his gaffe.

"I didn't say that. I didn't. I'm kidding," he said, trying to recover.

But we knew he had. It was heartbreaking how his efforts to fit in could make him an outcast.

Whitney spent the summer before high school on the Falcons. The coaches were strict and many of the fathers attended practice, watching their sons, calling out from the sidelines. This team in particular had a history of being made up of kids whose dads were former NFL players, and this summer was no different. Todd thought the competitive atmosphere would be a good challenge and would prepare him to try out for the Watterson team. Whitney was very attuned to his environment and to the people around him, so Todd thought these teammates would spur him to action.

I agreed to give it a try, but I was worried about how it would work out. Should I tell the coach Whitney's history or just throw him in with the kids? The first day of practice, I heard one of the kids scream out, "Hey, what's that white kid doing here?" Here was yet another reason for Whitney to be considered different. The team was made up of all black players. Whitney headed off to play but I knew he was nervous about fitting in. When I came back to pick him up, I asked the coach how practice was.

"Great," he answered. "See you tomorrow."

Whitney was all smiles on the ride home. He'd had a ball. "I am a football player!" he said to me, his eyes gleaming with joy. I was relieved.

This euphoria did not last long. Three days later, the coach pulled me aside. "I don't think Whitney is right for the team," he said.

"Why not?" I asked, feeling my defenses rising.

"He is too self-centered and wants everything his way. I am trying to build a team that thinks like one person, and Whitney thinks he knows more than everyone else." I knew there might be issues with Whitney on this team, but this wasn't one I'd have predicted. It didn't sound right at all. "What is he doing?" I asked.

"He is running off and doing the opposite of what I am telling him, and when I put him on the bench to teach him to pay attention and follow directions, he gets upset. Then the next time I put him on the field, he is even more defiant. He has to have his own way," said the coach.

I had a feeling I knew what the problem was, but I wasn't quite sure how to phrase it. "I think it might be the way you are talking," I said meekly. "Whitney used to be deaf, and in new situations, he mis-hears things and gets the directions mixed up."

The coach looked perplexed, as if he were reconsidering his opinion. Then he said, "I wear a hearing aid during the day at work, but not out here on the field. I think I understand what you mean."

The next day, the coach made sure Whitney heard him and saw his face when he gave directions, and I noticed he was careful not to scream instructions while Whitney was running off in the other direction. It worked like a charm. The following week the coaches voted Whitney team captain because of his team-building skills and good sportsmanship.

One afternoon, William and my father were sitting in the stands waiting for the game to begin. All of a sudden they heard an odd barking sound on the sidelines. It sounded familiar to William. Finally, he spotted Whitney, off on his own—barking and howling.

William turned to his grandfather slowly. "Is he barking?"

My father looked quizzically at his grandson, howling on the sidelines. "I think so."

William just shook his head in wonderment. *What now?* he thought.

After the game, William gave Whitney a hard time. "Why were you barking?" he asked.

"The coach told me to," Whitney replied.

"The coach told you to bark." William was skeptical.

"Yeah, he said, 'I want you to be barking and howling like a dog before every game.'"

It turned out the coach *had* taken Whitney aside and told him he wanted him to get revved up before every game. Of course, the coach had been speaking metaphorically when he said he wanted him to bark like a dog—but Whitney took the advice to heart.

During his seventh- and eighth-grade years, Whitney had learned a lot about fitting in. Perhaps it was his combination of fearlessness in saying what was on his mind, coupled with his strong intuitive sense that alerted him when he'd said something that people found odd, that helped him start to navigate the social world and learn about social cues. Regardless, we were now ready to try out these new skills in high school.

17

Leaving

Home

Hagley Field was packed with football fans eagerly awaiting the start of the Dublin Coffman vs. Watterson game. My parents and my friend John Stang had joined Vanessa, Whitney, and me to watch William play. The stadium was buzzing with excitement and nervous anticipation that mimicked my state of mind these days. Whitney had made it to ninth grade and was a freshman—a goal we had all worked toward for fourteen years. For me, his academic progress was our family touchdown victory.

With one week of school completed, it was now time for the Friday night football game, first game of the season; the football team had been practicing rigorously since July. William was psyched. It was his junior year, and he was starting on the defensive line for Watterson. Whitney had made the freshman team and their first game was the next day, also against Dublin Coffman. So if the varsity team lost on Friday, Watterson had a chance for a sort of rematch with the two junior varsity teams the following day. Dublin was twice the size of Watterson and was in Division 1, whereas Watterson was Division 3. Dublin had

everything money could buy in terms of athletic equipment and training areas; Watterson had a dirt field and coaches with heart. Although
Watterson was the underdog, the team still often made it to the finals.
So did Dublin. The stands were packed on both sides with proud,
competitive-minded parents and fans.

Minutes after kickoff, I heard my name called over the loudspeaker.
"Dr. Florance—please come to the north end of the stadium."

My mind raced through a quick inventory of my kids, the way any
mother's does at the sign of trouble. Vanessa was with me, I could see
William on the sidelines. But Whitney had asked if he could sit with
his new classmates, and we'd agreed to meet at the hotdog stand after
the game.

Oh dear I sighed. John and I made our way past the other parents
and students in the bleachers to see what had happened. When we
arrived, Whitney was sobbing uncontrollably. He was rocking in a fetal
position under the stands on a dark cement walkway behind the con-
cession stand. Marion Hutson was explaining that he was suspended
for a week. "You'll get a zero for each of these days, so your grades for
first quarter are in serious jeopardy," she reported matter-of-factly. The
Dean of Men stood behind her.

I could see the deep concern on both their faces. Seeing a child
behave in this abnormal way was quite disturbing, and this was not the
Whitney she knew. The more he cried, the more she tried to justify his
punishment. She was gentle but firm, using clear reasoning to explain
that they couldn't have people fighting at games. I knew that more
explaining was not going to help. It was as if all of Whitney's autism
was returning before my eyes—the more she talked, the more Whitney
fell apart.

I couldn't imagine what had happened. I knelt down on the ground
beside Whitney and tried to guide him nonverbally to get up and come
back to the family seats with me. In spite of recognizing a few speech
and behavioral eccentricities, John Stang had also never known Whitney as autistic and found our stories of the past hard to believe.

Stunned, he was now trying to help him up also, gently taking his arm and trying to get him to stand.

For about fifteen minutes, I could not get Whitney to focus on me. I hadn't seen Whitney like this in a long time, and was more scared than I'd been in years. Would the Watterson administration let him go to their school after all? They were clear that they could not accept students with special needs because they were not equipped or trained to handle anyone who is not ready for college prep; the academic work is too hard for someone with special circumstances.

Finally, I got Whitney to look at me. Once he focused on my face, I was able to break through to him and get him to agree that going to sit with Grandma and Grandpa to watch Will play was the thing to do. After we got him to come sit with us, he slowly calmed down and returned to our world and his usual self. I chose to focus on my sense of relief and push aside the anxiety and fear that came with the realization that these old behaviors could still resurface.

It took me a few days to sort out what had transpired. Apparently Whitney had gone over to the Dublin side of the stadium to see if any of his old friends were there. Some kids starting calling him "retard," and Whitney decided to stand up for himself.

"I'm not in special ed anymore. I'm going to Watterson now." They laughed at him, convinced he was lying.

Whitney wouldn't back down. "No, I'm not in special ed anymore. I'm doing great."

One of the boys leaned in and dared him. "If you're not a retard anymore, touch that girl on the shoulder and say 'Hi.'"

To most teenagers, that would reek of a setup, but to Whitney, it sounded like an easy way to prove himself. What he didn't know was that before he'd gotten there, they'd been teasing the girl and her boyfriend, an athlete, giving them a hard time about kissing in the stands. When Whitney went up to the girl and touched her, her boyfriend was fed up—and he wheeled around and punched Whitney.

Shocked, Whitney punched him back.

The police grabbed both boys, pulled them apart, and escorted Whitney back to the Watterson side of the stadium. They called Ms. Hutson and told her to keep her students on their own side.

"There hasn't been a fight at a Watterson game in years," said the policeman. The officer seemed to be telling Ms. Hutson that she must take control of the situation and make a statement. In order to send a strong message about fighting at games, Whitney was suspended for a week.

I thought about challenging his suspension. I didn't want him to start out with that mark on his record and I was seriously concerned that the faculty would think Whitney was a bad kid. I knew that the first couple of weeks in a new school could set up your reputation, and after that it could be hard to change. I had done "back-to-school" local TV news spots, written newspaper articles, and given workshops in the community for many years on how to get off on the right foot during the first six weeks of the school year so that the rest of the year would go smoothly. In my practice, I have a back-to-school program to help children transition from the summer to the school year. Then again, I didn't want to start off his high school years fighting his fights for him. I calmed down and decided it was best to accept his punishment.

It was a rough week. Whitney took to his bed and we had a hard time getting him to come to dinner. John Stang talked to him for a long time, explaining that no one was mad at him and that school would be fine when he returned. William and Vanessa brought Whitney's home-work everyday and tutored him at home. They had already taken these classes so they were able to "homeschool" him at night. I knew it would be hard to walk into his classes as the kid who was suspended after his first week. I met with Ms. Hutson prior to his return and, after dis-cussing it with her, sent a letter to each of his teachers explaining his history and what happened at the game. I asked that they give him a helping hand back into the classroom.

He was nervous when he reentered the school. But his teachers were very accommodating. Whitney quickly charmed them with his eagerness and open warmth, along with his hard work. His first weeks back, he came home with stories each day about how much he liked his teachers and how nice they were. Returning to football cheered him further; he was happy to be doing sports again with his brother.

I still was concerned about how Whitney would handle his academic load. Watterson is a very hard, aggressive academic school, and the teachers demand a great deal of the students. Everyone is college prep, and the students, teachers, and families put a huge premium on learning and academic excellence. Could Whitney do this? It was a huge jump from his little twelve-member eighth-grade class. But even though the zeros pulled him down, he was able to get pretty good grades on his first report card. More important, he was learning—and learning on his own, with no help from me, his brother or sister, or any tutors. With the rocky start he had had and the more advanced placement in many of his classes, this was a major accomplishment.

When I analyzed the situation, I realized that Whitney's episode was caused by his not understanding why people were lashing out at him— once again, a communication problem. The Mavericks often have emotional responses to things that seem out of proportion to the "50–50s" (those in the middle of the bell curve). Whitney now had a very strong sense of right and wrong. He didn't want to make mistakes, break rules, or upset anyone. However, he still didn't have an intuitive sense of the correct response expected at all times. He was still baffled by what is often the right thing to say or do, as it doesn't always fit into his pattern recognition and associative thinking.

Although Whitney has never had another relapse like this one, he still has some moments when I can tell that his language processing is more like that of someone who learned English as a second language.

I recently accompanied Whitney on a school trip to France and Italy. I quickly noticed that the guides would say things that were off a step. For example, the French guide said, "I explain you the Nôtre Dame. You see they have the plenty of gargoyles." These mistakes are not that noticeable in someone you know is using a language that is not his or her native tongue. Whitney also learned language after the primary language development period of the first five years of life. If he uses language incorrectly, though, it is not viewed with the same sense of "forgiveness" as if he were speaking French and used a word too literally, or colloquially, by mistake.

The last night of his school trip, I bought everyone a gift and asked each person to say something nice about another. When it was ViVi's turn to talk about Whitney, she said, "I was surprised you are so intelligent. I really didn't know you that well except for the fact that you are on the football team. So I thought you were a little weird, a dumb jock. I was happy to get to know you better and to share my ideas with you. You are really a cool guy." Whitney responded, "ViVi has been to Europe before, so she took all of the girls under her wing to go shopping. The girls really loved shopping with ViVi." ViVi smiled. Then Whitney said, "And she didn't turn them into sluts, either. She really did a good job of making everyone comfortable." Everyone smiled. Later Whitney proudly repeated his comment to me, saying, "I really wanted ViVi to know that she had done a good job." He had no idea that the "slut" commentary wasn't necessary. I don't consider this a relapse, but more due to the fact that he learned to be verbal after the natural language acquisition period.

When he was rocking in the fetal position at the football game, I think it was, as it turned out, not a relapse but a regression to earlier behavior as a temporary defense mechanism. When stress goes up, we cope if we can, defend if we must, and if all else fails, we fragment. Whitney was falling apart after being called a "retard," tricked into inappropriate social behavior by some cocky kids teasing, in a fight, reprimanded by the police, and his school's administrators during his brother's big rivalry football game in his first week of school. If you gave points for each stressor, as is commonly done on stress scales, this would break the bank. Whitney's response to stress was to regress. Dr. Stang had been horrified. "I had never seen Whitney like this. I couldn't imagine what it would be like for Whitney not to be Whitney," he said. Since Whitney bounced back, I knew that prognostically that was a hopeful sign. At the time, there was no way to know if he would relapse again, or have more permanent problems along the way. But now, three years later, I feel confident that those days are behind us.

I realized that grasping the subtext and subtleties of human language was going to be more important than any academic lesson he could learn in high school. Language is more than comprehending or producing words. It is understanding body language, nonverbal cues, and the pragmatic use of language, knowing intuitively how to say the right thing at the right time. How to interpret inflection, how the words are stressed, and all the little nuances that you use to infer meaning—all that is language too.

High school has no shortage of lessons in this—especially for a football player. As I thought about this, I realized a lesson that Whitney had "learned" in preseason football practice had probably added to his confusion about what to react to and what to ignore when it came to aggression. I'd always prefer the boys ignore aggression, but I have learned that especially when they play football, a certain amount of aggression is part of the game—on and off the field.

That summer, just before school started, Whitney attended "two-a-days," a grueling back-to-back schedule of football practices. He was trying out for the team, and the varsity quarterback honored him with a rite of passage: he "pantsed" Whitney. In this ritual, a more senior player initiates a new player by tackling him and pulling his pants down in the locker room. Whitney, being good-natured, took it in stride.

The next day after practice, Whitney pantsed the quarterback, and the quarterback punched him. Whitney started to punch him back.

William was out of the locker room when it happened, but when he heard what was going on, he ran back inside to discover the quarterback punching Whitney. Apparently it wasn't full-blown fighting, but more of a lesson that Whitney was being taught. William watched for a moment and when Whitney started to punch back, he laughed and said, "Well, now you are a real member of the team, Whit!" He put his arm around his shoulders and moved him away. The quarterback laughed too, so Whitney took his cue from them and laughed, realizing he was now officially one of the guys.

When I heard the story, I objected. "Why didn't you stop Spence right away from hitting Whitney?" I asked William.

"Mom, this was a locker room thing," William explained. "Spence was pissed. If I had jumped in too early to save him, Whitney would never hear the end of it. It would always be: 'Is your brother gonna come and save you?' I told Whit, 'You started this, you gotta finish it.' It was the best thing to do, Mom, I promise. Don't worry—Spence was only punching him a couple of times to show him that he was an upper classmate and Whitney is a freshman."

Whitney was surprised by this lesson. To him, his action was totally logical. "He pantsed me, I pantsed him back," Whitney said, bemused.

"You're a freshman, he's a senior. You don't do that! Freshman are not allowed to feel equal to seniors—it's the rule," William explained.

Once his brother had explained the rite of passage and the rule: Freshmen aren't equal to seniors, Whitney was proud of being one of the guys. "Yeah, Mom—you just don't understand football," he agreed.

So William let his brother learn a lesson about social standing. In a funny way, I think Whitney taught William something too. "It was pretty funny," William confided to me later. "I never would've done that. I'm always concerned with social standing and what people think. Sometimes I'm afraid I'll spend my life doing stuff because other people want me to. He just walked up and did it. I think Whitney's gonna be pretty happy. He just does what he thinks is right and fair. I admire that."

Whitney's confusion in this situation reminded me of the little boy who wanted to check out puppets the way other people checked out books in the library or buy the deluxe train set when others were loading their carts with things at the store—it all seemed equally logical to him. Now he was learning why a behavior might be OK in one situation, but not in another.

When you consider the social rules that we intuitively pick up, you gain an appreciation for the complexity of our species. I had to admit, social rules surrounding sports were hard even for me to understand. The kids say a prayer before the game to do their best, yet William's nickname was "Killer" and Whitney's therefore became "Little Killer." I found it bizarre that the coaches and the teachers called the boys by these names. When it was time for Will to go on the field, Coach Golden would scream, "Okay, Killer, go!" And off William would run to "kill" the opponent. Spence was allowed to hit Whitney in the locker room, but Whitney couldn't fight back because he was an underling. Yet he was also not allowed to defend himself at the game with a peer when he was called a "retard."

It is extremely difficult to learn the nuance of language, what are called the "supra-segmentals"—the extras on top of the words, including inflection, prosody, body language—all the factors that stimulate proper immediate interpretation of the nuance of language and the learning of the code of language as it applies in various situations. It is not consistent. The English language is ambiguous most of the time. We instinctively use inference and deductive verbal reasoning very rapidly to understand the intention of the speaker and to respond appropriately.

The way a visual thinker misunderstands language is illustrated by another story from Whitney's school trip to Europe. We were visiting Versailles and our guide, Helen, said, "Everyone has to wait in that really long line, heh heh heh,—no no—I cheated and will get you in the back door follow me and when you get done go out to the fountain and we will meet as a group and then we will walk down to the end of the gardens where you can get a snack, un café au lait, du chocolat, un croissant, les glace, visit Madame PeePee and enjoy the view."

I was worried how Whitney would decode this. After a ten-day trip, we all were used to the quirks of the way "Helen from Scotland," as Whitney named her, communicated. But initially I thought her jokes and sarcasm were hard to register. She had an accent; she gave many instructions at a time; she was a complex communicator.

Sure enough, we got to the fountain and Whitney was not there. "Where do you think he is?" she asked me.

I told her he was probably at the snack shop because that had been the final meeting point in her instructions. Knowing Whitney's excellent sense of direction and his visual scanning of the scenario in front of him, I thought it was very likely he had jumped to the bottom line and completed the task without addressing each intermediate step. We walked down the garden path, and sure enough, here was Whitney on his way back. Once he got to the snack area, he realized he was the only one there and that there must have been a step he had skipped, so he started to backtrack. He had heard all the words—some French, some English, some made up. And with all of that to decode, he pulled out what he perceived to be most important from this sea of words and attempted to act on it.

The visual thinker who is using a picture language is scanning for consistent patterns and algorithms—the logical analysis that generalizes from situation to situation. That is how Whitney operates at the heart of his intelligence.

With Whitney settling in at Watterson academically and socially, it was time to turn our attention to the next looming change in our lives: Vanessa was deciding where to apply to college. The summer before, she'd taken a class at Southern Methodist University in Dallas.

Vanessa thrived being away from home. She loved SMU and came home very excited about the prospect of college. Her excitement tore at me. I knew she was ready to go off on her own, and she'd certainly earned her independence. I also knew we'd all miss her terribly. She'd been confidante and right-hand to me, best friend to William, and Whitney's friend and special therapist. What would we do without her?

One morning she announced she'd had a dream that she was at college in New York City. For the first time, I became excited about Vanessa going to college. New York was easy to get to, and I thought it would be an exciting city to study in.

We started planning family trips to New York so we could evaluate the colleges. We went to *Rocky Horror Picture Show* on Broadway and to Madame Tussaud's wax museum and spent some time at the U.N. After much deliberation and many college visits to New York and elsewhere, Vanessa decided to apply to Manhattan College, a highly rated liberal arts college in Riverdale, a beautiful area just north of the city but still on the subway line.

We all helped her with her application at family meetings and anxiously waited to see if she was accepted. Sure enough, in early January, a letter sat waiting on the dining room table inviting her to become a Manhattan College Jasper.

William, Vanessa, and I shouted with excitement.

Whitney sat quietly.

"Aren't you happy for me, Whit?" said Vanessa.

"That city is big, Nessa," he said. "I think you should go to Michigan."

"But I love New York—and you can come visit," she said, addressing what we all knew was his real concern.

"Whatever. I hope it works out," he mumbled and disappeared to play video games.

We all knew what he was thinking. He did not want his sister to leave home. He was missing her already.

I knew I had to give Whitney extra attention to help ease him through the big changes that were coming up with his sister and brother starting to leave home. The summer before Vanessa went to college, William took summer courses in psychology and expository writing at Georgetown in Washington, D.C. Whitney and I flew in for the Fourth of July to bring William home. While Will took his finals, Whitney and I spent most of our time together exploring the city, learning the subway, going to the comedy club and blues alley, hanging around the Smithsonian and the museums, taking a tour of the Kennedy Center, and listening to free concerts every evening at six p.m.

By now I was feeling just like Whitney felt about Vanessa leaving; I couldn't bear to have them all growing up. I could still remember grabbing Whitney in a big hug and telling him, "I'm never gonna let you go." Now I could barely wrap my arms around this hulking young man.

With high school underway successfully, the next step would be getting ready for college. By this time, I had seen about fifty medical students who had failed their national board exams or flunked out of school. As a result, I was learning what problems were causing this academic failure and how to help the students improve so that they could return successfully. I wanted to teach Whitney what I was teaching the med students so that leaving home for college was not such a big step for him. Both William and Vanessa had taken college classes away from home while still in high school, which made the transition much easier for them.

I decided we should start with the idea of doing something nonacademic in a college away from home. That same summer, at our family meeting, we decided Whitney should try football camps at OSU and the University of Michigan for one week each. Could he live in a dorm for two weeks at two different universities without the guidance of his brother or sister?

Going off to OSU was the first gamble. We told Whitney, "If you don't like it, call and we will come get you." OSU is only a fifteen-minute drive from our house, so we all felt comfortable with this plan. I figured it would be a lot easier to get him home from the OSU campus than Ann Arbor, Michigan.

We had been building a foundation for this camp for many years. William had done these camps before and Whitney had done day camps, so the routine of a sports camp was familiar. Still, staying away from home and the network of support we created for Whitney would be a major change. He would not be in his own bed. He would have meals on a schedule perhaps different from ours. He would have to follow instructions without our coaching or reinterpreting for him at night at family meetings. He would have to pick up on the social nuances that were common to the traditions of these college football camps but foreign to us. Whitney, too, was somewhat uncomfortable—I think because we planned the OSU camp first, and then if that went well, he would go to the University of Michigan camp.

At first, Whitney insisted that he go to OSU as a day camper and come home each night. His reasoning was it was "dumb to pay for housing" when he lived only a few miles away. William convinced him that it would be a ton more fun to stay overnight in the dorms. A lot of the OSU players would stop by to give pep talks and answer questions, and he would have the chance to make new friends.

William and Vanessa helped pack his bag. All he needed was shorts, T-shirts, and socks and underwear, so there was not much that could go wrong with the dress code. By now, Whitney was a tall, lanky, muscular kid with a strong, well-defined body. A good runner and a good all-around athlete, when he ran Whitney looked like a deer to me: fluid and graceful and amazing after so many years of occupational and physical therapy.

William and I decided that if Whitney had fun at OSU, then Michigan would be the next step. And so it was. Whitney had a blast at OSU

and even more fun at the Michigan camp. We did not hear a peep out of
him until he returned home. Then, he and William discussed the plays
and the drills. From a mom's perspective, William and Whitney seemed
happy with the result. I also felt he had transitioned to these new envi-
ronments with no apparent problems, which I thought was a good step
forward. Now Whitney's challenges were beginning to seem more like
those faced by his peers.

Meanwhile, Vanessa was getting ready to leave for college. She was
excited and happy about her new life in the Big Apple, but William,
Whitney, and I were all dreading her departure. We knew how our
home life would radically change with her gone, and we were sad.

It seemed the tight-knit years of the four of us bonding together
through adversity were now coming to an end. It was with good reason
and good results—but we faced the change with bittersweet happiness.

The morning after we put Vanessa on the plane for New York,
William and I both cried. Whitney stood stoically,

As soon as we walked in the front door of our house, I felt a vast
emptiness. I immediately made the boys help me move furniture all day.
Eight hours later, exhausted from rearranging everything, I was still
not consoled. I couldn't get rid of the feeling of how much I missed my
daughter. I was very happy for her but I missed her and I dreaded all of
them growing up and leaving.

Whitney knew I was sad so he came to me and said, "Mom, let's go
see a movie."

I was reminded of the afternoon years ago when I'd tried to comfort
Whitney, who had withdrawn to his firetruck bed after his failed swim
demonstration at camp. A movie and popcorn was always a good cure-
all in our family. Off we went.

A few hours later we emerged from the theater.

"You were right, that helped," I said.

Whitney looked at me with anticipation as he put his arm around my shoulder.

Gone was the little boy whose hand I had trouble grasping. Long gone was the hollow boy who didn't respond to anyone around him. Instead, a young man towered above me.

"See, I fixed *you*!" he said. And his face burst into a proud grin.

18

The Florance

Maverick Syndrome

With Vanessa gone, William leaving in a few months, and Whitney to follow soon, for the first time in nearly two decades I had time to think about what I wanted to do, rather than doing what I needed to do to survive. I was spending a lot of mental time contemplating where I wanted to live, what work I wanted to do, and what direction I wanted my career to take.

In the meantime, every Wednesday night William, Whitney, fifteen medical students and other high achievers, and I were sitting down to dinner and an excruciating verbal workout, a new program I called "Building the Champion Brain." These Mavericks were what is termed "twice exceptional." "Twice exceptional" means that you are in the superior range in certain abilities and have problems in others: the hyper/hypo brain of the Mavericks, who are above the ninety-ninth percentile in visual thinking but had communication disabilities with verbal scores below the first percentile, fits this definition, although it was created to describe a host of out-of-balance strengths and weaknesses, not high visual/low verbal imbalances.

Both boys were participating in the program. William had decided to join us in our verbal workouts with the medical student Mavericks because he wanted to prepare for college. He'd been awarded the Presidential Scholarship at Manhattan College, the highest award given for an incoming freshman, and invited to be a member of the LaSallian Honor Society. He planned to major in chemical engineering and was thinking about medical school after college.

We invited guest professors to lecture, authority figures from the community to ask questions—all as part of our workout for our verbal and visual brains. This was the most difficult communication skills–building exercise I had created: a therapy program for my twice-exceptional genius Mavericks to improve their verbal abilities and become the best they could be. Whitney assisted with this program and helped me modify it for the high school and middle school kids. He worked as a tutor for the elementary Mavericks, assisting in the classroom simulators, as did Vanessa and William. We also began to develop more Internet-driven augmentative systems that involved Power Point presentations, for which the kids helped scan in documents. Whitney began searching the Internet for streaming video that I could use in auditory and visual quick-thinking drills. He enjoyed being involved in helping others who had problems similar to his.

I wanted to know how unique my work with Whitney and the Mavericks was. Dr. Stang told me he thought I might have discovered a new syndrome: "No one has identified these medical problems as you have, and you have also figured out how to treat them. I think you have discovered the Florance Maverick Syndrome," he said. Dr. Stang has written over two thousand questions for the national board exams and is considered an excellent physician on the national talk circuits. He was a frequent keynote speaker at medical meetings, especially those that involved preparation for the various board examinations that simulate diagnosing patients. He had received numerous teacher or professor of the year awards as an outstanding teacher, and literally hundreds of physicians consider him to be one of the premier diagnosticians in the country. I took his praise seriously.

So when it was time for William to go on college interviews in New York and D.C., I scheduled a series of visits with scientists at the National Institutes of Health. After being very prolific professionally, I had not written anything for sixteen years, so I was nervous about how to present my ideas to them in a way that would make sense. I also wanted to know, from their perspective, how unique my work was.

I knew once we went to NIH, the response of the scientists there could have a major impact on my post-child-rearing career. My days as Whitney's doctor-therapist were nearing an end, and my days as the primary caregiver and provider for all three children were also ending. I wanted to gain some ideas about my future direction professionally.

On the Metro en route to my meetings, William, who was accompanying me, could sense my tension. "We don't have to do this, Mom," he said.

"I know. But what have we got to lose?"

If in my work with Whitney we had discovered a new disease model for a new syndrome and its treatment, I wanted to find that out, even if it meant taking the risk that I wouldn't be taken seriously.

Before we'd left, I'd asked Whitney if he thought I should go to NIH. He hadn't hesitated. "Mom, all you have to do is tell them about me. The schools said I was retarded for years. And I am not retarded. The doctors said I would always be autistic and I am not autistic. I couldn't hear. And now I can hear."

I reminded myself of Whitney's reassurances as William and I walked into the conference room and told our story. I laid out how others whom I highly respected thought I'd identified a new syndrome, suggesting the possibility of a Florance Maverick Syndrome. I had prepared some professional documents for them to evaluate, with reviews of literature and interpretations of cognitive models well organized in a binder to show the progression of my thinking. However, what the scientists were most interested in, and what we spent the most time talking about, was the physiology of what was wrong with Whitney initially and how I was able to correct it.

We had a wonderful brain-storming session. William loved our visit so much that he is hoping that one day he will work at the NIH.

One of the scientists outlined exactly what he thought we should do next—a five-year plan to research this syndrome so that we could share the information with other scientists. His advice echoed in my ears: *First you need to mobilize local support and build yourself a portable lab that can move with you. Next you need to find an academic home.* He offered to help with a proposal and future grants when I got a lab up and running.

Until now, despite my success, the best we had heard from authority figures was something like, "Hmm, how odd," or "What a strange developmental profile." Other than doctors Cantwell and Stang, no one had really understood the science of what I was talking about.

As we were leaving for our next meetings, one of the doctors shook our hands. "You know, I have children too. I can't imagine how hard it must have been—" He turned to William. "For both of you. What you have done is remarkable."

I could barely look at William. Here was a respected scientist congratulating us on a job well done. And my kids were part of the equation.

After we left, we made a quick phone call to Whitney and Vanessa. I handed the phone to William and I could hear him talking a mile a minute, first to his brother and then his sister. *And then guess what they said . . . and then . . . and then . . .* He recounted the whole story. My head buzzed with possibilities of research collaborations.

As we rode back to our hotel, I could tell William was feeling great about our day. Later that night we had dinner with Peter Swire and his wife, Anne. Peter Swire was hired by the White House to create Internet law and policy for health care delivery over the Internet. We spoke to him about an idea I'd been wanting to implement to provide assessment and training of auditory and visual processing via the Internet.

That night I could barely sleep. I couldn't quite believe that my dreams of expanding this research and treatment might become reality.

When we returned home, I met with officials from the Ohio governor's Developmental Disabilities Council, along with William and one of the med students. We presented a proposal to test all of the first-year medical students to determine how many of them have "Florance Maverick Syndrome" and to learn more about brain engineering. The grant was approved, and the officials at OSU medical school agreed that I could test all of the medical students in the incoming class.

William, Vanessa, and Whitney spent the summer helping me build a virtual "eBrain Laboratory," where we could test the students and collect data over the Internet. We also were considering how a professor could create a self-regulatory classroom where the students could sculpt their learning experiences to match their brain type. To explore this idea further, I asked Whitney, who was now just completing tenth grade, to enroll in a human biology class at Columbus State taught by Dr. Keith Meske. Dr. Meske was a former television director and an excellent teacher who used slides, streaming video, and movies to illustrate his points made in lectures and books. The only course that would work with his football schedule was an advanced course for juniors in college. Dr. Meske allowed Whitney to take it. We decided to give it a try, and if it was too hard we would drop it. I also had some patients who had flunked out of college and some who wanted to prepare for college, so we formed a study group and they all enrolled in Dr. Meske's class.

Since I had re-engineered Whitney's brain, I knew how I had designed his verbal pathway for learning to work. I had also taught him to harness his visual thinking systems for maximal effectiveness. I thought I could coach Whitney—and the other Mavericks—to learn how to sculpt a class to match his most intuitive ways of learning.

I taught the group that they have what I was now calling an "opticoder system" (for thinking in pictures) and a "lexicoder system" (for

thinking in words), my terms for the visual and verbal thinking systems. I explained that when they are learning something new, they can
use the "central executive" function of their brain to access the system
that will be most effective for the task at hand.

Whitney absolutely dove head first into this experience. He was by
far the youngest student in the class. He was hungry to try my every
idea, and he advanced them to the max. By the end of the summer,
Whitney had the highest grade in the class. Here was a deaf-mute autistic "retarded" kid who was unable to speak for seven years working at
the top of the class in a third-year college-level course. How did this
happen? His success is due to the power of the visual brain. What a
superior thinking system it is! Dr. Cantwell's view that nothing would
change until the doctors, classroom teachers, and therapists understand each other was true. The medical student patients can be some of
the best advocates for better understanding communication issues
because they will enter into the world of health care with their own
personal knowledge of what happened to them.

Pete, a med student who was making incredible progress, said,
"Whitney keeps me going. When others doubt me or when I doubt
myself, I think of Whitney and what he has accomplished, and I think,
I can do it." Pete had to pass three tests or get kicked out of med
school. On the last test he got a score of 90—one of the highest in
the class. Rob, another med student misdiagnosed with ADD, was accepted to his first choice for residency in Florida. He said, "When you
think about Whitney and the fact that he couldn't hear and now he
can—it can stop you in your tracks—but then I look around this room
and hear everyone talking about how they 'couldn't hear' either—they
couldn't listen—and now they are learning to function in a verbal
world."

The old adage—that there's something to be learned from every
problem—is certainly true in our case. If I hadn't had the life I had, I
wouldn't have been able to figure out how to help Whitney. I was lucky
to be able to tackle his problem from a multidisciplinary viewpoint.

Working with Head Start and stroke patients and executives with stuttering problems back-to-back made me see a pattern that otherwise
wouldn't have occurred to me: that Whitney's problem was due to his
high visual thinking. It was my cross-training that enabled me to best
help the Mavericks: academic training in speech and hearing science
and psychology at the doctoral level; a post-doctoral fellowship at NIH
in brain disorders with a Freudian psychologist mentor; senior fellow-
ships in psychiatry and medicine. Perhaps more important than my
academic training, though, were the societal and school issues I had to
live through as a mother. Only Whitney could have taught me that.

In many ways, the experience of the past sixteen years turned
me from an extrovert to an introvert. Outside of my patients and my
children, I haven't spoken to many people until recently. I might rather
have worked quietly via word of mouth, helping one visual person at a
time if it hadn't been for the process of writing this book, and the
encouragement from those who have believed in my work. These have
been important steps in my decision to move ahead with my work with
Mavericks.

At times people thought I was way out on a limb about my interpretation of what went on with Whitney. There are times when I feel like I
have a communication disorder myself when I try to explain what we
did to fix him. The process of writing this book has helped me clarify
the journey. I've now helped well over four hundred highly visual people
with low verbal ability.

Watterson sophomores are required to participate in a service-to-
humanity project. Although they are directed to choose from a preap-
proved list, Whitney wrote a proposal to his religion teacher petitioning
to be allowed to return to Clintonville Academy for his project. Whitney
wrote, "I learned how to be a human during my years at Clintonville
Academy." He had learned how to feel like a normal person. How to
make friends. How to play sports. How to become a high school kid and

leave special education behind. "Now it is time for me to help the next child. I need to do my service to humanity for the little kids at C.A."

To our surprise, his proposal was approved, and Whitney went once a week to Clintonville.

Terry, one of my medical student patients, had volunteered to pick up Whitney on one of his service days. When she walked into the school, she found Whitney telling a story to all the kids in the after-school program sitting around him cross-legged, hanging on his every word. When he finished his story, Terry waved at him. "Time to go study, Whitney."

"OK, see ya, kids," Whitney called back. As he rose to leave, the kids shouted, "No, no, no! Tell us more stories—don't go!"

"The kids were hanging all over Whitney," Terry told me later. "Knowing his history, it was such a touching sight."

To think that a boy who had seemed so inhuman as a baby, who had been unable to cuddle or communicate in any way, was now giving his service to humanity through language!

Epilogue

Vanessa is completing her sophomore year with honor grades in college in pre-law. She is interning with U.S. Congressman Engle from the Bronx and swimming on the Manhattan College swim team, and has been selected to serve as a resident advisor. She calls Whitney to give him sisterly advice on girls and studies and chats with him on the Internet.

William has a job at the Manhattan College gym to pay for his expenses. He is the Presidential Scholar and in an honors program in chemical engineering, which he loves. This summer he will be interning at the OSU College of Medicine and Public Health.

Whitney played on the state championship football team and was a singer-dancer in the school play, *Carousel*. He plans to continue to take college classes this summer, and in his senior year, he will attend high school half a day and college half a day.

I have set up The Brain Clinic at OSU Medical School, a full-functioning clinical research center to study the Florance Maverick

Syndrome. I have an ongoing eBrain scholars program for training therapists through the City University of New York.

All four of us would agree that the story of how helping a little boy overcome giant obstacles has become the foundation for helping executives and surgeons. Whitney's Maverick Mind has changed our lives and enriched us all.